Effective Objective-C 2.0

The Effective Software Development Series

Scott Meyers, Consulting Editor

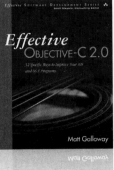

⋀ **Addison-Wesley**

Visit **informit.com/esds** for a complete list of available publications.

The **Effective Software Development Series** provides expert advice on all aspects of modern software development. Titles in the series are well written, technically sound, and of lasting value. Each describes the critical things experts always do — or always avoid — to produce outstanding software.

Scott Meyers, author of the best-selling books *Effective C++* (now in its third edition), *More Effective C++*, and *Effective STL* (all available in both print and electronic versions), conceived of the series and acts as its consulting editor. Authors in the series work with Meyers to create essential reading in a format that is familiar and accessible for software developers of every stripe.

Make sure to connect with us!
informit.com/socialconnect

 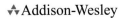

informIT.com
the trusted technology learning source

⋀ Addison-Wesley

Safari
Books Online

Effective Objective-C 2.0

52 SPECIFIC WAYS TO IMPROVE YOUR iOS AND OS X PROGRAMS

Matt Galloway

✦✦Addison-Wesley

Upper Saddle River, NJ • Boston • Indianapolis • San Francisco
New York • Toronto • Montreal • London • Munich • Paris • Madrid
Capetown • Sydney • Tokyo • Singapore • Mexico City

The publisher offers excellent discounts on this book when ordered in quantity for bulk purchases or special sales, which may include electronic versions and/or custom covers and content particular to your business, training goals, marketing focus, and branding interests. For more information, please contact:

U.S. Corporate and Government Sales
(800) 382-3419
corpsales@pearsontechgroup.com

For sales outside the United States, please contact:

International Sales
international@pearsoned.com

Visit us on the Web: informit.com/aw

The Cataloging-in-Publication Data is on file with the Library of Congress.

ISBN-13: 978-0-321-91701-0
ISBN-10:   0-321-91701-4
Text printed in the United States at R.R. Donnelley in Crawfordsville, Indiana.
First printing, May 2013

Editor-in-Chief
Mark Taub

Acquisitions Editor
Trina MacDonald

Development Editor
Chris Zahn

Managing Editor
John Fuller

Project Editor
Elizabeth Ryan

Packager
Vicki Rowland

Copy Editor
Evelyn W. Pyle

Indexer
Sharon Hilgenberg

Proofreader
Archie Brodsky

Technical Reviewers
Anthony Herron
Cesare Rocchi
Chris Wagner

Editorial Assistant
Olivia Bassegio

Cover Designer
Chuti Prasertsith

Compositor
Vicki Rowland

To Rosie

Contents

Preface

Objective-C is verbose. Objective-C is clunky. Objective-C is ugly. I have heard all these things said about Objective-C. On the contrary, I find it elegant, flexible, and beautiful. However, to get it to be these things, you must understand not only the fundamentals but also the quirks, pitfalls, and intricacies: the topic of this book.

About This Book

This book doesn't teach you the syntax of Objective-C. It is assumed that you know this already. Instead, this book teaches you how to use the language to its full potential to write good code. Objective-C is extremely dynamic, thanks to having its roots in Smalltalk. Much of the work that's usually done by a compiler in other languages ends up being done by the runtime in Objective-C. This leads to a potential for code to function fine during testing but to break in strange ways later down the line in production, perhaps when processing invalid data. Avoiding these problems by writing good code in the first place is, of course, the best solution.

Many of the topics are not, strictly speaking, related to core Objective-C. Reference is made to items found in system libraries, such as Grand Central Dispatch, which is part of libdispatch. Similarly, many classes from the Foundation framework are referred to, not least the root class, NSObject, because developing with modern Objective-C means developing for Mac OS X or iOS. When developing for either, you will undoubtedly be using the system frameworks, collectively known as Cocoa and Cocoa Touch, respectively.

Since the rise of iOS, developers have been flocking to join the ranks of Objective-C development. Some of these developers are new to programming, some have come from Java or C++ backgrounds, and some have come from web-development backgrounds. In any case, all developers should take the time to learn how to use a language effectively.

Doing so will yield code that is more efficient, easier to maintain, and less likely to contain bugs.

Even though I have been writing this book for only around six months, it has been years in the making. I bought an iPod Touch on a whim; then, when the first SDK for it was released, I decided to have a play with development. That led to me build my first "app," which I released as Subnet Calc, which immediately got many more downloads than I could have imagined. I became certain that my future was in this beautiful language I had come to know. Since then, I have been researching Objective-C, regularly blogging about it on my web site, www.galloway. me.uk/. I am most interested in the inner workings, such as the guts of blocks and how ARC works. When I got the opportunity to write a book about this language, I jumped at the chance.

In order to get the full potential from this book, I encourage you to jump around it, hunting for the topics that are of most interest or relevant to what you're working on right now. Each item can be read individually, and you can use the cross-references to go to related topics. Each chapter collates items that are related, so you can use the chapter headings to quickly find items relevant to a certain language feature.

Audience for This Book

This book is aimed at developers who wish to further their knowledge of Objective-C and learn to write code that will be maintainable, efficient, and less likely to contain bugs. Even if you are not already an Objective-C developer but come from another object-oriented language, such as Java or C++, you should still be able to learn. In this case, reading about the syntax of Objective-C first would be prudent.

What This Book Covers

It is not the aim of this book to teach the basics of Objective-C, which you can learn from many other books and resources. Instead, this book teaches how to use the language effectively. The book comprises Items, each of which is a bite-sized chunk of information. These Items are logically grouped into topic areas, arranged as follows:

+ **Chapter 1: Accustoming Yourself to Objective-C**

  + Core concepts relating to the language in general are featured here.

+ **Chapter 2: Objects, Messaging, and the Runtime**

  + Important features of any object-oriented language are how objects relate to one another and how they interact. This chapter deals with these features and delves into parts of the runtime.

✦ Chapter 3: Interface and API Design

✦ Code is rarely written once and never reused. Even if it is not released to the wider community, you will likely use your code in more than one project. This chapter explains how to write classes that feel right at home in Objective-C.

✦ Chapter 4: Protocols and Categories

✦ Protocols and categories are both important language features to master. Effective use of them can make your code much easier to read, more maintainable, and less prone to bugs. This chapter helps you achieve mastery.

✦ Chapter 5: Memory Management

✦ Objective-C's memory-management model uses reference counting, which has long been a sticky point for beginners, especially if they have come from a background of a language that uses a garbage collector. The introduction of Automatic Reference Counting (ARC) has made life easier, but you need to be aware of a lot of important things to ensure that you have a correct object model that doesn't suffer from leaks. This chapter fosters awareness of common memory-management pitfalls.

✦ Chapter 6: Blocks and Grand Central Dispatch

✦ Blocks are lexical closures for C, introduced by Apple. Blocks are commonly used in Objective-C to achieve what used to involve much boilerplate code and introduced code separation. Grand Central Dispatch (GCD) provides a simple interface to threading. Blocks are seen as GCD tasks that can be executed, perhaps in parallel, depending on system resources. This chapter enables you to make the most from these two core technologies.

✦ Chapter 7: The System Frameworks

✦ You will usually be writing Objective-C code for Mac OS X or iOS. In those cases, you will have the full system frameworks stack at your disposal: Cocoa and Cocoa Touch, respectively. This chapter gives a brief overview of the frameworks and delves into some of their classes.

If you have any questions, comments, or remarks about this book, I encourage you to contact me. You can find my full contact details on the web site for this book at www.effectiveobjectivec.com.

Acknowledgments

When asked whether I would like to write a book about Objective-C, I instantly became excited. I had already read other books in this series and knew that the task of creating one for Objective-C would be a challenge. But with the help of many people, this book became a reality.

Much inspiration for this book has come from the many excellent blogs that are dedicated to Objective-C. Mike Ash, Matt Gallagher, and "bbum" are a few of the individuals whose blogs I read. These blogs have helped me over the years to gain a deeper understanding of the language. *NSHipster* by Mattt Thompson has also provided excellent articles that gave me food for thought while compiling this book. Finally, the excellent documentation provided by Apple has also been extremely useful.

I would not have been in a position to write this book had it not been for the excellent mentoring and knowledge transfer that happened while I was working at MX Telecom. Matthew Hodgson in particular gave me the opportunity to develop the company's first iOS application, building on top of a mature C++ code base. The knowledge I picked up from this project formed the basis of much of my subsequent work.

Over the years, I have had many excellent colleagues with whom I have always stayed in touch either for academic reasons or purely just being there for a beer and a chat. All have helped me while writing this book.

I've had a fantastic experience with the team from Pearson. Trina MacDonald, Olivia Basegio, Scott Meyers, and Chris Zahn have all provided help and encouragement when required. They have provided the tools for me to get the book written without distraction and answered my queries when necessary.

The technical editors I have had the pleasure of working with have been incredibly helpful. Their eagle eyes have pushed the content of the book to be the very best. They should all be proud of the level of detail they used when analyzing the manuscript.

Finally, I could not have written this book without the understanding and support from Helen. Our first child was born the day I was supposed to start writing, so I naturally postponed for a short time. Both Helen and Rosie have been fantastic at keeping me going throughout.

About the Author

Matt Galloway is an iOS developer from London, UK. He graduated from the University of Cambridge, Pembroke College, in 2007, having completed an M.Eng. degree, specializing in electrical and information sciences. Since then, he has been programming, mostly in Objective-C. He has been developing for iOS ever since the first SDK was released. You'll find him on Twitter as @mattjgalloway, and he is a regular contributor to *Stack Overflow* (http://stackoverflow.com).

Accustoming Yourself to Objective-C

Objective-C brings object-oriented features to C through an entirely new syntax. Often described as verbose, Objective-C syntax makes use of a lot of square brackets and isn't shy about using extremely long method names. The resulting source code is very readable but is often difficult for C++ or Java developers to master.

Writing Objective-C can be learned quickly but has many intricacies to be aware of and features that are often overlooked. Similarly, some features are abused or not fully understood, yielding code that is difficult to maintain or to debug. This chapter covers fundamental topics; subsequent chapters cover specific areas of the language and associated frameworks.

Item 1: Familiarize Yourself with Objective-C's Roots

Objective-C is similar to other object-oriented languages, such as C++ and Java, but also differs in many ways. If you have experience in another object-oriented language, you'll understand many of the paradigms and patterns used. However, the syntax may appear alien because it uses a messaging structure rather than function calling. Objective-C evolved from Smalltalk, the origin of messaging. The difference between messaging and function calling looks like this:

```
// Messaging (Objective-C)
Object *obj = [Object new];
[obj performWith:parameter1 and:parameter2];

// Function calling (C++)
Object *obj = new Object;
obj->perform(parameter1, parameter2);
```

The key difference is that in the messaging structure, the runtime decides which code gets executed. With function calling, the compiler decides which code will be executed. When polymorphism is introduced to the function-calling example, a form of runtime lookup is involved through what is known as a virtual table. But with messaging, the lookup is always at runtime. In fact, the compiler doesn't even care about the type of the object being messaged. That is looked up at runtime as well, through a process known as dynamic binding, covered in more detail in Item 11.

The Objective-C runtime component, rather than the compiler, does most of the heavy lifting. The runtime contains all the data structures and functions that are required for the object-oriented features of Objective-C to work. For example, the runtime includes all the memory-management methods. Essentially, the runtime is the set of code that glues together all your code and comes in the form of a dynamic library to which your code is linked. Thus, whenever the runtime is updated, your application benefits from the performance improvements. A language that does more work at compile time needs to be recompiled to benefit from such performance improvements.

Objective-C is a superset of C, so all the features in the C language are available when writing Objective-C. Therefore, to write effective Objective-C, you need to understand the core concepts of both C and Objective-C. In particular, understanding the memory model of C will help you to understand the memory model of Objective-C and why reference counting works the way it does. This involves understanding that a pointer is used to denote an object in Objective-C. When you declare a variable that is to hold a reference to an object, the syntax looks like this:

```
NSString *someString = @"The string";
```

This syntax, mostly lifted straight from C, declares a variable called someString whose type is NSString*. This means that it is a pointer to an NSString. All Objective-C objects must be declared in this way because the memory for objects is always allocated in heap space and never on the stack. It is illegal to declare a stack-allocated Objective-C object:

```
NSString stackString;
// error: interface type cannot be statically allocated
```

The someString variable points to some memory, allocated in the heap, containing an NSString object. This means that creating another variable pointing to the same location does not create a copy but rather yields two variables pointing to the same object:

```
NSString *someString = @"The string";
NSString *anotherString = someString;
```

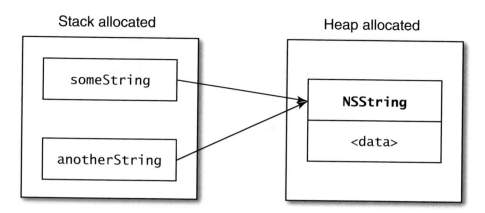

Figure 1.1 Memory layout showing a heap-allocated NSString instance and two stack-allocated pointers to it

There is only one NSString instance here, but two variables are pointing to the same instance. These two variables are of type NSString*, meaning that the current stack frame has allocated 2 bits of memory the size of a pointer (4 bytes for a 32-bit architecture, 8 bytes for a 64-bit architecture). These bits of memory will contain the same value: the memory address of the NSString instance.

Figure 1.1 illustrates this layout. The data stored for the NSString instance includes the bytes needed to represent the actual string.

The memory allocated in the heap has to be managed directly, whereas the stack-allocated memory to hold the variables is automatically cleaned up when the stack frame on which they are allocated is popped.

Memory management of the heap memory is abstracted away by Objective-C. You do not need to use malloc and free to allocate and deallocate the memory for objects. The Objective-C runtime abstracts this out of the way through a memory-management architecture known as reference counting (see Item 29).

Sometimes in Objective-C, you will encounter variables that don't have a * in the definition and might use stack space. These variables are not holding Objective-C objects. An example is CGRect, from the CoreGraphics framework:

```
CGRect frame;
frame.origin.x = 0.0f;
frame.origin.y = 10.0f;
frame.size.width = 100.0f;
```

```
frame.size.height = 150.0f;
```

A CGRect is a C structure, defined like so:

```
struct CGRect {
  CGPoint origin;
  CGSize size;
};
typedef struct CGRect CGRect;
```

These types of structures are used throughout the system frameworks, where the overhead of using Objective-C objects could affect performance. Creating objects incurs overhead that using structures does not, such as allocating and deallocating heap memory. When nonobject types (int, float, double, char, etc.) are the only data to be held, a structure, such as CGRect, is usually used.

Before embarking on writing anything in Objective-C, I encourage you to read texts about the C language and become familiar with the syntax. If you dive straight into Objective-C, you may find certain parts of the syntax confusing.

Things to Remember

✦ Objective-C is a superset of C, adding object-oriented features. Objective-C uses a messaging structure with dynamic binding, meaning that the type of an object is discovered at runtime. The runtime, rather than the compiler, works out what code to run for a given message.

✦ Understanding the core concepts of C will help you write effective Objective-C. In particular, you need to understand the memory model and pointers.

Item 2: Minimize Importing Headers in Headers

Objective-C, just like C and C++, makes use of header files and implementation files. When a class is written in Objective-C, the standard approach is to create one of each of these files named after the class, suffixed with .h for the header file and .m for the implementation file. When you create a class, it might end up looking like this:

```
// EOCPerson.h
#import <Foundation/Foundation.h>

@interface EOCPerson : NSObject
@property (nonatomic, copy) NSString *firstName;
@property (nonatomic, copy) NSString *lastName;
```

```
@end

// EOCPerson.m
#import "EOCPerson.h"

@implementation EOCPerson
// Implementation of methods
@end
```

The importing of Foundation.h is required pretty much for all classes you will ever make in Objective-C. Either that, or you will import the base header file for the framework in which the class's superclass lives. For example, if you were creating an iOS application, you would subclass UIViewController often. These classes' header files will import UIKit.h.

As it stands, this class is fine. It imports the entirety of Foundation, but that doesn't matter. Given that this class inherits from a class that's part of Foundation, it's likely that a large proportion of it will be used by consumers of EOCPerson. The same goes for a class that inherits from UIViewController. Its consumers will make use of most of UIKit.

As time goes on, you may create a new class called EOCEmployer. Then you decide that an EOCPerson instance should have one of those. So you go ahead and add a property for it:

```
// EOCPerson.h
#import <Foundation/Foundation.h>

@interface EOCPerson : NSObject
@property (nonatomic, copy) NSString *firstName;
@property (nonatomic, copy) NSString *lastName;
@property (nonatomic, strong) EOCEmployer *employer;
@end
```

A problem with this, though, is that the EOCEmployer class is not visible when compiling anything that imports EOCPerson.h. It would be wrong to mandate that anyone importing EOCPerson.h must also import EOCEmployer.h. So the common thing to do is to add the following at the top of EOCPerson.h:

```
#import "EOCEmployer.h"
```

This would work, but it's bad practice. To compile anything that uses EOCPerson, you don't need to know the full details about what an EOCEmployer is. All you need to know is that a class called EOCEmployer exists. Fortunately, there is a way to tell the compiler this:

```
@class EOCEmployer;
```

This is called forward declaring the class. The resulting header file for EOCPerson would look like this:

```
// EOCPerson.h
#import <Foundation/Foundation.h>

@class EOCEmployer;

@interface EOCPerson : NSObject
@property (nonatomic, copy) NSString *firstName;
@property (nonatomic, copy) NSString *lastName;
@property (nonatomic, strong) EOCEmployer *employer;
@end
```

The implementation file for EOCPerson would then need to import the header file of EOCEmployer, as it would need to know the full interface details of the class in order to use it. So the implementation file would end up looking like this:

```
// EOCPerson.m
#import "EOCPerson.h"
#import "EOCEmployer.h"

@implementation EOCPerson
// Implementation of methods
@end
```

Deferring the import to where it is required enables you to limit the scope of what a consumer of your class needs to import. In the example, if EOCEmployer.h were imported in EOCPerson.h, anything importing EOCPerson.h would also import all of EOCEmployer.h. If the chain of importing continues, you could end up importing a lot more than you bargained for, which will certainly increase compile time.

Using forward declaration also alleviates the problem of both classes referring to each other. Consider what would happen if EOCEmployer had methods to add and remove employees, defined like this in its header file:

```
- (void)addEmployee:(EOCPerson*)person;
- (void)removeEmployee:(EOCPerson*)person;
```

This time, the EOCPerson class needs to be visible to the compiler, for the same reasons as in the opposite case. However, achieving this by importing the other header in each header would create a chicken-and-egg situation. When one header is parsed, it imports the other, which imports the first. The use of #import rather than #include doesn't end in an infinite loop but does mean that one of the classes won't compile correctly. Try it for yourself if you don't believe me!

Sometimes, though, you need to import a header in a header. You must import the header that defines the superclass from which you are inheriting. Similarly, if you declare any protocols that your class conforms to, they have to be fully defined and not forward declared. The compiler needs to be able to see the methods the protocol defines rather than simply that a protocol does exist from a forward declaration.

For example, suppose that a rectangle class inherits from a shape class and conforms to a protocol allowing it to be drawn:

```
// EOCRectangle.h
#import "EOCShape.h"
#import "EOCDrawable.h"

@interface EOCRectangle : EOCShape <EOCDrawable>
@property (nonatomic, assign) float width;
@property (nonatomic, assign) float height;
@end
```

The extra import is unavoidable. For such protocols, it is prudent to put them in their own header file for this reason. If the EOCDrawable protocol were part of a larger header file, you'd have to import all of that, thereby creating the same dependency and extra compilation-time problems as described before.

That said, not all protocols, such as delegate protocols (see Item 23), need to go in their own files. In such cases, the protocol makes sense only when defined alongside the class for which it is a delegate. In these cases, it is often best to declare that your class implements the delegate in the class-continuation category (see Item 27). This means that the import of the header containing the delegate protocol can go in the implementation file rather than in the public header file.

When writing an import into a header file, always ask yourself whether it's really necessary. If the import can be forward declared, prefer that. If the import is for something used in a property, instance variable, or protocol conformance and can be moved to the class-continuation category (see Item 27), prefer that. Doing so will keep compile time as low as possible and reduce interdependency, which can cause problems with maintenance or with exposing only parts of your code in a public API should ever you want to do that.

Things to Remember

+ Always import headers at the very deepest point possible. This usually means forward declaring classes in a header and importing their corresponding headers in an implementation. Doing so avoids coupling classes together as much as possible.

+ Sometimes, forward declaration is not possible, as when declaring protocol conformance. In such cases, consider moving the protocol-conformance declaration to the class-continuation category, if possible. Otherwise, import a header that defines only the protocol.

Item 3: Prefer Literal Syntax over the Equivalent Methods

While using Objective-C, you will come across a few classes all the time. They are all part of the Foundation framework. Although technically, you do not have to use Foundation to write Objective-C code, you usually do in practice. The classes are NSString, NSNumber, NSArray, and NSDictionary. The data structures that each represent are self-explanatory.

Objective-C is well known for having a verbose syntax. That's true. However, ever since Objective-C 1.0, there has been a very simple way to create an NSString object. It is known as a string literal and looks like this:

```
NSString *someString = @"Effective Objective-C 2.0";
```

Without this type of syntax, creating an NSString object would require allocating and initializing an NSString object in the usual alloc and then init method call. Fortunately, this syntax, known as literals, has been extended in recent versions of the compiler to cover NSNumber, NSArray, and NSDictionary instances as well. Using the literal syntax reduces source code size and makes it much easier to read.

Literal Numbers

Sometimes, you need to wrap an integer, floating-point, or Boolean value in an Objective-C object. You do so by using the NSNumber class, which can handle a range of number types. Without literals, you create an instance like this:

```
NSNumber *someNumber = [NSNumber numberWithInt:1];
```

This creates a number that is set to the integer 1. However, using literals makes this cleaner:

```
NSNumber *someNumber = @1;
```

As you can see, the literal syntax is much more concise. But there's more to it than that. The syntax also covers all the other types of data that NSNumber instances can represent. For example:

```
NSNumber *intNumber = @1;
NSNumber *floatNumber = @2.5f;
NSNumber *doubleNumber = @3.14159;
NSNumber *boolNumber = @YES;
NSNumber *charNumber = @'a';
```

The literal syntax also works for expressions:

```
int x = 5;
float y = 6.32f;
NSNumber *expressionNumber = @(x * y);
```

Making use of literals for numbers is extremely useful. Doing so makes using NSNumber objects much clearer, as the bulk of the declaration is the value rather than superfluous syntax.

Literal Arrays

Arrays are a commonly used data structure. Before literals, you would create an array as follows:

```
NSArray *animals =
    [NSArray arrayWithObjects:@"cat", @"dog",
                              @"mouse", @"badger", nil];
```

Using literals, however, requires only the following syntax:

```
NSArray *animals = @[@"cat", @"dog", @"mouse", @"badger"];
```

But even though this is a much simpler syntax, there's more to it than that with arrays. A common operation on an array is to get the object at a certain index. This also is made easier using literals. Usually, you would use the objectAtIndex: method:

```
NSString *dog = [animals objectAtIndex:1];
```

With literals, it's a matter of doing the following:

```
NSString *dog = animals[1];
```

This is known as subscripting, and just like the rest of the literal syntax, it is more concise and much easier to see what's being done. Moreover, it looks very similar to the way arrays are indexed in other languages.

However, you need to be aware of one thing when creating arrays using the literal syntax. If any of the objects is nil, an exception is thrown, since literal syntax is really just syntactic sugar around creating an array and then adding all the objects within the square brackets. The exception you get looks like this:

```
*** Terminating app due to uncaught exception
'NSInvalidArgumentException', reason: '***
-[__NSPlaceholderArray initWithObjects:count:]: attempt to
insert nil object from objects[0]'
```

This brings to light a common problem when switching to using literals. The following code creates two arrays, one in each syntax:

```
id object1 = /* … */;
id object2 = /* … */;
id object3 = /* … */;

NSArray *arrayA = [NSArray arrayWithObjects:
                          object1, object2, object3, nil];
NSArray *arrayB = @[object1, object2, object3];
```

Now consider the scenario in which object1 and object3 point to valid Objective-C objects, but object2 is nil. The literal array, arrayB, will cause the exception to be thrown. However, arrayA will still be created but will contain only object1. The reason is that the arrayWithObjects: method looks through the variadic arguments until it hits nil, which is sooner than expected.

This subtle difference means that literals are much safer. It's much better that an exception is thrown, causing a probable application crash, rather than creating an array having fewer than the expected number of objects in it. A programmer error most likely caused nil to be inserted into the array, and the exception means that the bug can be found more easily.

Literal Dictionaries

Dictionaries provide a map data structure in which you add key-value pairs. Like arrays, dictionaries are commonly used in Objective-C code. Creating one used to look like this:

```
NSDictionary *personData =
    [NSDictionary dictionaryWithObjectsAndKeys:
        @"Matt", @"firstName",
        @"Galloway", @"lastName",
        [NSNumber numberWithInt:28], @"age",
        nil];
```

This is rather confusing, because the order is <object>, <key>, <object>, <key>, and so on. However, you usually think about dictionaries the other way round, as in key to object. Therefore, it doesn't read particularly well. However, literals once again make the syntax much clearer:

```
NSDictionary *personData =
    @{@"firstName" : @"Matt",
      @"lastName" : @"Galloway",
      @"age" : @28};
```

This is much more concise, and the keys are before the objects, just as you'd expect. Also note that the literal number in the example shows where literal numbers are useful. The objects and keys have to all be Objective-C objects, so you couldn't store the integer 28; instead, it must be wrapped in an NSNumber instance. But the literal syntax means that it's simply one extra character.

Just like arrays, the literal syntax for dictionaries suffers from an exception being thrown if any values are nil. However, for the same reason, this is a good thing. It means that instead of creating a dictionary with missing values, owing to the dictionaryWithObjectsAndKeys: method stopping at the first nil, an exception is thrown.

Also similar to arrays, dictionaries can be accessed using literal syntax. The old way of accessing a value for a certain key is as follows:

```
NSString *lastName = [personData objectForKey:@"lastName"];
```

The equivalent literal syntax is:

```
NSString *lastName = personData[@"lastName"];
```

Once again, the amount of superfluous syntax is reduced, leaving an easy-to-read line of code.

Mutable Arrays and Dictionaries

In the same way that you can access indexes in an array or keys in a dictionary through subscripting, you can also set them if the object is mutable. Setting through the normal methods on mutable arrays and dictionaries looks like this:

```
[mutableArray replaceObjectAtIndex:1 withObject:@"dog"];
[mutableDictionary setObject:@"Galloway" forKey:@"lastName"];
```

Setting through subscripting looks like this:

```
mutableArray[1] = @"dog";
mutableDictionary[@"lastName"] = @"Galloway";
```

Limitations

A minor limitation with the literal syntax is that with the exception of strings, the class of the created object must be the one from the Foundation framework. There's no way to specify your own custom subclass that should be created instead. If you wanted to create an instance of your own custom subclass, you'd need to use the nonliteral syntax. However, since NSArray, NSDictionary, and NSNumber are class clusters (see Item 9), they are rarely subclassed, as it's nontrivial to do so. Also, the standard implementations are usually good enough. Strings can use a custom class, but it must be changed through a compiler option. Use of this option is discouraged because unless you know what you are doing, you will always want to use NSString anyway.

Also, in the case of strings, arrays, and dictionaries, only immutable variants can be created with the literal syntax. If a mutable variant is required, a mutable copy must be taken, like so:

```
NSMutableArray *mutable = [@[@1, @2, @3, @4, @5] mutableCopy];
```

This adds an extra method call, and an extra object is created, but the benefits of using the literal syntax outweigh these disadvantages.

Things to Remember

- ✦ Use the literal syntax to create strings, numbers, arrays, and dictionaries. It is clearer and more succinct than creating them using the normal object-creation methods.

- ✦ Access indexes of an array or keys in a dictionary through the subscripting methods.

- ✦ Attempting to insert nil into an array or dictionary with literal syntax will cause an exception to be thrown. Therefore, always ensure that such values cannot be nil.

Item 4: Prefer Typed Constants to Preprocessor #define

When writing code, you will often want to define a constant. For example, consider a UI view class that presents and dismisses itself using animations. A typical constant that you'd likely want to factor out is the animation duration. You've learned all about Objective-C and its C foundations, and so you take the approach of defining the constant like this:

```
#define ANIMATION_DURATION 0.3
```

This is a preprocessor directive; whenever the string ANIMATION_DURATION is found in your source code, it is replaced with 0.3. This might seem exactly what you want, but this definition has no type information. It is likely that something declared as a "duration" means that the value is related to time, but it's not made explicit. Also, the preprocessor will blindly replace all occurrences of ANIMATION_DURATION, so if that were declared in a header file, anything else that imported that header would see the replacement done.

To solve these problems, you should make use of the compiler. There is always a better way to define a constant than using a preprocessor define. For example, the following defines a constant of type NSTimeInterval:

```
static const NSTimeInterval kAnimationDuration = 0.3;
```

Note that with this style, there is type information, which is beneficial because it clearly defines what the constant is. The type is NSTimeInterval, and so it helps to document the use of that variable. If you have a lot of constants to define, this will certainly help you and other people who read the code later.

Also note how the constant is named. The usual convention for constants is to prefix with the letter k for constants that are local to a translation unit (implementation file). For constants that are exposed outside of a class, it is usual to prefix with the class name. Item 19 explains more about naming conventions.

It is important where you define your constants. Sometimes, it is tempting to declare preprocessor defines in header files, but that is extremely bad practice, especially if the defines are not named in such a way that they won't clash. For example, the ANIMATION_DURATION constant would be a bad name to appear in a header file. It would be present in all other files that imported the header. Even the static const as it stands should not appear in a header file. Since Objective-C has no namespaces, it would declare a global variable called kAnimationDuration. Its name should be prefixed with something that scopes it to the class it is to be used with, such as EOCViewClassAnimationDuration. Item 19 explains more about using a clear naming scheme.

A constant that does not need to be exposed to the outside world should be defined in the implementation file where it is used. For example, if the animation duration constant were used in a UIView subclass, for use in an iOS application that uses UIKit, it would look like this:

```
// EOCAnimatedView.h
#import <UIKit/UIKit.h>

@interface EOCAnimatedView : UIView
- (void)animate;
@end

// EOCAnimatedView.m
#import "EOCAnimatedView.h"

static const NSTimeInterval kAnimationDuration = 0.3;

@implementation EOCAnimatedView
- (void)animate {
    [UIView animateWithDuration:kAnimationDuration
                     animations:^(){
                         // Perform animations
                     }];

}
@end
```

It is important that the variable is declared as both static and const. The const qualifier means that the compiler will throw an error if you try to alter the value. In this scenario, that's exactly what is required. The value shouldn't be allowed to change. The static qualifier means that the variable is local to the translation unit in which it is defined. A translation unit is the input the compiler receives to generate one object file. In the case of Objective-C, this usually means that there is one translation unit per class: every implementation (.m) file. So in the preceding example, kAnimationDuration will be declared locally to the object file generated from EOCAnimatedView.m. If the variable were not declared static, the compiler would create an external symbol for it. If another translation unit also declared a variable with the same name, the linker would throw an error with a message similar to this:

```
duplicate symbol _kAnimationDuration in:
    EOCAnimatedView.o
    EOCOtherView.o
```

In fact, when declaring the variable as both static and const, the compiler doesn't end up creating a symbol at all but instead replaces occurrences just like a preprocessor define does. Remember, however, the benefit is that the type information is present.

Sometimes, you will want to expose a constant externally. For example, you might want to do this if your class will notify others using

NSNotificationCenter. This works by one object posting notifications and others registering to receive them. Notifications have a string name, and this is what you might want to declare as an externally visible constant variable. Doing so means that anyone wanting to register to receive such notifications does not need to know the actual string name but can simply use the constant variable.

Such constants need to appear in the global symbol table to be used from outside the translation unit in which they are defined. Therefore, these constants need to be declared in a different way from the static const example. These constants should be defined like so:

```
// In the header file
extern NSString *const EOCStringConstant;

// In the implementation file
NSString *const EOCStringConstant = @"VALUE";
```

The constant is "declared" in the header file and "defined" in the implementation file. In the constant's type, the placement of the const qualifier is important. These definitions are read backward, meaning that in this case, EOCStringConstant is a "constant pointer to an NSString." This is what we want; the constant should not be allowed to change to point to a different NSString object.

The extern keyword in the header tells the compiler what to do when it encounters the constant being used in a file that imports it. The keyword tells the compiler that there will be a symbol for EOCStringConstant in the global symbol table. This means that the constant can be used without the compiler's being able to see the definition for it. The compiler simply knows that the constant will exist when the binary is linked.

The constant has to be defined once and only once. It is usually defined in the implementation file that relates to the header file in which it is declared. The compiler will allocate storage for the string in the data section of the object file that is generated from this implementation file. When this object file is linked with other object files to produce the final binary, the linker will be able to resolve the global symbol for EOCStringConstant wherever else it has been used.

The fact that the symbol appears in the global symbol table means that you should name such constants carefully. For example, a class that handles login for an application may have a notification that is fired after login has finished. The notification may look like this:

```
// EOCLoginManager.h
#import <Foundation/Foundation.h>
```

```
extern NSString *const EOCLoginManagerDidLoginNotification;

@interface EOCLoginManager : NSObject
- (void)login;
@end

// EOCLoginManager.m
#import "EOCLoginManager.h"

NSString *const EOCLoginManagerDidLoginNotification =
    @"EOCLoginManagerDidLoginNotification";

@implementation EOCLoginManager

- (void)login {
    // Perform login asynchronously, then call 'p_didLogin'.
}

- (void)p_didLogin {
    [[NSNotificationCenter defaultCenter]
        postNotificationName:EOCLoginManagerDidLoginNotification
                      object:nil];
}

@end
```

Note the name given to the constant. Prefixing with the class name that the constant relates to is prudent and will help you avoid potential clashes. This is common throughout the system frameworks as well. UIKit, for example, declares notification names as global constants in the same way. The names include UIApplicationDidEnterBackgroundNotification and UIApplicationWillEnterForegroundNotification.

The same can be done with constants of other types. If the animation duration needed to be exposed outside of the EOCAnimatedView class in the preceding examples, you could declare it like so:

```
// EOCAnimatedView.h
extern const NSTimeInterval EOCAnimatedViewAnimationDuration;

// EOCAnimatedView.m
const NSTimeInterval EOCAnimatedViewAnimationDuration = 0.3;
```

Defining a constant in this way is much better than a preprocessor define because the compiler is used to ensure that the value cannot change. Once defined in EOCAnimatedView.m, that value is used everywhere. A preprocessor define could be redefined by mistake, meaning that different parts of an application end up using different values.

In conclusion, avoid using preprocessor defines for constants. Instead, use constants that are seen by the compiler, such as static const globals declared in implementation files.

Things to Remember

✦ Avoid preprocessor defines. They don't contain any type information and are simply a find and replace executed before compilation. They could be redefined without warning, yielding inconsistent values throughout an application.

✦ Define translation-unit-specific constants within an implementation file as static const. These constants will not be exposed in the global symbol table, so their names do not need to be namespaced.

✦ Define global constants as external in a header file, and define them in the associated implementation file. These constants will appear in the global symbol table, so their names should be namespaced, usually by prefixing them with the class name to which they correspond.

Item 5: Use Enumerations for States, Options, and Status Codes

Since Objective-C is based on C, all the features of C are available. One of these is the enumeration type, enum. It is used extensively throughout the system frameworks but is often overlooked by developers. It is an extremely useful way to define named constants that can be used, for example, as error status codes and to define options that can be combined. Thanks to the additions of the C++11 standard, recent versions of the system frameworks include a way to strongly type such enumeration types. Yes, Objective-C has benefitted from the C++11 standard as well!

An enumeration is nothing more than a way of naming constant values. A simple enumeration set might be used to define the states through which an object goes. For example, a socket connection might use the following enumeration:

```
enum EOCConnectionState {
    EOCConnectionStateDisconnected,
    EOCConnectionStateConnecting,
    EOCConnectionStateConnected,
};
```

Using an enumeration means that code is readable, since each state can be referred to by an easy-to-read value. The compiler gives a unique value to each member of the enumeration, starting at 0 and increasing by 1 for each member. The type that backs such an enumeration is compiler dependent but must have at least enough bits to represent the enumeration fully. In the case of the preceding enumeration, this would simply need to be a char (1 byte), since the maximum value is 2.

This style of defining an enumeration is not particularly useful, though, and requires the following syntax:

enum EOCConnectionState state = EOCConnectionStateDisconnected;

It would be much easier if you didn't have to type enum each time but rather use EOCConnectionState on its own. To do this, you add a typedef to the enumeration definition:

```
enum EOCConnectionState {
    EOCConnectionStateDisconnected,
    EOCConnectionStateConnecting,
    EOCConnectionStateConnected,
};
typedef enum EOCConnectionState EOCConnectionState;
```

This means that EOCConnectionState can be used instead of the full enum EOCConnectionState:

EOCConnectionState state = EOCConnectionStateDisconnected;

The advent of the C++11 standard brought some changes to enumerations. One such change is the capability to dictate the underlying type used to store variables of the enumerated type. The benefit of doing this is that you can forward declare enumeration types. Without specifying the underlying type, an enumeration type cannot be forward declared, since the compiler cannot know what size the underlying type will end up being. Therefore, when the type is used, the compiler doesn't know how much space to allocate for the variable.

To specify the type, you use the following syntax:

enum EOCConnectionStateConnectionState : NSInteger { /* … */ };

This means that the value backing the enumeration will be guaranteed to be an NSInteger. If you so wished, the type could be forward declared like so:

enum EOCConnectionStateConnectionState : NSInteger;

It's also possible to define the value a certain enumeration member relates to rather than letting the compiler choose for you. The syntax looks like this:

```
enum EOCConnectionStateConnectionState {
    EOCConnectionStateDisconnected = 1,
    EOCConnectionStateConnecting,
    EOCConnectionStateConnected,
};
```

This means that EOCConnectionStateDisconnected will use the value 1 rather than 0. The other values follow, incrementing by 1 each time, just as before. Thus, EOCConnectionStateConnected will use the value 3, for example.

Another reason to use enumeration types is to define options, especially when the options can be combined. If the enumeration is defined correctly, the options can be combined using the bitwise OR operator. For example, consider the following enumeration type, found in the iOS UI framework, used to define which dimensions of a view can be resized:

```
enum UIViewAutoresizing {
    UIViewAutoresizingNone              = 0,
    UIViewAutoresizingFlexibleLeftMargin   = 1 << 0,
    UIViewAutoresizingFlexibleWidth        = 1 << 1,
    UIViewAutoresizingFlexibleRightMargin  = 1 << 2,
    UIViewAutoresizingFlexibleTopMargin    = 1 << 3,
    UIViewAutoresizingFlexibleHeight       = 1 << 4,
    UIViewAutoresizingFlexibleBottomMargin = 1 << 5,
}
```

Each option can be either on or off, and using the preceding syntax enables this because each option has just a single bit set in the value represented by it. Multiple options can be bitwise OR'ed together: for example, UIViewAutoResizingFlexibleWidth | UIViewAutoresizingFlexibleHeight. Figure 1.2 shows the bit layout of each enumeration member and the combination of two of the members.

It's then possible to determine whether one of the options is set by using the bitwise AND operator:

```
enum UIVewAutoresizing resizing =
    UIViewAutoresizingFlexibleWidth |
    UIViewAutoresizingFlexibleHeight;
if (resizing & UIViewAutoresizingFlexibleWidth) {
    // UIViewAutoresizingFlexibleWidth is set
}
```

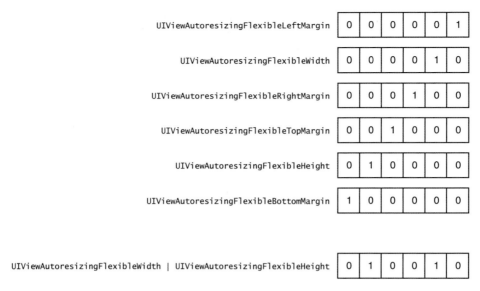

Figure 1.2 Binary representation of three options values and two of those values bitwise OR'ed together

This is used extensively throughout the system libraries. Another example from UIKit, the iOS UI framework, uses it as a way of telling the system what device orientations your view supports. It does this with an enumerated type called UIInterfaceOrientationMask, and you implement a method called supportedInterfaceOrientations to indicate the supported orientations:

```
- (NSUInteger)supportedInterfaceOrientations {
    return UIInterfaceOrientationMaskPortrait |
        UIInterfaceOrientationMaskLandscapeLeft;
}
```

A couple of helpers defined within the Foundation framework help define enumeration types that also allow you to specify the integral type that will be used to store values that use the enumeration type. These helpers provide backward compatibility such that if you're targeting a compiler that supports the new standard, that syntax is used, but it falls back to the old syntax if not. The helpers are provided in the form of preprocessor #define macros. One is provided for normal enumeration types, such as the EOCConnectionState example. The other is provided for the case in which the enumeration defines a list of options like the UIViewAutoresizing example. You use them as follows:

```
typedef NS_ENUM(NSUInteger, EOCConnectionState) {
    EOCConnectionStateDisconnected,
    EOCConnectionStateConnecting,
    EOCConnectionStateConnected,
};
typedef NS_OPTIONS(NSUInteger, EOCPermittedDirection) {
    EOCPermittedDirectionUp    = 1 << 0,
    EOCPermittedDirectionDown  = 1 << 1,
    EOCPermittedDirectionLeft  = 1 << 2,
    EOCPermittedDirectionRight = 1 << 3,
};
```

This is what the macro definitions look like:

```
#if (__cplusplus && __cplusplus >= 201103L &&
        (__has_extension(cxx_strong_enums) ||
         __has_feature(objc_fixed_enum))
    ) ||
    (!__cplusplus && __has_feature(objc_fixed_enum))
    #define NS_ENUM(_type, _name)
            enum _name : _type _name; enum _name : _type
    #if (__cplusplus)
        #define NS_OPTIONS(_type, _name)
                _type _name; enum : _type
    #else
        #define NS_OPTIONS(_type, _name)
                enum _name : _type _name; enum _name : _type
    #endif
#else
    #define NS_ENUM(_type, _name) _type _name; enum
    #define NS_OPTIONS(_type, _name) _type _name; enum
#endif
```

The reason for the various ways of defining the macros is that there are different scenarios. The first case that is checked is whether the compiler supports the new style enumerations at all. This is checked with what looks like some rather complex Boolean logic, but all that it's checking is that the feature is there. If the feature is not there, it defines the enumeration by using the old style.

If the feature is available, the NS_ENUM type is defined such that it expands out like this:

```
typedef enum EOCConnectionState : NSUInteger EOCConnectionState;
enum EOCConnectionState : NSUInteger {
    EOCConnectionStateDisconnected,
    EOCConnectionStateConnecting,
```

```
        EOCConnectionStateConnected,
};
```

The NS_OPTIONS macro is defined in different ways if compiling as C++ or not. If it's not C++, it's expanded out the same as NS_ENUM. However, if it is C++, it's expanded out slightly differently. Why? The C++ compiler acts differently when two enumeration values are bitwise OR'ed together. This is something, as shown earlier, that is commonly done with the options type of enumeration. When two values are OR'ed together, C++ considers the resulting value to be of the type the enumeration represents: NSUInteger. It also doesn't allow the implicit cast to the enumeration type. To illustrate this, consider what would happen if the EOCPermittedDirection enumeration were expanded out as NS_ENUM:

```
typedef enum EOCPermittedDirection : int EOCPermittedDirection;
enum EOCPermittedDirection : int {
    EOCPermittedDirectionUp    = 1 << 0,
    EOCPermittedDirectionDown  = 1 << 1,
    EOCPermittedDirectionLeft  = 1 << 2,
    EOCPermittedDirectionRight = 1 << 3,
};
```

Then consider attempting the following:

```
EOCPermittedDirection permittedDirections =
    EOCPermittedDirectionLeft | EOCPermittedDirectionUp;
```

If the compiler were in C++ mode (or potentially Objective-C++), this would result in the following error:

```
error: cannot initialize a variable of type
'EOCPermittedDirection' with an rvalue of type 'int'
```

You would be required to put in an explicit cast to the result of the ORing, back to EOCPermittedDirection. So the NS_OPTIONS enumeration is defined differently for C++ such that this does not have to be done. For this reason, you should always use NS_OPTIONS if you are going to be ORing together the enumeration values. If not, you should use NS_ENUM.

An enumeration can be used in many scenarios. Options and states have been shown previously; however, many other scenarios exist. Status codes for errors are a good candidate as well. Instead of using preprocessor defines or constants, enumerations provide a means for grouping together logically similar status codes into one enumeration. Another good candidate is styles. For example, if you have a UI element that can be created with different styles, an enumeration type is perfect for that situation.

One final extra point about enumerations has to do with using a switch statement. Sometimes, you will want to do the following:

```
typedef NS_ENUM(NSUInteger, EOCConnectionState) {
    EOCConnectionStateDisconnected,
    EOCConnectionStateConnecting,
    EOCConnectionStateConnected,
};

switch (_currentState) {
    EOCConnectionStateDisconnected:
        // Handle disconnected state
        break;
    EOCConnectionStateConnecting:
        // Handle connecting state
        break;
    EOCConnectionStateConnected:
        // Handle connected state
        break;
}
```

It is tempting to have a default entry in the switch statement. However, when used for switching on an enumeration that defines a state machine, it is best not to have a default entry. The reason is that if you add a state later on, the compiler will helpfully warn that the newly added state has not been cared for in the switch statement. A default block handles the new state, so the compiler won't warn. The same applies to any other type of enumeration defined using the NS_ENUM macro. For example, if used to define styles of a UI element, you would usually want to make sure that switch statements handled all styles.

Things to Remember

✦ Use enumerations to give readable names to values used for the states of a state machine, options passed to methods, or error status codes.

✦ If an enumeration type defines options to a method in which multiple options can be used at the same time, define its values as powers of 2 so that multiple values can be bitwise OR'ed together.

✦ Use the NS_ENUM and NS_OPTIONS macros to define enumeration types with an explicit type. Doing so means that the type is guaranteed to be the one chosen rather than a type chosen by the compiler.

✦ Do not implement a default case in switch statements that handle enumerated types. This helps if you add to the enumeration, because the compiler will warn that the switch does not handle all the values.

Objects, Messaging, and the Runtime

Objects are the building blocks of programming in an object-oriented language such as Objective-C, providing the means by which data is stored and moved around. Messaging is the process by which objects talk to each other to move data around and make things happen. A deep understanding of how both of these features work is crucial to building efficient and maintainable code.

The Objective-C runtime is the code that powers the language once an application is running. The runtime provides the crucial functions that enable messaging between objects to work and all the logic behind how instances of classes are created. Understanding how all this fits together makes you a better developer.

Item 6: Understand Properties

Properties are an Objective-C feature providing encapsulation of the data an object contains. Objects in Objective-C will usually contain a set of instance variables to store the data they need to work. Instance variables are usually accessed through accessor methods. A getter is used to read the variable, and a setter is used to write the variable. This concept was standardized and became part of the Objective-C 2.0 release through a feature called properties, which allow the developer to tell the compiler to write accessor methods automatically. This feature introduced a new "dot syntax" to make accessing the data stored by classes less verbose. You have probably used properties already, but you may not know about all the options. Also, you may not be aware of some of the intricacies surrounding properties. Item 6 illustrates the background surrounding the problem solved by properties and points out their key features.

A class to describe a person might store the person's name, date of birth, address, and so on. You can declare instance variables in the public interface for a class as follows:

```
@interface EOCPerson : NSObject {
@public
    NSString *_firstName;
    NSString *_lastName;
@private
    NSString *_someInternalData;
}
@end
```

This will be familiar if you are coming from the worlds of Java or C++, where you can define the scope of instance variables. However, this technique is rarely used in modern Objective-C. The problem with the approach is that the layout of an object is defined at compile time. Whenever the _firstName variable is accessed, the compiler hard-codes the offset into the memory region where the object is stored. This works fine until you add another instance variable. For example, suppose that another instance variable were added above _firstName:

```
@interface EOCPerson : NSObject {
@public
    NSDate *_dateOfBirth;
    NSString *_firstName;
    NSString *_lastName;
@private
    NSString *_someInternalData;
}
@end
```

The offset that was once pointing to _firstName is now pointing to _dateOfBirth. Any code that had the offset hardcoded would end up reading the wrong value. To illustrate that point, Figure 2.1 shows the memory layout of the class, assuming 4-byte pointers, before and after adding the _dateOfBirth instance variable.

Code that makes use of calculating the offset at compile time will break unless recompiled when the class definition changes. For example, code may exist in a library that uses an old class defini-tion. If linked with code using the new class definition, there will be an incompatibility at runtime. To overcome this problem, languages have invented a variety of techniques. The approach Objective-C has taken is to make instance variables special variables held by class objects (see Item 14 for more on class objects) storing the offset. Then at runtime, the offset is looked up so that if the class defini-tion changes, the offset stored is updated; whenever an access to the instance variable is made, the correct offset is used. You can even add instance variables to classes at runtime. This is known as the

	Person
+0	_firstName
+4	_lastName
+8	_someInternalData

	Person
+0	_dateOfBirth
+4	_firstName
+8	_lastName
+12	_someInternalData

Figure 2.1 Class data layout before and after adding another instance variable

nonfragile Application Binary Interface (ABI). An ABI defines, among other things, the conventions for how code should be generated. The nonfragile ABI also means that instance variables can be defined in a class-continuation category (see Item 27) or in the implementation. So you don't have to have all your instance variables declared in the interface anymore, and you therefore don't leak internal information about your implementation in the public interface.

Encouraging the use of accessor methods rather than accessing instance variables directly is another factor overcoming this problem. Properties are backed by instance variables, but they provide a neat abstraction. You could write accessors yourself, but in true Objective-C style, accessors follow strict naming patterns. Because of this strict naming, it was possible to introduce a language construct to provide a means of automatically creating accessor methods. This is where the @property syntax comes in.

You use properties in the definition of an object interface to provide a standard means of accessing the data encapsulated by an object. As such, properties can also be thought of as shorthand for saying that there are going to be accessors to a variable of a given type and a given name. For example, consider the following class:

```
@interface EOCPerson : NSObject
@property NSString *firstName;
@property NSString *lastName;
@end
```

To a consumer of the class, this is equivalent to writing the class like this:

```
@interface EOCPerson : NSObject
- (NSString*)firstName;
- (void)setFirstName:(NSString*)firstName;
- (NSString*)lastName;
- (void)setLastName:(NSString*)lastName;
@end
```

To use a property, you use the dot syntax, similar to how you would access a member of a stack-allocated struct in plain C. The compiler turns the dot syntax into calls to the accessors, just as if you had invoked them directly. Thus, there is absolutely no difference between using the dot syntax and calling the accessors directly. The following code sample shows the equivalence:

```
EOCPerson *aPerson = [Person new];

aPerson.firstName = @"Bob"; // Same as:
[aPerson setFirstName:@"Bob"];

NSString *lastName = aPerson.lastName; // Same as:
NSString *lastName = [aPerson lastName];
```

But there's more to properties than that. If you let it, the compiler will automatically write the code for you for these methods through a process called autosynthesis. It is important to note that it's the compiler doing this, at compile time, so you won't see source code in your editor for the synthesized methods. Along with generating the code, the compiler also automatically adds an instance variable to the class, of the required type with the name of the property prefixed with an underscore. In the preceding example, there would be two instance variables: _firstName and _lastName. It is possible to control the name of this instance variable by using the @synthesize syntax within the class's implementation, like so:

```
@implementation EOCPerson
@synthesize firstName = _myFirstName;
@synthesize lastName = _myLastName;
@end
```

Using the preceding syntax would yield instance variables called _myFirstName and _myLastName instead of the defaults. It is unusual to want to change the name of the instance variable from the default; however, if you are not a fan of using the underscore approach to naming instance variables, you can use this to name them however you want. But I encourage you to use the default naming scheme, as it makes code readable by everyone if everyone sticks to the same conventions.

If you don't want the compiler to synthesize the accessor methods for you, you can implement the methods yourself. However, if you implement only one of the accessors, the compiler will still synthesize the other for you. Another way to stop it from synthesizing is to use the @dynamic keyword, which tells the compiler to not automatically create an instance variable to back the property and to not create the accessors for you. Also, when compiling code that accesses the property, the compiler will ignore the fact that the accessors have not been defined and trust you that they will be available at runtime. For example, this is used when subclassing CoreData's NSManagedObject, where the accessors are dynamically created at runtime. NSManagedObject opts for this approach because the properties are not instance variables. The data comes from whatever database back end is being used. For example:

```
@interface EOCPerson : NSManagedObject
@property NSString *firstName;
@property NSString *lastName;
@end
```

```
@implementation EOCPerson
@dynamic firstName, lastName;
@end
```

In this class, no accessors or instance variables would be synthesized. Nor would the compiler warn if you attempted to access either property.

Property Attributes

Another aspect of properties that you should be aware of is all the attributes that can be used to control the accessors generated by the compiler. An example using three attributes looks like this:

```
@property (nonatomic, readwrite, copy) NSString *firstName;
```

Four categories of attributes can be applied.

Atomicity

By default, synthesized accessors include locking to make them atomic. If you supply the attribute nonatomic, no locking is used. Note that although there is no atomic attribute (atomic is assumed by the lack of the nonatomic attribute), it can still be applied with no compiler errors in case you want to be explicit. If you define the accessors yourself, you should provide the specified atomicity.

Read/Write

✦ **readwrite** Both a getter and a setter are available. If the property is synthesized, the compiler will generate both methods.

✦ **readonly** Only a getter is available, and the compiler will generate it only if the property is synthesized. You may want to use this if you expose a property only for read externally but redeclare it as read/write internally in the class-continuation category. See Item 27 for more information.

Memory-Management Semantics

Properties encapsulate data, and that data needs to have concrete ownership semantics. This affects only the setter. For example, should the setter retain the new value or simply assign it to the underlying instance variable? When the compiler synthesizes the accessors, it uses these attributes to determine what code to write for you. If you create your own accessors, you must stick to what you specify for this attribute.

✦ **assign** The setter is a simple assign operation used for scalar types, such as CGFloat or NSInteger.

✦ **strong** This designates that the property defines an owning relationship. When a new value is set, it is first retained, the old value is released, and then the value is set.

✦ **weak** This designates that the property defines a nonowning relationship. When a new value is set, it is not retained; nor is the old value released. This is similar to what assign does, but the value is also nilled out when the object pointed to by the property at any time is destroyed.

✦ **unsafe_unretained** This has the same semantics as assign but is used where the type is an object type to indicate a nonowning relationship (unretained) that is not nilled out (unsafe) when the target is destroyed, unlike weak.

✦ **copy** This designates an owning relationship similar to strong; however, instead of retaining the value, it is copied. This is often used when the type is NSString* to preserve encapsulation, since the value passed into the setter might be an instance of the subclass NSMutableString. If it's this mutable variant, the value could be mutated after the property is set, without the object's knowing. So an immutable copy is taken to ensure that the string cannot change from underneath the object. Any object that may be mutable should take a copy.

Method Names

The names of the accessor methods can be controlled by using the following attributes:

✦ **getter=<name>** Specifies the name of the getter. This method is usually used for Boolean properties where you want the getter to be prefixed with is. For example, on the UISwitch class, the property for whether the switch is on or off is defined like so:

```
@property (nonatomic, getter=isOn) BOOL on;
```

✦ **setter=<name>** Specifies the name of the setter. This method is not commonly used.

You can use these attributes to get fine-grained control over the synthesized accessors. However, you should note that if you implement your own accessors, you should make them adhere to the specified attributes yourself. For example, a property declared as copy should ensure that a copy of the object is taken in the setter. Otherwise, users of the property would be under false impressions, and bugs could be introduced from the contract's not being upheld.

Ensuring that you adhere to the semantics laid out in the property definition is important even in other methods that may set the property. For example, consider an extension of the EOCPerson class. It declares the properties' memory-management semantics as copy because the value might be mutable. It also adds an initializer that sets up the initial values of the first and last names:

```
@interface EOCPerson : NSManagedObject

@property (copy) NSString *firstName;
@property (copy) NSString *lastName;

- (id)initWithFirstName:(NSString*)firstName
               lastName:(NSString*)lastName;

@end
```

In the implementation of the custom initializer, it is important to adhere to the copy semantics laid out in the property definitions. The reason is that the property definitions document the contract that the class has with the values that are set. So an implementation of the initializer would look like this:

```
- (id)initWithFirstName:(NSString*)firstName
              lastName:(NSString*)lastName
{
    if ((self = [super init])) {
        _firstName = [firstName copy];
        _lastName = [lastName copy];
    }
    return self;
}
```

You may wonder why you can't simply use the properties' setter methods instead, which will always ensure that the correct semantics are used. You should never use your own accessors in an init (or dealloc) method, as explained further in Item 7.

If you've read Item 18, you'll know that, if possible, it's best to make an object immutable. Applied to EOCPerson, you'd make both properties read-only. The initializer will set the values, after which they cannot be changed. In this scenario, it is important to still declare what memory-management semantics you use for the values. So the property definitions would end up looking like this:

```
@property (copy, readonly) NSString *firstName;
@property (copy, readonly) NSString *lastName;
```

Even though no setters are created, because the properties are read-only, it is still important to document what the semantics are when the initializer is run to set the values. Without this documented, a consumer of the class could not assume that it takes a copy and therefore might make an extra copy before calling the initializer. Doing so would be both redundant and less efficient.

You may wonder how atomic and nonatomic differ. As described earlier, atomic accessors include locks to ensure atomicity. This means that if two threads are reading and writing the same property, the value of the property at any given point in time is valid. Without the locks, or nonatomic, the property value may be read on one thread while another thread is midway through writing to it. If this happens, the value that's read could be invalid.

If you've been developing for iOS at all, you'll notice that all properties are declared nonatomic. The reason is that, historically, the locking introduces such an overhead on iOS that it becomes a performance problem. Usually, atomicity is not required anyway, since it does not ensure thread safety, which usually requires a deeper level of locking. For example, even with atomicity, a single thread might read a property multiple times immediately after one another and obtain different values if another thread is writing to it at the same time. Therefore, you will usually want to use nonatomic properties on iOS. But on Mac OS X, you don't usually find that atomic property access is a performance bottleneck.

Things to Remember

✦ The @property syntax provides a way of defining what data an object encapsulates.

✦ Use attributes to provide the right semantics for the data being stored.

✦ Ensure that anywhere a property's backing instance variable is set, the declared semantics are adhered to.

✦ Use nonatomic on iOS, since performance is severely impacted if atomic is used.

Item 7: Access Instance Variables Primarily Directly When Accessing Them Internally

Properties should always be used to access instance variables of an object externally, but how you access instance variables internally is a hotly debated topic within the Objective-C community. Some suggest always using a property to access instance variables, some suggest always accessing the instance variable directly, and some suggest a mixture of the two. I strongly encourage you to read instance variables using direct access but to set them using the property, with a few caveats.

Consider the following class:

```
@interface EOCPerson : NSObject
@property (nonatomic, copy) NSString *firstName;
@property (nonatomic, copy) NSString *lastName;

// Convenience for firstName + " " + lastName:
- (NSString*)fullName;
- (void)setFullName:(NSString*)fullName;
@end
```

The convenience methods fullName and setFullName: might be implemented like this:

```
- (NSString*)fullName {
    return [NSString stringWithFormat:@"%@ %@",
            self.firstName, self.lastName];
```

```
}

/** The following assumes all full names have exactly 2
 *  parts. The method could be rewritten to support more
 *  exotic names.
 */
- (void)setFullName:(NSString*)fullName {
    NSArray *components =
        [fullName componentsSeparatedByString:@" "];
    self.firstName = [components objectAtIndex:0];
    self.lastName = [components objectAtIndex:1];
}
```

In both the getter and the setter, we access the instance variables via the accessor methods, using the property dot syntax. Now suppose that you rewrote both methods to access the instance variables directly:

```
- (NSString*)fullName {
    return [NSString stringWithFormat:@"%@ %@",
            _firstName, _lastName];
}
```

```
- (void)setFullName:(NSString*)fullName {
    NSArray *components =
        [fullName componentsSeparatedByString:@" "];
    _firstName = [components objectAtIndex:0];
    _lastName = [components objectAtIndex:1];
}
```

The two styles have a few differences.

✦ Direct access to the instance variables will undoubtedly be faster, as it does not have to go through Objective-C method dispatch (see Item 11). The compiler will emit code that directly accesses the memory where the object's instance variables are stored.

✦ Direct access bypasses the property's memory-management semantics defined by the setter. For example, if your property is declared as copy, directly setting the instance variable will not cause a copy to be made. The new value will be retained and the old value released.

✦ Key-Value Observing (KVO) notifications would not be fired when accessing the instance variables directly. This may or may not be a problem, depending on how you want your objects to behave.

✦ Accessing through properties can make it easier to debug issues surrounding a property, since you can add a breakpoint to the getter and/or setter to determine who is accessing the properties and when.

A good compromise is to write instance variables using the setter and to read using direct access. Doing so has the benefit of fast reading and not losing the control of writing via properties. The most important reason for writing via the setter is that you will ensure that the memory-management semantics are upheld. There are, however, a few caveats to that approach.

The first caveat is when values are set within an initializer method. Here, you should always use direct instance variable access, because subclasses could override the setter. Consider that EOCPerson has a subclass EOCSmithPerson that is designed to be used only for people whose last name is "Smith." This subclass might override the setter for lastName like so:

```
- (void)setLastName:(NSString*)lastName {
    if (![lastName isEqualToString:@"Smith"]) {
        [NSException raise:NSInvalidArgumentException
                    format:@"Last name must be Smith"];
    }
    self.lastName = lastname;
}
```

The base class EOCPerson might set the last name to the empty string in its default initializer. If it did this through the setter, the subclass's setter would be called and throw an exception. However, there are some cases in which you must use the setter in an initializer. This is when the instance variable is declared within a superclass; you cannot access the instance variable directly anyway, so you must use the setter.

Another caveat is when the property uses lazy initialization. In this case, you have to go via the getter; if you don't, the instance variable will never get a chance to be initialized. For example, the EOCPerson class might have a property to give access to a complex object representing each person's brain. If this property is infrequently accessed and expensive to set up, you might initialize it lazily in the getter, like this:

```
- (EOCBrain*)brain {
    if (!_brain) {
        _brain = [Brain new];
    }
    return _brain;
}
```

If you were to access the instance variable directly and the getter had not been called yet, brain would not have been set up, and you would need to call the accessor for all accesses to the brain property.

Things to Remember

- ✦ Prefer to read data directly through instance variables internally and to write data through properties internally.

- ✦ Within initializers and dealloc, always read and write data directly through instance variables.

- ✦ Sometimes, you will need to read data through properties when that data is being lazily initialized.

Item 8: Understand Object Equality

Being able to compare objects for equality is extremely useful. However, comparing using the == operator is usually not what you want to do, since doing so compares the pointers themselves rather than the objects to which they point. Instead, you should use the isEqual: method declared within the NSObject protocol to check any two objects for equality. Usually, however, two objects of a different class are always determined to be unequal. Some objects also provide special equality-checking methods that you can use if you already know that the two objects you are checking are of the same class. Take, for example, the following code:

```
NSString *foo = @"Badger 123";
NSString *bar = [NSString stringWithFormat:@"Badger %i", 123];
BOOL equalA = (foo == bar); //< equalA = NO
BOOL equalB = [foo isEqual:bar]; //< equalB = YES
BOOL equalC = [foo isEqualToString:bar]; //< equalC = YES
```

Here, you can see the difference between == and using equality methods. NSString is an example of a class that implements its own equality-checking method, called isEqualToString:. The object passed to this method must also be an NSString; otherwise, the results are undefined. This method is designed to be faster than calling isEqual:, which has to do extra steps because it doesn't know the class of the object being compared.

The two methods at the heart of equality checking from the NSObject protocol are as follows:

```
- (BOOL)isEqual:(id)object;
- (NSUInteger)hash;
```

The default implementations of these methods from the NSObject class itself work such that two objects are equal if and only if their pointer values are exactly the same. To understand how to override these for your own objects, it's important to understand the contract. Any two objects determined to be equal using the isEqual: method must return the same value from the hash method. However, two objects that return the same value from the hash method do not have to be equal according to the isEqual: method.

For example, consider the following class:

```
@interface EOCPerson : NSObject
@property (nonatomic, copy) NSString *firstName;
@property (nonatomic, copy) NSString *lastName;
@property (nonatomic, assign) NSUInteger age;
@end
```

Two EOCPerson objects are equal if all the fields are equal. So the isEqual: method would look like this:

```
- (BOOL)isEqual:(id)object {
    if (self == object) return YES;
    if ([self class] != [object class]) return NO;

    EOCPerson *otherPerson = (EOCPerson*)object;
    if (![_firstName isEqualToString:otherPerson.firstName])
        return NO;
    if (![_lastName isEqualToString:otherPerson.lastName])
        return NO;
    if (_age != otherPerson.age)
        return NO;
    return YES;
}
```

First, the object is checked for direct pointer equality to self. If the pointers are equal, the objects must be equal, since they are the same object! Next, the class of the two objects is compared. If the class is not the same, the two objects cannot be equal. After all, an EOCPerson cannot be equal to an EOCDog. Of course, you may want an instance of EOCPerson to be equal to an instance of a subclass of it: for example, EOCSmithPerson. This illustrates a common problem in inheritance hierarchies with equality. You should consider this when implementing your isEqual: methods. Last, each property is checked for equality. If any of them are not equal, the two objects are deemed unequal; otherwise, they are equal.

That leaves the hash method. Recall the contract whereby equal objects must return the same hash, but objects with the same hash do not necessarily need to be equal. Therefore, this is essential to override if you override isEqual:. A perfectly acceptable hash method would be the following:

```
- (NSUInteger)hash {
    return 1337;
}
```

However, this could lead to performance problems if you ever put these objects in a collection, since the hash is used as an index within the hash tables that collections use. A set implementation might use the hash to bin objects into different arrays. Then when an object is added to the set, the array corresponding to its hash is enumerated to see whether any objects in that array are equal. If they are, the object is already in the set. Therefore, if you return the same hash value for every object and you add 1,000,000 objects to the set, each further addition to the set has to scan each of those 1,000,000 objects.

Another implementation of the hash method might be:

```
- (NSUInteger)hash {
    NSString *stringToHash =
        [NSString stringWithFormat:@"%@:%@:%i",
            _firstName, _lastName, _age];
    return [stringToHash hash];
}
```

This time, the algorithm of NSString's hash method is piggybacked by creating a string and returning the hash of that. Doing so adheres to the contract, since two EOCPerson objects that are equal will always return the same hash. However, the downside of this approach is that it is much slower than returning a single value, since you have the overhead of creating a string. This can again cause performance issues when adding the object to a collection, since the hash has to be calculated for the object being added to the collection.

A third and final approach is to create a hash like this:

```
- (NSUInteger)hash {
    NSUInteger firstNameHash = [_firstName hash];
    NSUInteger lastNameHash = [_lastName hash];
    NSUInteger ageHash = _age;
    return firstNameHash ^ lastNameHash ^ ageHash;
}
```

This approach is a middle ground between efficiency and creating at least some range of hashes. There will, of course, be collisions with hashes created using this algorithm, but at least multiple return values are possible. The tradeoff between collision frequency and a computationally intensive hash method is something that you should experiment with and see what works for your object.

Class-Specific Equality Methods

Other than NSString as described earlier, classes that provide a specific equality method include NSArray (isEqualToArray:) and NSDictionary (isEqualToDictionary:), both of which will throw an exception if the object being compared is not an array or a dictionary, respectively. Objective-C has is no strong type checking at compile time, so you could easily accidentally pass in an object of the wrong type. Therefore, you need to be sure that the object you're passing in is indeed of the correct type.

You may decide to create your own equality method if equality is likely to be checked frequently; therefore, the extra speed from not having to check types is significant. Another reason for providing a specific method is purely cosmetic where you think that it looks better and is more readable, which is likely part of the motivation for NSString's isEqualToString: method. Code that uses this method is easier to read, as you don't have to hunt for the types of the two objects being compared.

If you do create a specific method, you should override the isEqual: method also and pass through if the class of the object being compared is the same as the receiver. If it's not, passing through to the superclass implementation is common practice. For example, the EOCPerson class could implement the following:

```
- (BOOL)isEqualToPerson:(EOCPerson*)otherPerson {
    if (self == object) return YES;

    if (![_firstName isEqualToString:otherPerson.firstName])
        return NO;
    if (![_lastName isEqualToString:otherPerson.lastName])
        return NO;
    if (_age != otherPerson.age)
        return NO;
    return YES;
}
```

```
- (BOOL)isEqual:(id)object {
    if ([self class] == [object class]) {
        return [self isEqualToPerson:(EOCPerson*)object];
    } else {
        return [super isEqual:object];
    }
}
```

Deep versus Shallow Equality

When you create an equality method, you need to decide whether to check the whole object for equality or simply a few fields. NSArray checks whether the two arrays being compared contain the same number of objects and if so, iterates through them and calls isEqual: on each. If all objects are equal, the two arrays are deemed to be equal, known as deep equality. Sometimes, however, if you know that only a selection of the data determines equality, it is valid to not check every bit of data for equality.

For example, using the EOCPerson class, if instances had come from a database, they might have another property added with a unique identifier used as the primary key in the database:

@property NSUInteger identifier;

In such a scenario, you may decide to check only that the identifiers match, especially if the properties were declared readonly externally such that you can be certain that if two objects have the same identifier, they are indeed representing the same object and are therefore equal. This would save on having to check through every single bit of data that the EOCPerson object contains when you can assert that if the identifiers match, so must the rest of the data, since it came from the same data source.

Whether or not you check all fields in your equality method depends entirely on the object in question. Only you can know what it means for two instances of your object to be equal.

Equality of Mutable Classes in Containers

An important scenario to consider is when mutable classes are put into containers. Once you add an object to a collection, its hash should not change. Earlier, I explained how objects are binned according to their hash. If their hash changes once in a bin, the objects would be in the wrong bin. To get around this problem, you can either ensure that the hash is not dependent on the mutable portions of the object or simply not mutate objects once they are in collections. In Item 18,

I explain why you should make objects immutable. This is a great example of such a reason.

You can see this problem in action by testing with an NSMutableSet and a few NSMutableArrays. Start by adding one array to the set:

```
NSMutableSet *set = [NSMutableSet new];

NSMutableArray *arrayA = [@[@1, @2] mutableCopy];
[set addObject:arrayA];
NSLog(@"set = %@", set);
// Output: set = {((1,2))}
```

The set contains one object: an array with two objects in it. Now add an array that contains equal objects in the same order, such that the array already in the set and the new one are equal:

```
NSMutableArray *arrayB = [@[@1, @2] mutableCopy];
[set addObject:arrayB];
NSLog(@"set = %@", set);
// Output: set = {((1,2))}
```

The set still contains just a single object, since the object added is equal to the object already in there. Now we add to the set an array that is not equal to the array already in the set:

```
NSMutableArray *arrayC = [@[@1] mutableCopy];
[set addObject:arrayC];
NSLog(@"set = %@", set);
// Output: set = {((1),(1,2))}
```

As expected, the set now contains two arrays: the original one and the new one, since arrayC does not equal the one already in the set. Finally, we mutate arrayC to be equal to the other array already in the set:

```
[arrayC addObject:@2];
NSLog(@"set = %@", set);
// Output: set = {((1,2),(1,2))}
```

Ah, oh dear, now two arrays in the set are equal to each other! A set is not meant to allow this, but it has been unable to maintain its semantics because we've mutated one of the objects that was already in the set. What's even more awkward is if the set is then copied:

```
NSSet *setB = [set copy];
NSLog(@"setB = %@", setB);
// Output: setB = {((1,2))}
```

The copied set has only a single object in it, just as if the set had been created by making an empty set and one by one adding the entries from the original. This may or may not be what you expected. You may have thought that it would copy verbatim the original, with the corruption included. Or you may have thought that it would do what it did. Both would be valid copying algorithms, which further illustrates the point that the set had become corrupt and so all bets are off when dealing with it.

The moral of this story is to be aware of what can happen when you mutate an object that's in a collection. It's not to say you should never do it, but you should be aware of the potential problems and code accordingly.

Things to Remember

✦ Provide isEqual: and hash methods for objects that you will want to check for equality.

✦ Objects that are equal must have the same hash, but objects that have the same hash do not necessarily have to be equal.

✦ Determine what is necessary to test for equality rather than bluntly testing every property.

✦ Write hash methods that will be quick but provide a reasonably low level of collisions.

Item 9: Use the Class Cluster Pattern to Hide Implementation Detail

A class cluster is a great way to hide implementation detail behind an abstract base class. This pattern is prevalent within the Objective-C system frameworks. An example from UIKit, the user interface framework for iOS, is UIButton. To create a button, you call the following class method:

```
+ (UIButton*)buttonWithType:(UIButtonType)type;
```

The type of the object returned will depend on the button type passed in. However, all classes inherit from the same base class, UIButton. The point of doing this is that the consumer of the UIButton class does not care about the type of the button being created and the implementation detail behind how that button draws itself. All it needs to know is how to create a button; set attributes, such as the title; and add targets for touch actions.

Going back to basics, this problem could be solved by having a single class that handles all button drawing and switches based on the type:

```
- (void)drawRect:(CGRect)rect {
    if (_type == TypeA) {
        // Draw TypeA button
    } else if (_type == TypeB) {
        // Draw TypeB button
    } /* … */
}
```

It's clear, however, that this approach would become very cumbersome if many methods required switching on the type. A good programmer at this point might refactor such that there are multiple subclasses that do the specialist work required of each button type. However, doing so would require a user to know about all the different subclasses. This is where the Class Cluster pattern comes into its own and provides the flexibility of multiple subclasses while keeping a clean interface by hiding them away behind an abstract base class. You don't create instances of the subclasses; you let the base class create them for you.

Creating a Class Cluster

As an example of how to create a class cluster, consider a class for handling employees, all of whom have a name and salary and can be told to do a day's work. What happens when each does a day's work, however, is different for each type of employee. The manager of the business in which these employees are held doesn't care about what happens when each individual does his or her work but simply tells the employees to do it.

First, you need to define the abstract base class:

```
typedef NS_ENUM(NSUInteger, EOCEmployeeType) {
    EOCEmployeeTypeDeveloper,
    EOCEmployeeTypeDesigner,
    EOCEmployeeTypeFinance,
};

@interface EOCEmployee : NSObject

@property (copy) NSString *name;
@property NSUInteger salary;

// Helper for creating Employee objects
+ (EOCEmployee*)employeeWithType:(EOCEmployeeType)type;

// Make Employees do their respective day's work
```

```objc
- (void)doADaysWork;

@end

@implementation EOCEmployee

+ (EOCEmployee*)employeeWithType:(EOCEmployeeType)type {
    switch (type) {
        case EOCEmployeeTypeDeveloper:
            return [EOCEmployeeDeveloper new];
            break;
        case EOCEmployeeTypeDesigner:
            return [EOCEmployeeDesigner new];
            break;
        case EOCEmployeeTypeFinance:
            return [EOCEmployeeFinance new];
            break;
    }
}

- (void)doADaysWork {
    // Subclasses implement this.
}

@end
```

Each concrete subclass inherits from the base class. For example:

```objc
@interface EOCEmployeeDeveloper : EOCEmployee
@end

@implementation EOCEmployeeDeveloper

- (void)doADaysWork {
    [self writeCode];
}

@end
```

In this example, the base class implements a method declared as a class method, which switches based on the type of employee being created and allocates an instance of the required class. This Factory pattern is one way of creating a class cluster.

Unfortunately, Objective-C gives no language feature for designating that the base class is abstract. Instead, convention for how to use a class should be made in documentation. In this case, there is no init family method defined in the interface, which indicates that perhaps instances should not be created directly. Another way to ensure that instances of the base class are not used would be to throw an exception in doADaysWork in the base class. However, this is quite extreme and usually unnecessary.

It is important to take care when using objects that are members of a class cluster during introspection (see Item 14). The reason is that even though you think you have created an instance of one class, you have in fact created an instance of a subclass. In the Employee example, you might have thought that calling [employee isMemberOfClass:[EOCEmployee class]] would return YES, but it's not really an Employee that has been returned, so this call would return NO.

Class Clusters in Cocoa

There are many class clusters in the system frameworks. Most of the collection classes are class clusters, such as NSArray, and its mutable counterpart, NSMutableArray. So, in fact, there are two abstract base classes: one for immutable arrays and one for mutable arrays. It's still a class cluster but with two public interfaces. The immutable class defines the methods common to all arrays, and the mutable class defines the methods that are present only on mutable arrays. The fact that it is a class cluster means that it's easy to both share code behind the scenes between the two array types and support creating copies that change the mutability.

In the case of NSArray, when an instance is allocated, it's an instance of another class that's allocated (during a call to alloc), known as a placeholder array. This placeholder array is then converted to an instance of another class, which is a concrete subclass of NSArray. This is a pretty little dance but beyond the scope of this book to explain fully.

Being aware that classes like NSArray (and most of the other collection classes, for that matter) are class clusters is important because otherwise, you might write the following code:

```
id maybeAnArray = /* … */;
if ([maybeAnArray class] == [NSArray class]) {
    // Will never be hit
}
```

Knowing that NSArray is a class cluster should make you understand why this code is incorrect and the if statement will never be true. The class returned from [maybeAnArray class] will never be the NSArray class, since instances returned from NSArray's initializers are instances of internal types behind the class cluster public facade.

Note that it is still possible to check the class of an instance of a class cluster. Instead of the preceding, you should use the introspection methods. Item 14 illustrates these methods. Instead of checking equality of class objects, you should do the following:

```
id maybeAnArray = /* … */;
if ([maybeAnArray isKindOfClass:[NSArray class]]) {
    // Will be hit
}
```

Adding a concrete implementation into a class cluster is a common requirement, but caution should be observed when attempting it. In the case of the Employee example, adding a new employee type would be impossible without having the source of the factory method to add to. In the case of Cocoa's class clusters, such as NSArray, it can be done, but a few rules must be obeyed. They are as follows.

+ *The subclass should inherit from the class cluster's abstract base class.*

In the case of NSArray, this could be either the immutable or the mutable base class.

+ *The subclass should define its own storage.*

This part is often where people get stuck in subclassing something like NSArray. You must have inside your subclass an instance variable that holds the objects the array contains. This seems somewhat contrary to expectations, as surely that's what NSArray itself does. But remember that NSArray itself is simply a shim around other hidden objects that purely defines the interface to arrays. A good choice of object to use to hold the instances of a custom array subclass would be an NSArray itself.

+ *The subclass should override a documented set of methods of the superclass.*

Each abstract base class has a set of methods that subclasses must implement. In the case of NSArray, the methods that need to be implemented are count and objectAtIndex:. Other methods, such as lastObject, don't have to be implemented, since they use these two methods themselves.

All the specifics of how to subclass a class cluster should be defined in the class's documentation, so you should always read that first.

Things to Remember

+ The Class Cluster pattern can be used to hide implementation detail behind a simple public facade.

✦ Class clusters are commonly used in the system frameworks.

✦ Care should be taken when subclassing a class cluster's public abstract class, and documentation, if it exists, should always be read.

Item 10: Use Associated Objects to Attach Custom Data to Existing Classes

Sometimes, you want to associate information with an object. Normally, you would do this by subclassing the object's class and use that instead. However, you can't always do this, since instances of the class might be created for you by some means and you cannot tell it to create instances of your class instead. That's where the powerful Objective-C feature called Associated Objects comes in handy.

Objects are associated with other objects, using a key to identify them. They are also designated a storage policy to govern memory-management semantics of the stored value. The storage policies are defined by the enumeration objc_AssociationPolicy, which contains the values shown in Table 2.1 against the @property attribute for the equivalent if the association were a property (see Item 6 for further information on properties).

Management of associations is performed using the following methods:

✦ void objc_setAssociatedObject(id object, void *key, id value, objc_AssociationPolicy policy)

Sets up an association of object to value with the given key and policy.

✦ id objc_getAssociatedObject(id object, void *key)

Retrieves the value for the association on object with the given key.

Table 2.1 Object Association Types

Association Type	Equivalent @property attributes
OBJC_ASSOCIATION_ASSIGN	assign
OBJC_ASSOCIATION_RETAIN_NONATOMIC	nonatomic, retain
OBJC_ASSOCIATION_COPY_NONATOMIC	nonatomic, copy
OBJC_ASSOCIATION_RETAIN	retain
OBJC_ASSOCIATION_COPY	copy

✦ void objc_removeAssociatedObjects(id object)

Removes all associations against object.

The accessing of associated objects is functionally similar to imagining that the object is an NSDictionary and calling [object setObject:value forKey:key] and [object objectForKey:key]. An important difference to note, though, is that key is treated purely as an opaque pointer. Whereas with a dictionary, keys are regarded equal if they return YES for isEqual:, the key for associated objects must be the exact same pointer for them to match. For this reason, it is common to use static global variables for the keys.

An Example of Using Associated Objects

In iOS development, it's common to use the UIAlertView class, which provides a standard view for showing an alert to the user. There's a delegate protocol to handle when the user taps a button to close it; however, using delegation splits up the code of creation of the alert and handling the tap. This makes it slightly awkward to read, as the code is split between two places. Here is an example of what using a UIAlertView would look like normally:

```
- (void)askUserAQuestion {
    UIAlertView *alert = [[UIAlertView alloc]
                        initWithTitle:@"Question"
                          message:@"What do you want to do?"
                          delegate:self
                    cancelButtonTitle:@"Cancel"
                    otherButtonTitles:@"Continue", nil];
        [alert show];
}

// UIAlertViewDelegate protocol method
- (void)alertView:(UIAlertView *)alertView
        clickedButtonAtIndex:(NSInteger)buttonIndex
{
    if (buttonIndex == 0) {
        [self doCancel];
    } else {
        [self doContinue];
    }
}
```

This pattern gets even more complicated if you ever want to present more than one alert in the same class, since you then have to check the alertView parameter passed into the delegate method and switch based on that. It would be much simpler if the logic for what to do when each button is tapped could be decided when the alert is created. This is where an associated object can be used. A solution is to set a block against an alert when it is created and then read that block out when the delegate method is run. Implementing it would look like this:

```objc
#import <objc/runtime.h>

static void *EOCMyAlertViewKey = "EOCMyAlertViewKey";

- (void)askUserAQuestion {
    UIAlertView *alert = [[UIAlertView alloc]
                            initWithTitle:@"Question"
                              message:@"What do you want to do?"
                               delegate:self
                        cancelButtonTitle:@"Cancel"
                        otherButtonTitles:@"Continue", nil];

    void (^block)(NSInteger) = ^(NSInteger buttonIndex){
        if (buttonIndex == 0) {
            [self doCancel];
        } else {
            [self doContinue];
        }
    };

    objc_setAssociatedObject(alert,
                             EOCMyAlertViewKey,
                             block,
                             OBJC_ASSOCIATION_COPY);

    [alert show];
}

// UIAlertViewDelegate protocol method
- (void)alertView:(UIAlertView*)alertView
        clickedButtonAtIndex:(NSInteger)buttonIndex
{
    void (^block)(NSInteger) =
        objc_getAssociatedObject(alertView, EOCMyAlertViewKey);
    block(buttonIndex);
}
```

With this approach, the code for creating the alert and handling the result is all in one place, making it more readable than before, as you don't have to flick between two portions of code to understand why the alert view is being used. You would, however, need to be careful with this approach, as retain cycles could easily be introduced if the block captured. See Item 40 for more information on this problem.

As you can see, this approach is very powerful, but it should be used only when there's no other way of achieving what you need to do. Widespread use of this approach could get out of hand very quickly and make debugging difficult. Retain cycles become harder to reason, since there is no formal definition of the relationship between the associated objects, as the memory-management semantics are defined at association time rather than in an interface definition. So proceed with caution when using this approach, and do not use it purely because you can. An alternative way of achieving the same with UIAlertView would be to subclass it and add a property to store the block. I would suggest this approach over associated objects if the alert view were to be used more than once.

Things to Remember

+ Associated objects provide a means of linking two objects together.

+ The memory-management semantics of associated objects can be defined to mimic owning or nonowning relationships.

+ Associated objects should be used only when another approach is not possible, since they can easily introduce hard-to-find bugs.

Item 11: Understand the Role of objc_msgSend

One of the most common things you'll do in Objective-C is call methods on objects. In Objective-C terminology, this is called passing a message. Messages have names, or selectors, take arguments, and may return a value.

Since Objective-C is a superset of C, it's a good idea to start by understanding that calling a function in C uses what is known as static binding, which means that the function being called is known at compile time. For example, consider the following code:

```
#import <stdio.h>

void printHello() {
    printf("Hello, world!\n");
}
```

```
void printGoodbye() {
    printf("Goodbye, world!\n");
}

void doTheThing(int type) {
    if (type == 0) {
        printHello();
    } else {
        printGoodbye();
    }
    return 0;
}
```

Ignoring inlining, when this is compiled, printHello and printGoodbye are known, and the compiler emits instructions to directly call the functions. The addresses of the functions are effectively hardcoded into the instructions. Consider now if that had been written like this:

```
#import <stdio.h>

void printHello() {
    printf("Hello, world!\n");
}
void printGoodbye() {
    printf("Goodbye, world!\n");
}

void doTheThing(int type) {
    void (*fnc)();
    if (type == 0) {
        fnc = printHello;
    } else {
        fnc = printGoodbye;
    }
    fnc();
    return 0;
}
```

Here, dynamic binding is used, since the function being called is unknown until runtime. The difference in the instructions the compiler emits will be that in the first example, a function call is made inside both the if and the else statements. In the second example, only a single function call is made but at the cost of having to read the address of which function to call rather than being hardcoded.

Dynamic binding is the mechanism by which methods in Objective-C are invoked when a message is passed to an object. All methods are plain old C functions under the hood, but which one is invoked for a given message is decided entirely at runtime and can even change throughout the course of an app running, making Objective-C truly dynamic.

A message being called on an object looks like this:

```
id returnValue = [someObject messageName:parameter];
```

In this example, someObject is referred to as the receiver, and messageName is the selector. The selector combined with the parameters is known as the message. When it sees this message, the compiler turns it into a standard C function call to the function at the heart of messaging, objc_msgSend, which has the following prototype:

```
void objc_msgSend(id self, SEL cmd, ...)
```

This is a variadic function that takes two or more parameters. The first parameter is the receiver, the second parameter is the selector (SEL is the type of a selector), and the remaining parameters are the message parameters in the order they appear. A selector is the name that refers to a method. The term *selector* is often used interchangeably with the term *method*. The preceding example message will be converted to the following:

```
id returnValue = objc_msgSend(someObject,
                              @selector(messageName:),
                              parameter);
```

The objc_msgSend function calls the correct method, depending on the type of the receiver and the selector. In order to do this, the function looks through the list of methods implemented by the receiver's class and, if it finds a method that matches the selector name, jumps to its implementation. If not, the function traverses up the inheritance hierarchy to find the method to jump to. If no matching method is found, message forwarding kicks in. For further explanation on message forwarding, see Item 12.

This may all sound like a lot of work to go through whenever a method is invoked. Fortunately, objc_msgSend caches the result in a fast map, one for each class, so that future messages to the same class and selector combination are executed quickly. Even this fast path is slower than for a statically bound function call but not by very much once the selector is cached; in reality, message dispatch is not the bottleneck in an application. If it were, you could drop down to writing a C function anyway and call that, passing in any state from the Objective-C object as required.

The preceding stands only for certain messages. Additional functions are exposed by the Objective-C runtime to handle certain edge cases:

✦ `objc_msgSend_stret`

For sending messages that return a struct. This function can handle only messages that return a type that fits into CPU registers. If the return type doesn't fit—for example, if a struct is returned—another function is called to perform the dispatch. In this case, another function is called to handle returning the struct via a stack-allocated variable.

✦ `objc_msgSend_fpret`

For sending messages that return floating-point values. Some architectures require special handling of floating-point registers across function calls, meaning that the standard `objc_msgSend` is not good enough. This function exists to handle such slightly odd cases that crop up for such architectures as x86.

✦ `objc_msgSendSuper`

For sending messages to the superclass, such as [super message:parameter]. There are also equivalents of `objc_msgSend_stret` and `objc_msgSend_fpret` for calling super as well.

I alluded earlier to the fact that `objc_msgSend` and friends "jump to" the correct method implementation once it has been looked up. The way this works is that every method of an Objective-C object can be thought of as a simple C function, whose prototype is of the following form:

```
<return_type> Class_selector(id self, SEL _cmd, ...)
```

The name of the function is not quite like this, but I've shown it as a combination of the class and the selector just to illustrate the point. Pointers to functions like this are held in a table within each class, keyed against the selector name. It's this that the `objc_msgSend` family of methods looks through to find the implementation to jump to. Note that the prototype is strangely similar to the `objc_msgSend` function itself. This is no coincidence. It makes jumping to the method simpler and can make good use of tail-call optimizations.

Tail-call optimization occurs when the last thing a function does is call another function. Instead of pushing a new stack frame, the compiler can emit code to jump to the next function. This can be done only if the final thing a function does is call another function and does not need to use the return value for anything. Using this optimization is crucial for objc_msgSend because without it, the stack trace would show objc_msgSend right before every Objective-C method. Also, stack overflow would occur prematurely.

In reality, you do not need to worry about all this when writing Objective-C, but it is good to understand the fundamentals of what is going on under the hood. If you understand what happens when a message is invoked, you can appreciate how your code is executing and why you see objc_msgSend constantly in backtraces when debugging.

Things to Remember

+ A message consists of a receiver, a selector, and parameters. Invoking a message is synonymous with calling a method on an object.

+ When invoked, all messages go through the dynamic message dispatch system whereby the implementation is looked up and then run.

Item 12: Understand Message Forwarding

Item 11 explains why it's important to understand the way messages are sent to objects. Item 12 explores why it's important to understand what happens when a message is sent to an object that it doesn't understand.

A class can understand only messages that it has been programmed to understand, through implementing methods. But it's not a compile-time error to send a message to a class that it doesn't understand, since methods can be added to classes at runtime so the compiler has no way of knowing whether a method implementation is going to exist. When it receives a method that it doesn't understand, an object goes through message forwarding, a process designed to allow you as the developer to tell the message how to handle the unknown message.

Even if you are unaware of it, you will very likely already have encountered messages going through the message-forwarding pathways. Every time you've seen a message such as the following in the console, it's because you've sent a message to an object that it doesn't understand and the default NSObject implementation of the forwarding path has kicked in:

```
-[__NSCFNumber lowercaseString]: unrecognized selector sent to
instance 0x87
```

```
*** Terminating app due to uncaught exception
'NSInvalidArgumentException', reason: '-[__NSCFNumber
lowercaseString]: unrecognized selector sent to instance 0x87'
```

This is an exception being thrown from NSObject's method called doesNotRecognizeSelector: telling you that the receiver of the message is of type __NSCFNumber and that it doesn't understand the selector lowercaseString. That's not really surprising in this case, since NSNumber (__NSCFNumber is the internal class used in toll-free bridging—see Item 49—which is created when you allocate an NSNumber). In this case, the forwarding pathways ended in the application's crashing, but you can hook into the forwarding pathways in your own classes to perform any desired logic instead of crashing.

The forwarding pathways are split into two avenues. The first gives the class to which the receiver belongs a chance to dynamically add a method for the unknown selector. This is called dynamic method resolution. The second avenue is the full forwarding mechanism. If the runtime has made it this far, it knows that there's no longer a chance for the receiver itself to respond to the selector. So it asks the receiver to try to handle the invocation itself. It does this in two steps. First, it asks whether another object should receive the message instead. If there is, the runtime diverts the message, and everything proceeds as normal. If there is no replacement receiver, the full forwarding mechanism is put into effect, using the NSInvocation object to wrap up the full details about the message that is currently unhandled and gives the receiver one final chance to handle it.

Dynamic Method Resolution

The first method that's called when a message is passed to an object that it doesn't understand is a class method on the object's class:

```
+ (BOOL)resolveInstanceMethod:(SEL)selector
```

This method takes the selector that was not found and returns a Boolean to indicate whether an instance method was added to the class that can now handle that selector. Thus, the class is given a second opportunity to add an implementation before proceeding with the rest of the forwarding mechanism. A similar method, called resolveClassMethod:, is called when the unimplemented method is a class method rather than an instance method.

Using this approach requires the implementation of the method to already be available, ready to plug in to the class dynamically. This method is often used to implement @dynamic properties (see Item 6), such as occurs in CoreData for accessing properties of

NSManagedObjects, since the methods required to implement such prop-erties can be known at compile time.

Such an implementation of resolveInstanceMethod: for use with @dynamic properties might look like this:

```
id autoDictionaryGetter(id self, SEL _cmd);
void autoDictionarySetter(id self, SEL _cmd, id value);

+ (BOOL)resolveInstanceMethod:(SEL)selector {
    NSString *selectorString = NSStringFromSelector(selector);
    if ( /* selector is from a @dynamic property */ ) {
        if ([selectorString hasPrefix:@"set"]) {
            class_addMethod(self,
                            selector,
                            (IMP)autoDictionarySetter,
                            "v@:@");
        } else {
            class_addMethod(self,
                            selector,
                            (IMP)autoDictionaryGetter,
                            "@@:");
        }
        return YES;
    }
    return [super resolveInstanceMethod:selector];
}
```

The selector is obtained as a string and then checked to see whether it looks like a setter. If it is prefixed with set, it is assumed to be a setter; otherwise, it is assumed to be a getter. In each case, a method is added to the class for the given selector pointing to an implemen-tation defined as a pure C function. In these C functions there would be code to manipulate whatever data structure was being used by the class to store the properties' data. For example, in the case of Core-Data, these methods would talk to the database back end to retrieve or update values accordingly.

Replacement Receiver

The second attempt to handle an unknown selector is to ask the receiver whether a replacement receiver is available to handle the message instead. The method that handles this is:

```
- (id)forwardingTargetForSelector:(SEL)selector
```

The unknown selector is passed in, and the receiver is expected to return the object to act as its replacement or nil if no replacement can be found. This method can be used to provide some of the benefits of multiple inheritance by combining its use with composition. An object could own a range of other objects internally that it returns in this method for selectors that they handle, making it look as though it is itself handling them.

Note that there is no way to manipulate the message using this part of the forwarding path. If the message needs to be altered before sending to the replacement receiver, the full forwarding mechanism must be used.

Full Forwarding Mechanism

If the forwarding algorithm has come this far, the only thing left to do is to apply the full forwarding mechanism. This starts by creating an NSInvocation object to wrap up all the details about the message that is left unhandled. This object contains the selector, target, and arguments. An NSInvocation object can be invoked, which causes the message-dispatch system to whir into action and dispatch the message to its target.

The method that gets called to attempt forwarding this way is:

```
- (void)forwardInvocation:(NSInvocation*)invocation
```

A simple implementation would change the target of the invocation and invoke it. This would be equivalent to using the replacement receiver method, so such a simple implementation is rarely used. A more useful implementation would be to change the message in some way before invoking it, such as appending another argument or changing the selector.

An implementation of this method should always call its superclass's implementation for invocations it doesn't handle. This means that once all superclasses in the hierarchy have been given a chance to handle the invocation, NSObject's implementation will be called. This invokes doesNotRecognizeSelector: to raise the unhandled selector exception.

The Full Picture

The process through which forwarding is handled can be described by a flow diagram like that shown in Figure 2.2.

At each step, the receiver is given a chance to handle the message. Each step is more expensive than the one before it. The best scenario is that the method is resolved at the first step, since the method that was resolved will end up being cached by the runtime such that forwarding does not have to kick in at all next time the same selector

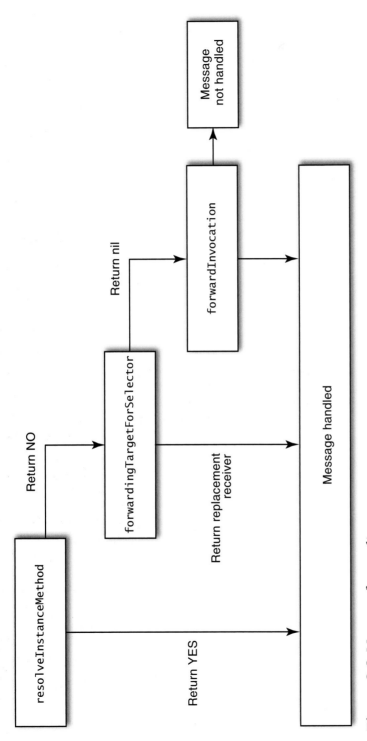

Figure 2.2 Message forwarding

is invoked on an instance of the same class. At the second step, forwarding a message to another receiver is simply an optimization of the third step for the case in which a replacement receiver can be found. In that case, the only thing that needs to be changed about the invocation is the target, which is much simpler to do than the final step, in which a complete NSInvocation needs to be created and handled.

Full Example of Dynamic Method Resolution

To illustrate how forwarding can be useful, the following example shows the use of dynamic method resolution to provide @dynamic properties. Consider an object that allows you to store any object in it, much like a dictionary, but provides access through properties. The idea of the class will be that you can add a property definition and declare it @dynamic, and the class will magically handle storing and retrieving that value. That would be pretty fantastic, right?

The interface for the class will be like this:

```objc
#import <Foundation/Foundation.h>

@interface EOCAutoDictionary : NSObject
@property (nonatomic, strong) NSString *string;
@property (nonatomic, strong) NSNumber *number;
@property (nonatomic, strong) NSDate *date;
@property (nonatomic, strong) id opaqueObject;
@end
```

It doesn't particularly matter for this example what the properties are. In fact, I've shown a variety of types just to illustrate the power of this feature. Internally, the values for each property will be held in a dictionary, so the start of the implementation of this class would look like the following, including declaring the properties as @dynamic such that instance variables and accessors are not automatically created for them:

```objc
#import "EOCAutoDictionary.h"
#import <objc/runtime.h>

@interface EOCAutoDictionary ()
@property (nonatomic, strong) NSMutableDictionary
*backingStore;
@end

@implementation EOCAutoDictionary

@dynamic string, number, date, opaqueObject;
```

```objc
- (id)init {
    if ((self = [super init])) {
        _backingStore = [NSMutableDictionary new];
    }
    return self;
}
```

Then comes the fun part: the resolveInstanceMethod: implementation:

```objc
+ (BOOL)resolveInstanceMethod:(SEL)selector {
    NSString *selectorString = NSStringFromSelector(selector);
    if ([selectorString hasPrefix:@"set"]) {
        class_addMethod(self,
                        selector,
                        (IMP)autoDictionarySetter,
                        "v@:@");
    } else {
        class_addMethod(self,
                        selector,
                        (IMP)autoDictionaryGetter,
                        "@@:");
    }
    return YES;
}
```

@end

The first time it encounters a call to a property on an instance of EOCAutoDictionary the runtime will not find the corresponding selector, since they're not implemented directly or synthesized. For example, if the opaqueObject property is written, the preceding method will be invoked with a selector of setOpaqueObject:. Similarly, if the property is read, it will be invoked with a selector of opaqueObject. The method detects the difference between set and get selectors by checking for a prefix of set. In each case, a method is added to the class for the given selector pointing to a function called either autoDictionarySetter or autoDictionaryGetter, as appropriate. This makes use of the runtime method class_addMethod, which adds a method dynamically to the class for the given selector, with the implementation given as a function pointer. The final parameter in this function is the type encoding of the implementation. The type encoding is made up from characters representing the return type, followed by the parameters that the function takes.

The getter function would then be implemented as follows:

```
id autoDictionaryGetter(id self, SEL _cmd) {
    // Get the backing store from the object
    EOCAutoDictionary *typedSelf = (EOCAutoDictionary*)self;
    NSMutableDictionary *backingStore = typedSelf.backingStore;

    // The key is simply the selector name
    NSString *key = NSStringFromSelector(_cmd);

    // Return the value
    return [backingStore objectForKey:key];
}
```

Finally, the setter function would be implemented like this:

```
void autoDictionarySetter(id self, SEL _cmd, id value) {
    // Get the backing store from the object
    EOCAutoDictionary *typedSelf = (EOCAutoDictionary*)self;
    NSMutableDictionary *backingStore = typedSelf.backingStore;

    /** The selector will be for example, "setOpaqueObject:".
     *  We need to remove the "set", ":" and lowercase the first
     *  letter of the remainder.
     */
    NSString *selectorString = NSStringFromSelector(_cmd);
    NSMutableString *key = [selectorString mutableCopy];

    // Remove the ':' at the end
    [key deleteCharactersInRange:NSMakeRange(key.length - 1, 1)];

    // Remove the 'set' prefix
    [key deleteCharactersInRange:NSMakeRange(0, 3)];

    // Lowercase the first character
    NSString *lowercaseFirstChar =
        [[key substringToIndex:1] lowercaseString];
    [key replaceCharactersInRange:NSMakeRange(0, 1)
                       withString:lowercaseFirstChar];

    if (value) {
        [backingStore setObject:value forKey:key];
    } else {
        [backingStore removeObjectForKey:key];
    }
}
```

Using EOCAutoDictionary is then a simple matter of the following:

```
EOCAutoDictionary *dict = [EOCAutoDictionary new];
dict.date = [NSDate dateWithTimeIntervalSince1970:475372800];
NSLog(@"dict.date = %@", dict.date);
// Output: dict.date = 1985-01-24 00:00:00 +0000
```

The other properties on the dictionary could be accessed just like the date property, and new properties could be introduced by adding a @property definition and declaring it @dynamic. A similar approach is employed by CALayer, part of the CoreAnimation framework on iOS. This approach allows CALayer to be a key-value-coding-compliant container class, meaning that it can store a value against any key. CALayer uses this ability to allow the addition of custom animatable properties whereby the storage of the property values is handled directly by the base class, but the property definition can be added in a subclass.

Things to Remember

+ Message forwarding is the process that an object goes through when it is found to not respond to a selector.

+ Dynamic method resolution is used to add methods to a class at runtime as and when they are used.

+ Objects can declare that another object is to handle certain selectors that it doesn't understand.

+ Full forwarding is invoked only when no previous way of handling a selector has been found.

Item 13: Consider Method Swizzling to Debug Opaque Methods

The method to call when a message is sent to an object in Objective-C is resolved at runtime, as explained in Item 11. It might then occur to you that perhaps the method invoked for a given selector name could be changed at runtime. You'd be correct. This feature can be used to great advantage, as it can be used to change functionality in classes for which you don't have the source code, without having to subclass and override methods. Thus, the new functionality can be used by all instances of the class rather than only instances of the subclass with overridden methods. Such an approach is often referred to as method swizzling.

A class's method list contains a list of selector names to implementation mappings, telling the dynamic messaging system where to find the implementation of a given method. The implementations are stored as function pointers called IMPs and have the following prototype:

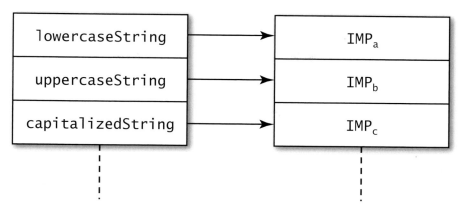

Figure 2.3 NSString's selector table

```
id (*IMP)(id, SEL, ...)
```

The NSString class responds to selectors called lowercaseString, uppercaseString, and capitalizedString, among others. Each selector points to a different IMP, making up a table like the one shown in Figure 2.3.

This table can be manipulated by using a few different functions exposed by the Objective-C runtime. You can add selectors to the list, change the implementation pointed to for a given selector, or swap the implementation pointed to by two selectors. After performing a few of these operations, the class's method table might look something like Figure 2.4.

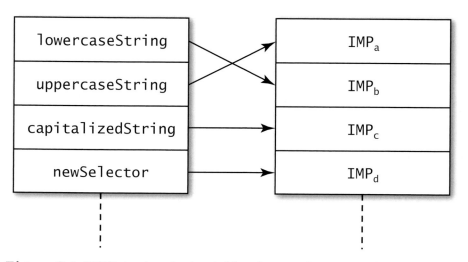

Figure 2.4 NSString's selector table after performing a few operations on it

A new selector called newSelector has been added, the implementation of capitalizedString has been changed, and the implementations of lowercaseString and uppercaseString have been swapped. All this can be done without writing a single subclass, and the new method table layout will be used for each instance of NSString in the application. A very powerful feature, I'm sure you'll agree!

The topic of this item refers to the process of exchanging implementations. In doing so, additional functionality can be added to a method. However, before explaining how it can be used to add functionality, I will explain how to simply swap two existing method implementations. To exchange implementations, you use the following function:

```
void method_exchangeImplementations(Method m1, Method m2)
```

This function takes as its arguments the two implementations to exchange, which can be obtained by using the following function:

```
Method class_getInstanceMethod(Class aClass, SEL aSelector)
```

This function retrieves a method from a class for the given selector. To swap the implementations of lowercaseString and uppercaseString as in the preceding example, you would perform the following:

```
Method originalMethod =
    class_getInstanceMethod([NSString class],
                            @selector(lowercaseString));
Method swappedMethod =
    class_getInstanceMethod([NSString class],
                            @selector(uppercaseString));
method_exchangeImplementations(originalMethod, swappedMethod);
```

From then on, whenever an NSString instance has lowercaseString called on it, the original implementation of uppercaseString will be invoked and vice versa:

```
NSString *string = @"ThIs iS tHe StRiNg";

NSString *lowercaseString = [string lowercaseString];
NSLog(@"lowercaseString = %@", lowercaseString);
// Output: lowercaseString = THIS IS THE STRING

NSString *uppercaseString = [string uppercaseString];
NSLog(@"uppercaseString = %@", uppercaseString);
// Output: uppercaseString = this is the string
```

That explains how to exchange method implementations, but in reality, simply swapping two implementations like that is not very useful. After all, there's a good reason why the implementation for

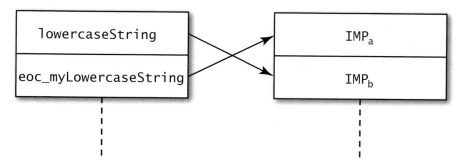

Figure 2.5 Swapping the implementations of `lowercaseString` and `eoc_myLowercaseString`

`uppercaseString` and `lowercaseString` do what they do! There's no reason why you'd want to swap them. But the same approach can be used to add functionality to an existing method implementation. What if you wanted to log something every time `lowercaseString` was called? The same approach can be used to achieve just that. It involves adding another method that implements the additional functionality and then calls through to the original implementation.

The additional method can be added using a category, like so:

```
@interface NSString (EOCMyAdditions)
- (NSString*)eoc_myLowercaseString;
@end
```

This method is going to be swapped with the original `lowercaseString` method, so the method table will end up looking like the one in Figure 2.5.

The implementation of this new method would look like this:

```
@implementation NSString (EOCMyAdditions)
- (NSString*)eoc_myLowercaseString {
    NSString *lowercase = [self eoc_myLowercaseString];
    NSLog(@"%@ => %@", self, lowercase);
    return lowercase;
}
@end
```

This might look like a recursive call, but remember that the implementations are going to be swapped. So at runtime, when the `eoc_myLowercaseString` selector is looked up, it's the implementation of `lowercaseString` that gets called. Finally, to swap the method implementations, the following is used:

```
Method originalMethod =
    class_getInstanceMethod([NSString class],
                            @selector(lowercaseString));
Method swappedMethod =
    class_getInstanceMethod([NSString class],
                            @selector(eoc_myLowercaseString));
method_exchangeImplementations(originalMethod, swappedMethod);
```

From then on, whenever any NSString has lowercaseString called on it, the log line will be printed out:

```
NSString *string = @"ThIs iS tHe StRiNg";
NSString *lowercaseString = [string lowercaseString];
// Output: ThIs iS tHe StRiNg => this is the string
```

Being able to add in logging like this to methods that are completely opaque to you can be a very useful debugging feature. However, this is usually useful only for debugging. Rarely will you find a need other than debugging to perform method swizzling like this to alter functionality of a class globally. Don't feel that you should use such a feature just because you can. Overuse can easily lead to code that is difficult to read and unmaintainable.

Things to Remember

✦ Method implementations for a given selector of a class can be added and replaced at runtime.

✦ Swizzling is the process of swapping one method implementation for another, usually to add functionality to the original implementation.

✦ Meddling with methods through the runtime is usually good only for debugging and should not be used just because it can.

Item 14: Understand What a Class Object Is

Objective-C is extremely dynamic in nature. Item 11 explains how the implementation for a given method call is looked up at runtime, and Item 12 explains how forwarding works when a class does not immediately respond to a certain selector. But what about the receiver of a message: the object itself? How does the runtime know what type an object is? The type of an object is not bound at compile time but rather is looked up at runtime. Moreover, a special type, id, can be used to denote any Objective-C object type. In general, though, you specify a type whenever possible so that the compiler can warn about sending messages that it thinks the receiver doesn't understand.

Conversely, any object that is of type id will be assumed to respond to all messages.

As you'll know from Item 12, though, the compiler cannot actually know all the selectors a certain type understands, since they can be dynamically inserted at runtime. However, even if this technique is used, the compiler expects to see the method prototype defined in a header somewhere such that it can know the full method signature to be able to emit the correct code to perform the message dispatch.

Inspecting the type of an object at runtime is known as introspection and is a powerful and useful feature baked into the Foundation framework as part of the NSObject protocol, to which all objects that inherit from the common root classes (NSObject and NSProxy) conform. Using these methods rather than directly comparing classes of objects is prudent, as I will explain. However, before looking at introspection techniques, here is some background as to what an Objective-C object is.

Every Objective-C object instance is a pointer to a blob of memory. That's why you see the * next to the type when declaring a variable:

```
NSString *pointerVariable = @"Some string";
```

If you've come from a C world of programming, you'll understand exactly what this means. For the non-C programmers among you, this means that pointerVariable is a variable holding a memory address, where the data stored at that memory address is the NSString itself. The variable therefore "points to" the NSString instance. This is how all Objective-C objects are referred to; if you tried to allocate the memory for an object on the stack instead, you would receive an error from the compiler:

```
NSString stackVariable = @"Some string";
// error: interface type cannot be statically allocated
```

The generic object type, id, is already a pointer in itself, so you use it like so:

```
id genericTypedString = @"Some string";
```

This definition is semantically the same as if the variable were of type NSString*. The only difference with specifying the type fully is that the compiler can help and warn if you attempt to call a method that doesn't exist for instances of that class.

The data structure behind every object is defined in the runtime headers along with the definition of the id type itself:

```
typedef struct objc_object {
    Class isa;
} *id;
```

Therefore, each object contains as its first member a variable of type Class. This variable defines the class of the object and is often referred to as the "is a" pointer. For example, the object "is a" NSString. The Class object is also defined in the runtime headers:

```
typedef struct objc_class *Class;
struct objc_class {
    Class isa;
    Class super_class;
    const char *name;
    long version;
    long info;
    long instance_size;
    struct objc_ivar_list *ivars;
    struct objc_method_list **methodLists;
    struct objc_cache *cache;
    struct objc_protocol_list *protocols;
};
```

This structure holds metadata about the class, such as what methods instances of the class implement and what instance variables instances have. The fact that this structure also has an isa pointer as its first variable means that a Class is itself an Objective-C object. This structure also has another variable, called super_class, which defines the class's parent. The type of a class (i.e., the class the isa pointer points to) is another class, known as the metaclass, which is used to describe the metadata about instances of the class itself. This is where class methods are defined, since they can be thought of as instance methods of instances of a class. There is only ever one instance of a class, though, and only one instance of its associated metaclass.

The hierarchy of a class called SomeClass that inherits from NSObject looks like the one shown in Figure 2.6.

The super_class pointer creates the hierarchy, and the isa pointer describes the type of an instance. You can manipulate this layout to perform introspection. You can find out whether an object responds to a certain selector and conforms to a certain protocol and determine information about what part of the class hierarchy the object belongs to.

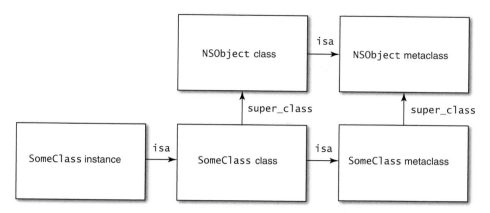

Figure 2.6 Class hierarchy for instances of SomeClass, which inherits from NSObject, including the metaclass hierarchy

Inspecting the Class Hierarchy

The introspection methods can be used to inspect the class hierarchy. You can check whether an object is an instance of a certain class by using isMemberOfClass: or whether an object is an instance of a certain class or any class that inherits from it by using isKindOfClass:. For example:

```
NSMutableDictionary *dict = [NSMutableDictionary new];
[dict isMemberOfClass:[NSDictionary class]]; ///< NO
[dict isMemberOfClass:[NSMutableDictionary class]]; ///< YES
[dict isKindOfClass:[NSDictionary class]]; ///< YES
[dict isKindOfClass:[NSArray class]]; ///< NO
```

This kind of introspection works by using the isa pointer to obtain the object's class and then walking the inheritance hierarchy, using the super_class pointer. Given the dynamic nature of objects, this feature is extremely important. You cannot ever fully know the type without introspection, unlike other languages with which you might be familiar.

Introspection of the class of an object is extremely useful given the dynamic typing used by Objective-C. Introspection is commonly used when retrieving objects from collections, since they are not strongly typed, meaning that when objects are retrieved from collections, they are usually of type id. Introspection can then be used if the type needs to be known: for example, when needing to generate a

comma-separated string from objects stored in an array to be saved
to a text file. The following code could be used in that scenario:

```
- (NSString*)commaSeparatedStringFromObjects:(NSArray*)array {
    NSMutableString *string = [NSMutableString new];
    for (id object in array) {
        if ([object isKindOfClass:[NSString class]]) {
            [string appendFormat:@"%@,", object];
        } else if ([object isKindOfClass:[NSNumber class]]) {
            [string appendFormat:@"%d,", [object intValue]];
        } else if ([object isKindOfClass:[NSData class]]) {
            NSString *base64Encoded = /* base64 encoded data */;
            [string appendFormat:@"%@,", base64Encoded];
        } else {
            // Type not supported
        }
    }
    return string;
}
```

It is also possible to check class objects for equality. You can do so by
using the == operator rather than an isEqual: method, as you would
usually use when comparing Objective-C objects (see Item 8). The
reason is that classes are singletons, and so only a single instance of
each class's Class object is within an application. Thus, another way
to test whether an object is exactly an instance of a class would be to
do the following:

```
id object = /* … */;
if ([object class] == [EOCSomeClass class]) {
    // 'object' is an instance of EOCSomeClass
}
```

However, you should always prefer the introspection methods to direct
equality of class object, because the introspection methods are able to
take into account objects that make use of message forwarding (see
Item 12). Consider an object that forwards all selectors to another.
Such an object is called a proxy, and NSProxy is a root class specifically for objects like that.

Usually, such proxy objects will return the proxy class (i.e., subclass of NSProxy) if the method class is called rather than the class
of the object being proxied. However, if introspection methods, such
as isKindOfClass:, are called on them, they will proxy the message
through to the proxied object. This means that the answer to the message will be as though the proxied object is being inspected. Therefore, this will yield a result different from inspecting the class object

returned from calling the class method, since that will be the proxy class itself rather than the class of the proxied object.

Things to Remember

+ The class hierarchy is modeled through Class objects that each instance has a pointer to in order to define its type.

+ Introspection should be used when the type of the object cannot be known for certain at compile time.

+ Always prefer introspection methods where possible, rather than direct comparison of class objects, since the object may implement message forwarding.

3

Interface and API Design

Once you have built an application, you are likely going to want to reuse parts of the code for future projects. You may even want to release some of the code for others to use. Even if you don't think that you're going to do either of these things, you probably will at some point. When you do, it'll help to write your interfaces in such a way that they fit in. This means using paradigms commonly used with Objective-C and understanding various pitfalls.

Over recent years, especially with the open-source community and components made popular with the advent of iOS, it is common to use other people's code in your own applications. Similarly, others may end up using your code, so writing in a clear way will enable them to quickly and easily integrate your code. And who knows, you may end up writing the next library that is used in thousands of applications!

Item 15: Use Prefix Names to Avoid Namespace Clashes

Unlike other languages, Objective-C has no built-in namespace feature. For this reason, it is easy for names to clash unless measures are taken to avoid the potential. The impact a naming clash has on an application is that it may not link, owing to duplicate symbol errors like this:

```
duplicate symbol _OBJC_METACLASS_$_EOCTheClass in:
    build/something.o
    build/something_else.o
duplicate symbol _OBJC_CLASS_$_EOCTheClass in:
    build/something.o
    build/something_else.o
```

This error results because the symbol for the class and metaclass (see Item 14) symbols for a class called EOCTheClass have been defined twice, from two implementations of a class called EOCTheClass in two separate parts of the application's code, perhaps from two separate libraries that you are pulling in.

Even worse than not linking would be if one of the libraries that contained one of the duplicates were loaded at runtime. In this case, the dynamic loader would encounter the duplicate symbol error and most likely bring down the entire application.

The only way to avoid this problem is to use a crude form of namespacing: prefixing all your names with a certain prefix. The prefix you choose should be relevant to your company, application, or both. For example, if your company were named Effective Widgets, you might decide to use the prefix EWS for code common to all your applications and EWB for code just for the application called Effective Browser. It's still not impossible to have clashes when you prefix your names, but it is much less likely.

If you are creating applications using Cocoa, it is important to note that Apple has stated that it reserves the right to use all two-letter prefixes, so you should definitely choose a three-letter prefix in this case. For example, an issue could have arisen by not following these guidelines and deciding to use the TW prefix. When the iOS 5.0 SDK came out, it brought along the Twitter framework, which too uses the TW prefix, which has a class called TWRequest for making HTTP requests to the Twitter API. You could very easily also have had a class called TWRequest if you had an API of your own, for a company called Tiny Widgets, for example.

The prefixing should not stop with class names but should apply to all names that you have within your application. Item 25 explains the importance of prefixing category names and the methods within them if the category is on an existing class. Another important and often overlooked potential for conflict is pure C functions or global variables you use within the implementation files of your classes. It's often easy to forget that these will appear as top-level symbols within your compiled object files. For example, the AudioToolbox framework in the iOS SDK has a function for playing a sound file. You can give it a callback that gets called when it finishes. You might decide to write a class to wrap this up into an Objective-C class that calls a delegate when the sound file finishes, like so:

```
// EOCSoundPlayer.h
#import <Foundation/Foundation.h>

@class EOCSoundPlayer;
@protocol EOCSoundPlayerDelegate <NSObject>
```

```objc
- (void)soundPlayerDidFinish:(EOCSoundPlayer*)player;
@end

@interface EOCSoundPlayer : NSObject
@property (nonatomic, weak) id <EOCSoundPlayerDelegate> delegate;
- (id)initWithURL:(NSURL*)url;
- (void)playSound;
@end
// EOCSoundPlayer.m
#import "EOCSoundPlayer.h"
#import <AudioToolbox/AudioToolbox.h>

void completion(SystemSoundID ssID, void *clientData) {
    EOCSoundPlayer *player =
        (__bridge EOCSoundPlayer*)clientData;
    if ([player.delegate
            respondsToSelector:@selector(soundPlayerDidFinish:)])
    {
        [player.delegate soundPlayerDidFinish:player];
    }
}

@implementation EOCSoundPlayer {
    SystemSoundID _systemSoundID;
}

- (id)initWithURL:(NSURL*)url {
    if ((self = [super init])) {
        AudioServicesCreateSystemSoundID((__bridge CFURLRef)url,
                                         &_systemSoundID);
    }
    return self;
}

- (void)dealloc {
    AudioServicesDisposeSystemSoundID(_systemSoundID);
}

- (void)playSound {
    AudioServicesAddSystemSoundCompletion(
        _systemSoundID,
        NULL,
        NULL,
```

```
        completion,
        (__bridge void*)self);
    AudioServicesPlaySystemSound(_systemSoundID);
}
```

@end

This looks completely innocuous, but looking at the symbol table for the object file created from this class, we find the following:

```
00000230 t -[EOCSoundPlayer .cxx_destruct]
0000014c t -[EOCSoundPlayer dealloc]
000001e0 t -[EOCSoundPlayer delegate]
0000009c t -[EOCSoundPlayer initWithURL:]
00000198 t -[EOCSoundPlayer playSound]
00000208 t -[EOCSoundPlayer setDelegate:]
00000b88 S _OBJC_CLASS_$_EOCSoundPlayer
00000bb8 S _OBJC_IVAR_$_EOCSoundPlayer._delegate
00000bb4 S _OBJC_IVAR_$_EOCSoundPlayer._systemSoundID
00000b9c S _OBJC_METACLASS_$_EOCSoundPlayer
00000000 T _completion
00000bf8 s l_OBJC_$_INSTANCE_METHODS_EOCSoundPlayer
00000c48 s l_OBJC_$_INSTANCE_VARIABLES_EOCSoundPlayer
00000c78 s l_OBJC_$_PROP_LIST_EOCSoundPlayer
00000c88 s l_OBJC_CLASS_RO_$_EOCSoundPlayer
00000bd0 s l_OBJC_METACLASS_RO_$_EOCSoundPlayer
```

Note the symbol lurking in the middle, called _completion. This is the completion function created to handle when the sound has finished playing. Even though it's defined in your implementation file and not declared in the header file, it still appears as a top-level symbol like this. Thus, if another function called completion is created somewhere, you'll end up with a duplicate-symbol error when linking, such as the following:

```
duplicate symbol _completion in:
    build/EOCSoundPlayer.o
    build/EOCAnotherClass.o
```

Worse still would be if you were shipping your code as a library for others to use in their own applications. If you exposed a symbol called _completion like this, anyone using your library would not be able to create a function called completion, which is a nasty thing for you to do.

So you should always prefix C functions like this as well. In the preceding example, you could call the completion handler

EOCSoundPlayerCompletion, for example. This also has the side effect that if the symbol ever appears in a backtrace, it's easy to determine what code the problem has come from.

You should be particularly careful of the duplicate-symbol problems when you use third-party libraries and ship your code as a library that others plug into their own applications. If the third-party libraries that you use are also going to be used by the application, it's easy for duplicate-symbol errors to arise. In that case, it's common to edit all the code of the libraries you use to prefix them with your own prefix. For example, if your library is called EOCLibrary and you pull in a library called XYZLibrary, you would go through and prefix all names in XYZLibrary with EOC. The application is then free to use XYZLibrary itself, without the chance of a naming collision, as shown in Figure 3.1.

Going through and changing all the names might seem like a rather tedious thing to do, but it's prudent if you want to avoid naming collisions. You may ask why it's necessary to do this at all and why the application can't simply not include XYZLibrary itself and use your implementation of it. It's possible to do that as well, but consider the scenario in which the application pulls in a third library, ABCLibrary, that has also decided to use XYZLibrary. In that case, if you and the author of ABCLibrary hadn't prefixed, the application would still get duplicate-symbol errors. Or if you use version X of XYZLibrary but the application requires features from version Y, it would want its own copy anyway. If you spend time using popular third-party libraries with iOS development, you will frequently see this kind of prefixing.

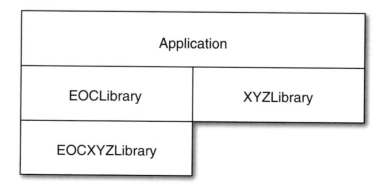

Figure 3.1 Avoiding naming clashes where a third-party library is included twice: once by the application itself and once by another library

Things to Remember

✦ Choose a class prefix that befits your company, application, or both. Then stick with that prefix throughout.

✦ If you use a third-party library as a dependency of your own library, consider prefixing its names with your own prefix.

Item 16: Have a Designated Initializer

All objects need to be initialized. When initializing an object, you sometimes don't need to give it any information, but often you do. This is usually the case if the object cannot perform its action without knowing this information. An example from UIKit, the iOS UI framework, is UITableViewCell, which requires being told its style and an identifier to group cells of different types, enabling efficient reuse of cell objects that are expensive to create. The term given to the initializer that gives the object the required amount of information to perform its task is the "designated initializer."

If there is more than one way to create an instance of a class, the class may have more than one initializer. This is perfectly fine, but there should still be just the one designated initializer through which all other initializers call. An example of this is NSDate, which has the following initializers:

```
- (id)init
- (id)initWithString:(NSString*)string
- (id)initWithTimeIntervalSinceNow:(NSTimeInterval)seconds
- (id)initWithTimeInterval:(NSTimeInterval)seconds
                 sinceDate:(NSDate*)refDate
- (id)initWithTimeIntervalSinceReferenceDate:
                            (NSTimeInterval)seconds
- (id)initWithTimeIntervalSince1970:(NSTimeInterval)seconds
```

The designated initializer in this case is initWithTimeInterval SinceReferenceDate:, as explained in the documentation for the class. This means that all the other initializers call through to this initializer. Thus, the designated initializer is the only place where internal data is stored. If the underlying data store is changed for any reason, only one place needs to be changed.

For example, consider a class that represents a rectangle. The interface would look like this:

```
#import <Foundation/Foundation.h>

@interface EOCRectangle : NSObject
@property (nonatomic, assign, readonly) float width;
```

```
@property (nonatomic, assign, readonly) float height;
@end
```

Taking heed of Item 18, the properties are read-only. But that means that there's no way in which a Rectangle object can ever have its properties set externally. So you might introduce an initializer:

```
- (id)initWithWidth:(float)width
          andHeight:(float)height
{
    if ((self = [super init])) {
        _width = width;
        _height = height;
    }
    return self;
}
```

But what if someone decides to create a rectangle by calling [[EOCRectangle alloc] init]? Doing so is legitimate, since EOCRectangle's superclass, NSObject, implements a method called init, which simply sets all instance variables to 0 (or equivalent of 0 for that data type). If that method is invoked, the width and height will stay set at 0 from when the EOCRectangle instance was allocated (in the call to alloc) in which all instance variables are set to 0. Although this might be what you want, you will more likely want to either set the default values yourself or throw an exception to indicate that an instance must be intialized using your designated initializer only. In the case of EOCRectangle, this would mean overriding the init method, like so:

```
// Using default values
- (id)init {
    return [self initWithWidth:5.0f andHeight:10.0f];
}


// Throwing an exception
- (id)init {
    @throw [NSException
            exceptionWithName:NSInternalInconsistencyException
             reason:@"Must use initWithWidth:andHeight: instead."
            userInfo:nil];

}
```

Note how the version that sets default values calls straight through to the designated initializer. This version could have been implemented by directly setting the _width and _height instance variables.

However, if the storage backing the class had changed—for example, by using a structure to hold the width and height together—the logic of how to set the data would have to be changed in both initializers. This wouldn't be too bad in this simple example, but imagine a more complicated class with many more initializers and more complicated data. It would be very easy to forget to change one of the initializers and end up with inconsistencies.

Now imagine that you want to subclass EOCRectangle and create a class called EOCSquare. It's clear that this hierarchy makes sense, but what should the initializer be? Clearly, the width and height should be forced to be equal, since that's what a square is! So you might decide to create an initializer like so:

```
#import "EOCRectangle.h"

@interface EOCSquare : EOCRectangle
- (id)initWithDimension:(float)dimension;
@end

@implementation EOCSquare

- (id)initWithDimension:(float)dimension {
    return [super initWithWidth:dimension andHeight:dimension];
}

@end
```

This would become EOCSquare's designated initializer. Note how it calls its superclass's designated initializer. If you look back to the implementation of EOCRectangle, you'll see that it too calls its superclass's designated initializer. This chain of designated initializers is important to maintain. However, it's still possible for callers to initialize an EOCSquare object by using either the initWithWidth:andHeight: or the init method. You don't really want to allow this, since someone could end up creating a square whose width and height don't match. This illustrates an important point when subclassing. You should always override the designated initializer of your superclass if you have a designated initializer with a different name. In the case of EOCSquare, you could override EOCRectangle's designated initializer like so:

```
- (id)initWithWidth:(float)width andHeight:(float)height {
    float dimension = MAX(width, height);
    return [self initWithDimension:dimension];
}
```

Note how the designated initializer of EOCSquare has been called. In implementing this, the method called init will also just magically work. Recall how in EOCRectangle, it was implemented to call through to EOCRectangle's designated initializer with default values. It will still do this, but since the initWithWidth:andHeight: method has been overridden, EOCSquare's implementation will be called, which in turn calls through to its designated initializer. So everything will still work, and there's no way of creating an EOCSquare with unequal sides.

Sometimes, you won't want to override the superclass's designated initializer, as it doesn't make sense. For example, you might decide that it's not very nice that an EOCSquare object created with the initWithWidth:andHeight: method has its dimension set to the maximum of the two values passed in. You might decide that it's a user error instead. In this case, the common pattern is to override the designated initializer and throw an exception:

```
- (id)initWithWidth:(float)width andHeight:(float)height {
    @throw [NSException
        exceptionWithName:NSInternalInconsistencyException
                reason:@"Must use initWithDimension: instead."
                userInfo:nil];
}
```

This might seem harsh, but it's sometimes required, since it would leave an object being created with inconsistent internal data. In the case of EOCRectangle and EOCSquare, it would mean that calling init would also cause the exception to be thrown, because init calls through to initWithWidth:andHeight:. In that case, you might decide to override init and call initWithDimension: with a sensible default:

```
- (id)init {
    return [self initWithDimension:5.0f];
}
```

However, throwing an exception in Objective-C should mean that the error is fatal (see Item 21), so throwing an exception from an initializer should be a last resort if the instance cannot be initialized otherwise.

In some situations, you may need to have more than one designated initializer. These situations arise when an instance of the object can be created in two distinct ways and must be handled separately. An example of this is the NSCoding protocol, a serialization mechanism that allows objects to dictate how they should be encoded and decoded. This mechanism is used extensively throughout AppKit and

UIKit, the two UI frameworks from Mac OS X and iOS, respectively, to provide the ability for objects to be serialized using an XML format called a NIB. These NIBs are usually used to store a view controller's layout of its views. When loaded from a NIB, the view controller goes through the unarchiving process.

The NSCoding protocol defines that the following initializer method should be implemented:

```
- (id)initWithCoder:(NSCoder*)decoder;
```

This method can't usually call through to your main designated initializer, because it has to do different work to unarchive the object through the decoder. Also, if the superclass implements NSCoding as well, its initWithCoder: method needs to be called. You would end up with two designated initializers in the strict sense of the term, because more than one initializer calls through to a superclass initializer.

Applying this to EOCRectangle would give the following:

```
#import <Foundation/Foundation.h>

@interface EOCRectangle : NSObject <NSCoding>
@property (nonatomic, assign, readonly) float width;
@property (nonatomic, assign, readonly) float height;
- (id)initWithWidth:(float)width
          andHeight:(float)height;
@end

@implementation EOCRectangle

// Designated initializer
- (id)initWithWidth:(float)width
          andHeight:(float)height
{
    if ((self = [super init])) {
        _width = width;
        _height = height;
    }
    return self;
}

// Superclass's designated initializer
- (id)init {
    return [self initWithWidth:5.0f andHeight:10.0f];
}
```

```objc
// Initializer from NSCoding
- (id)initWithCoder:(NSCoder*)decoder {
    // Call through to super's designated initializer
    if ((self = [super init])) {
        _width = [decoder decodeFloatForKey:@"width"];
        _height = [decoder decodeFloatForKey:@"height"];
    }
    return self;
}

@end
```

Note how the NSCoding initializer calls through to the superclass designated initializer rather than one of its own. However, if the superclass also implements NSCoding, it would call through to that initializer instead. For example, consider EOCSquare:

```objc
#import "EOCRectangle.h"

@interface EOCSquare : EOCRectangle
- (id)initWithDimension:(float)dimension;
@end

@implementation EOCSquare

// Designated initializer
- (id)initWithDimension:(float)dimension {
    return [super initWithWidth:dimension andHeight:dimension];
}

// Superclass designated initializer
- (id)initWithWidth:(float)width andHeight:(float)height {
    float dimension = MAX(width, height);
    return [self initWithDimension:dimension];
}

// NSCoding designated initializer
- (id)initWithCoder:(NSCoder*)decoder {
    if ((self = [super initWithCoder:decoder])) {
        // EOCSquare's specific initializer
    }
    return self;
}

@end
```

In the same way that any initializer is chained through to the super-class implementation, initWithCoder: calls it first before continuing to do anything specific that it needs to do. In this way, EOCSquare is also fully NSCoding compliant. If you called through to your own initializer here or to a different superclass initializer, EOCRectangle's initWithCoder: would never get called for EOCSquare instances, and so the _width and _height instance variables would not be decoded.

Things to Remember

✦ Implement a designated initializer in your classes, and document which one it is. All other initializers should call through to this one.

✦ If the designated initializer is different from the superclass, ensure that its designated initializer is overridden.

✦ Throw an exception in initializers overridden from superclasses that should not be used in the subclass.

Item 17: Implement the description **Method**

While debugging, you will often find it useful to print out an object to inspect it. One way is to write logging code to print out all the proper-ties of the object. But the most usual way is to do something like this:

```
NSLog(@"object = %@", object);
```

When the string to log is built up, object will be sent the descrip-tion message and put in place of the %@ in the format string. So, for instance, if the object were an array, the output might look like this:

```
NSArray *object = @[@"A string", @(123)];
NSLog(@"object = %@", object);
```

Which outputs this:

```
object = (
  "A string",
  123
)
```

However, if you try this on a class of your own, you'll often see some-thing that looks more like this:

```
object = <EOCPerson: 0x7fd9a1600600>
```

That is not as helpful as the array! Unless you override description in your own class, the default implementation from NSObject will be invoked. The method is defined on the NSObject protocol, but the NSObject class implements it. Many methods are part of the NSObject protocol, and it's done this way because NSObject is not the only root class. NSProxy is an example of another root class, which conforms to the NSObject protocol. Because methods like description are defined within the protocol, subclasses of these other root classes also must implement them. That implementation doesn't do much, as you can see. What it does do is show the class name alongside the memory address of the object. This would be useful to you only if you wanted to see whether two objects were exactly the same object. However, you can't tell any more about the objects than that. It's more likely that you are going to want to know some more information about the object.

To make the output more useful, all you need to do is override description to return the string you want to represent your object. For example, consider a class to describe a person:

```
#import <Foundation/Foundation.h>

@interface EOCPerson : NSObject

@property (nonatomic, copy, readonly) NSString *firstName;
@property (nonatomic, copy, readonly) NSString *lastName;

- (id)initWithFirstName:(NSString*)firstName
               lastName:(NSString*)lastName;

@end

@implementation EOCPerson

- (id)initWithFirstName:(NSString*)firstName
               lastName:(NSString*)lastName
{
    if ((self = [super init])) {
        _firstName = [firstName copy];
        _lastName = [lastName copy];
    }
    return self;
}

@end
```

A typical `description` method implementation for this would be as follows:

```
- (NSString*)description {
    return [NSString stringWithFormat:@"<%@: %p, \"%@ %@\">",
            [self class], self, _firstName, _lastName];
}
```

If this were to be used, the output for an object of type `EOCPerson` would now look like the following:

```
EOCPerson *person = [[EOCPerson alloc]
                        initWithFirstName:@"Bob"
                                 lastName:@"Smith"];
NSLog(@"person = %@", person);
// Output:
// person = <EOCPerson: 0x7fb249c030f0, "Bob Smith">
```

This is clear and contains much more useful information. I suggest displaying the class name and pointer address just like the default implementation, simply because it's useful to see sometimes. Although as you saw earlier, NSArray doesn't do this, and there certainly is no rule about it. What you choose to put in the description is whatever makes sense for the object in question.

A simple way to write a `description` method containing a lot of different bits of information is to piggyback on NSDictionary's description method. It returns something that looks like this:

```
{
    key: value;
    foo: bar;
}
```

This compact description can be used by forming a dictionary within your own `description` method and returning a string containing this dictionary's description method. For example, the following class describes a location with a title and coordinates (latitude and longitude):

```
#import <Foundation/Foundation.h>

@interface EOCLocation : NSObject
@property (nonatomic, copy, readonly) NSString *title;
@property (nonatomic, assign, readonly) float latitude;
@property (nonatomic, assign, readonly) float longitude;
- (id)initWithTitle:(NSString*)title
           latitude:(float)latitude
          longitude:(float)longitude;
```

```
@end

@implementation EOCLocation

- (id)initWithTitle:(NSString*)title
          latitude:(float)latitude
          longitude:(float)longitude
{
      if ((self = [super init])) {
            _title = [title copy];
            _latitude = latitude;
            _longitude = longitude;
      }
      return self;
}

@end
```

It would be nice if the description method for this showed the title as well as the latitude and longitude. If an NSDictionary were used, the description method would look like this:

```
- (NSString*)description {
    return [NSString stringWithFormat:@"<%@: %p, %@>",
            [self class],
            self,
            @{@"title":_title,
              @"latitude":@(_latitude),
              @"longitude":@(_longitude)}
           ];
}
```

The output would look like this:

```
location = <EOCLocation: 0x7f98f2e01d20, {
    latitude = "51.506";
    longitude = 0;
    title = London;
}>
```

This is much more useful than just the pointer and class name, and all the properties of the object are nicely presented. You could also have used a string format that was formed of each of the instance variables, but the NSDictionary approach is easier to maintain when more properties are added to the class and want to form part of the description method.

Another method to be aware of, also part of the NSObject protocol, is debugDescription, whose purpose is very similar to description. The difference is that debugDescription is the method called when you invoke the print-object command within the debugger. The default implementation within the NSObject class simply calls directly through to description. For example, taking the EOCPerson class, running an application in the debugger (LLDB in this case), and pausing at a breakpoint just after creating an instance looks like this:

```
EOCPerson *person = [[EOCPerson alloc]
                        initWithFirstName:@"Bob"
                                 lastName:@"Smith"];
NSLog(@"person = %@", person);
// Breakpoint here
```

When the breakpoint has been hit, the debug console will be ready to receive input. The command po in LLDB will perform the print-object function, yielding the following:

```
EOCTest[640:c07] person = <EOCPerson: 0x712a4d0, "Bob Smith">
(lldb) po person
(EOCPerson *) $1 = 0x0712a4d0 <EOCPerson: 0x712a4d0, "Bob Smith">
```

Note that the (EOCPerson *) $1 = 0x712a4d0 is added by the debugger. The portion after that is what is returned from the debug-description method.

You may decide to make the normal description of an EOCPerson to be just the person's name and then implement the debug-description method to provide the more thorough description. In that case, the two methods would look like this:

```
- (NSString*)description {
    return [NSString stringWithFormat:@"%@ %@",
            _firstName, _lastName];
}

- (NSString*)debugDescription {
    return [NSString stringWithFormat:@"<%@: %p, \"%@ %@\">",
            [self class], self, _firstName, _lastName];
}
```

This time, running the same code as previously and using the print-object command will yield the following:

```
EOCTest[640:c07] person = Bob Smith
(lldb) po person
(EOCPerson *) $1 = 0x07117fb0 <EOCPerson: 0x7117fb0, "Bob Smith">
```

This output can be particularly useful when you don't want all that extra information about the class name and pointer address to be visible in the normal description but still want the ability to access it easily during debugging. An example of a class that does this from the Foundation framework is NSArray. For example:

```
NSArray *array = @[@"Effective Objective-C 2.0", @(123), @(YES)];
NSLog(@"array = %@", array);
// Breakpoint here
```

In that case, running, stopping at the breakpoint, and printing out the array object looks like this:

```
EOCTest[713:c07] array = (
    "Effective Objective-C 2.0",
    123,
    1
)
(lldb) po array
(NSArray *) $1 = 0x071275b0 <__NSArrayI 0x71275b0>(
Effective Objective-C 2.0,
123,
1
)
```

Things to Remember

+ Implement the description method to provide a meaningful string description of instances.

+ If the object description could do with more detail for use during debugging, implement debugDescription.

Item 18: Prefer Immutable Objects

When designing a class, you will, ideally, be making good use of properties (see Item 6) to encapsulate data. When using properties, you can limit the property to read-only. Keeping properties at the default, read-write, makes all your classes mutable. Often, however, the data being modeled does not need to be mutable. For example, if the data represents an object that has come from a read-only web service, such as a list of points of interest to display on a map, it makes no sense for such objects to be mutable. If such an object is mutated, the data will never be pushed back to the server. As illustrated in Item 8, if mutable objects are stored in collections, a set's internal data structures can easily become inconsistent if objects held in the set are mutated. Therefore, I recommend making objects only as mutable as they need to be.

In practice, this means making properties read-only externally and exposing only the data that needs to be exposed. For example, consider a class to handle points of interest on a map where the data comes in from a web service. You might start out with a class that looks like this:

```
#import <Foundation/Foundation.h>

@interface EOCPointOfInterest : NSObject

@property (nonatomic, copy) NSString *identifier;
@property (nonatomic, copy) NSString *title;
@property (nonatomic, assign) float latitude;
@property (nonatomic, assign) float longitude;

- (id)initWithIdentifier:(NSString*)identifier
                   title:(NSString*)title
                latitude:(float)latitude
               longitude:(float)longitude;

@end
```

All the values come from the web service, and the identifier is to be used to refer to a point of interest in communications with the service. Once a point of interest has been created from a communication with the web service, it doesn't make any sense to be able to change any of the values. In other languages, you would probably have created the instance variables as private, using whatever language construct were available, and have only a get accessor for the variable. However, in using properties in Objective-C, it is incredibly easy to be lazy and not consider private variables at all.

In order to make the EOCPointOfInterest class immutable, you would add the readonly attribute to all the properties:

```
#import <Foundation/Foundation.h>

@interface EOCPointOfInterest : NSObject

@property (nonatomic, copy, readonly) NSString *identifier;
@property (nonatomic, copy, readonly) NSString *title;
@property (nonatomic, assign, readonly) float latitude;
@property (nonatomic, assign, readonly) float longitude;
```

```
- (id)initWithIdentifier:(NSString*)identifier
                    title:(NSString*)title
                 latitude:(float)latitude
                longitude:(float)longitude;
```

@end

This now ensures that if anyone tries to change one of the properties' values, a compiler error will be generated. The values can still be read but cannot be changed, so the data of an EOCPointOfInterest cannot become inconsistent. Thus, anyone making use of this object can be assured that the data is not going to be changed from underneath it. The object's own data structures won't become inconsistent. In the case of a map view displaying EOCPointOfInterest objects, the latitude and longitude of displayed points of interest are not going to change from underneath.

You might wonder why you need to bother setting the memory-management semantic attributes on the property, since there is not going to be a setter. Well, you could simply leave it as the default, like this:

```
@property (nonatomic, readonly) NSString *identifier;
@property (nonatomic, readonly) NSString *title;
@property (nonatomic, readonly) float latitude;
@property (nonatomic, readonly) float longitude;
```

However, it's useful to document what memory-management semantics you are using in the implementation, and it makes it easier to make the property read-write later if you need to.

You may want to be able to alter the data encapsulated by an object within the object itself but not from the outside. In this case, the usual procedure is to redeclare the readonly property internally as readwrite. Of course, this opens up the possibility of race conditions when the property is nonatomic. It's possible for an observer to read the property at the same time it is being written internally. This possibility should be overcome by ensuring that all access, including internally, is synchronized, if necessary, by using, for example, a dispatch queue (see Item 41).

Redeclaring the property as readwrite internally can be done by using the class-continuation category (see Item 27) whereby you can declare the same property as found in the public interface so long as it has the same attributes and expands on the readonly versus readwrite status. In the case of EOCPointOfInterest, for example, the class-continuation category might look like this:

```
#import "EOCPointOfInterest.h"

@interface EOCPointOfInterest ()
@property (nonatomic, copy, readwrite) NSString *identifier;
@property (nonatomic, copy, readwrite) NSString *title;
@property (nonatomic, assign, readwrite) float latitude;
@property (nonatomic, assign, readwrite) float longitude;
@end

@implementation EOCPointOfInterest

/* … */

@end
```

Now, the properties can be set internally only within the EOCPointOfInterest implementation. More accurately, it is still possible for something external to the object to set those properties through the use of Key-Value Coding (KVC), whereby they could use setValue:forKey: like so:

```
[pointOfInterest setValue:@"abc" forKey:@"identifier"];
```

This would set the value of the identifier property because KVC would look through your class for a setIdentifier: method that does exist even though it's not exposed through the public interface. However, this would be seen as an intrusion of your class's API, and if anything goes wrong from doing a hack like this, it's left up to that developer to pick up the pieces.

A brutal developer could even get around not having a setter by using introspection on the class to determine the offset of the property's instance variable within the instance's memory layout. The developer could then manually set the instance variable this way. But that would be even more of an invasion of your public API. So just because it is technically possible to work around the lack of a public setter, you shouldn't ignore the advice to make your objects immutable.

Another thing to keep in mind when defining the public API to your classes is whether collection-class properties should be mutable or immutable. If, for instance, you have a person represented by a class that can store references to the person's friends, you might want a property to get a list of all the friends of that person. If friends can be added and removed from the person, you would have a mutable set backing the property. In such a case, the usual way of exposing the friends set would be to have a readonly property that returns an immutable set that is a copy of the internal mutable set. For example, the following defines such a class:

```
// EOCPerson.h
#import <Foundation/Foundation.h>

@interface EOCPerson : NSObject

@property (nonatomic, copy, readonly) NSString *firstName;
@property (nonatomic, copy, readonly) NSString *lastName;
@property (nonatomic, strong, readonly) NSSet *friends;

- (id)initWithFirstName:(NSString*)firstName
            andLastName:(NSString*)lastName;
- (void)addFriend:(EOCPerson*)person;
- (void)removeFriend:(EOCPerson*)person;

@end
```

```
// EOCPerson.m
#import "EOCPerson.h"

@interface EOCPerson ()
@property (nonatomic, copy, readwrite) NSString *firstName;
@property (nonatomic, copy, readwrite) NSString *lastName;
@end

@implementation EOCPerson {
    NSMutableSet *_internalFriends;
}

- (NSSet*)friends {
    return [_internalFriends copy];
}

- (void)addFriend:(EOCPerson*)person {
    [_internalFriends addObject:person];
}

- (void)removeFriend:(EOCPerson*)person {
    [_internalFriends removeObject:person];
}

- (id)initWithFirstName:(NSString*)firstName
            andLastName:(NSString*)lastName {
```

```
    if ((self = [super init])) {
        _firstName = firstName;
        _lastName = lastName;
        _internalFriends = [NSMutableSet new];
    }
    return self;
}
```

@end

You could have declared the friends property as an NSMutableSet and let users of the class add people directly to that set themselves rather than going through the addFriend: and removeFriend: methods. But this would decouple the data too much and is an easy way for bugs to arise. If you had chosen to do this, an EOCPerson's internal set of friends could be changed from underneath it, potentially causing issues if, for example, the person object wanted to do something else when a friend is added or removed. If the set is altered from underneath it, without its knowing, the object would become inconsistent.

On that note, it is also important not to introspect any object returned to you to find out whether it's mutable. For example, you might be interfacing with a library that contains the EOCPerson class. The developer of that library might not have bothered to hand back a copy of the internal mutable set but instead opted to return the internal mutable set itself. This is legitimate and might be desirable if the set is likely to be extremely large, in which case taking a copy could be costly. It is legal to return an NSMutableSet, since it is a subclass of NSSet, in which case you might be tempted to do something like this:

```
EOCPerson *person = /* … */;
NSSet *friends = person.friends;
if ([friends isKindOfClass:[NSMutableSet class]]) {
    NSMutableSet *mutableFriends = (NSMutableSet*)friends;
    /* mutate the set */
}
```

However, you should avoid that at all costs. It is not the contract that you have with the EOCPerson class, so you should not use introspection techniques like this. The point still stands that the object might not be able to cope with its data changing from beneath it. Therefore, you should not assume that you can.

Things to Remember

✦ When possible, create objects that are immutable.

✦ Extend read-only properties in a class-continuation category to read-write if the property will be set internally.

✦ Provide methods to mutate collections held by objects rather than exposing a mutable collection as a property.

Item 19: Use Clear and Consistent Naming

The naming of classes, methods, variables, and so on is an important factor in Objective-C. Newcomers often consider the language verbose because it uses a syntax structure that ensures that the code can be read like a sentence. Names often include prepositions ("in," "for," "with," etc.), whereas other languages consider their use somewhat superfluous. For example, consider the following section of code:

```
NSString *text = @"The quick brown fox jumped over the lazy dog";
NSString *newText =
    [text stringByReplacingOccurrencesOfString:@"fox"
                                    withString:@"cat"];
```

This code could be considered a long-winded way to write what seems such a simple expression. After all, the method to perform the replacing is 48 characters long. But this definitely reads just like a sentence:

> "Take text and give me a new string by replacing the occurrences of the string "fox" with the string "cat"."

That sentence perfectly describes what is going on. In languages that are less verbose, a similar procedure might look like this:

```
string text = "The quick brown fox jumped over the lazy dog";
string newText = text.replace("fox", "cat");
```

But in which order are the parameters to `text.replace()`? Will "fox" be replaced by "cat" or vice versa? Also, does the `replace` function replace all occurrences or just the first one? It's not very clear. The Objective-C way of naming, however, is completely clear at the expense of more verbosity.

You will also note the use of camel casing—with a lowercase first letter—in method and variable names. Also, class names are always camel cased with an uppercase first letter and are also usually prefixed with two or three letters (see Item 15). This is the style most commonly used throughout Objective-C code. You could use your own style if you so wished, but using camel case will ensure that your names fit and feel right in the Objective-C world.

Method Naming

If you have come from a language such as C++ or Java, you'll be used to functions being fairly concise in name and having to look at the function prototype in order to determine what the parameters do. This makes it very difficult to read code, though, since you often have to refer back to the prototype to remember what the function does. For example, consider a class that represents a rectangle. In C++, you might define it like so:

```
class Rectangle {
public:
    Rectangle(float width, float height);
    float getWidth();
    float getHeight();
private:
    float width;
    float height;
};
```

If you're not familiar with C++, that doesn't matter. All you need to be aware of is that this defines a class that has two instance variables: width and height. It also has a single way to create an instance of the class, called a constructor, that takes the dimensions. It also has accessors for the dimensions. When using the class, you would create an instance like this:

```
Rectangle *aRectangle = new Rectangle(5.0f, 10.0f);
```

When you come to look back at this code, it is not obvious what the 5.0f and the 10.0f represent. You could probably assume that it's the dimensions of the rectangle, but is it the width or the height first? You would need to look back at the definition of the function to find out.

Objective-C overcomes this problem by being much more verbose in the naming of methods. A first effort at an equivalent class in Objective-C from someone familiar with C++ might be as follows:

```
#import <Foundation/Foundation.h>

@interface EOCRectangle : NSObject

@property (nonatomic, assign, readonly) float width;
@property (nonatomic, assign, readonly) float height;

- (id)initWithSize:(float)width :(float)height;

@end
```

The person writing the class like this has obviously seen that the equivalent of constructors is the `init-` family of methods and chosen to use the method name `initWithSize::`. This might already look strange to you, and perhaps you think that having no characters before the second semicolon is syntactically incorrect. In fact, the syntax is perfectly sound, although it looks wrong because it suffers from the same problem as the C++ function name in that if you used the class, you'd be in the same position of not knowing which variable is which:

```
EOCRectangle *aRectangle =
    [[EOCRectangle alloc] initWithSize:5.0f :10.0f];
```

A much better method name is the following:

```
- (id)initWithWidth:(float)width andHeight:(float)height;
```

This is verbose, but there is absolutely no ambiguity over what each variable is when it is used like so:

```
EOCRectangle *aRectangle =
    [[EOCRectangle alloc] initWithWidth:5.0f andHeight:10.0f];
```

Newcomers to Objective-C often have difficulty getting used to the verbose naming of methods, although using verbose naming enhances the readability of code. Don't be afraid to use long method names. Ensuring that method names are as long as they need to be means that they do precisely what they say. But you shouldn't have incredibly long names either. Your method names should be concise and precise.

Take, for example, the `EOCRectangle` class. Well-named methods would include the following:

```
- (EOCRectangle*)unionRectangle:(EOCRectangle*)rectangle
- (float)area
```

However, badly named versions of those methods would include:

```
- (EOCRectangle*)union:(EOCRectangle*)rectangle // Unclear
- (float)calculateTheArea // Too verbose
```

Clearly named methods will read left to right in a manner that flows just as if you were reading a passage of text. Following the many rules that define how methods should be named is not mandatory, but doing so will certainly make your code maintainable and more readable by others.

The `NSString` class is a great place to look for a class that follows good naming-convention guidelines. Here are a few of the methods and why they are named the way they are:

◆ + `string`

Factory method to create a new, empty string. The type of the return value is indicated clearly by the method name.

◆ + `stringWithString:`

Factory method to create a new string that is identical to another string. Just as with the factory method to create an empty string, the return type is indicated by the first word in the method.

◆ + `localizedStringWithFormat:`

Factory method to create a new, localized string with the specified format. The return type is indicated as the second word of the method name here because a modifier is applied to the logical return type. Even though it's still a "string" being returned, it is a more specific kind of string because it has been localized.

◆ - `lowercaseString`

Convert a string by converting all uppercase characters into lowercase. It creates a new string rather than transforming the receiver, so it follows the rule of the return type being part of the method name. A modifier is applied, though, so that precedes the type.

◆ - `intValue`

Parse a string as an integer. Because the return type is `int`, that is the first word. Usually, you would not abbreviate types like this; for example, `string` is never shortened to `str`, but `int` is the type name, so it is fine here. The method name is suffixed with `Value` to make it other than a single word. Single words are usually used for properties. Since `int` is not a property of the string, `Value` is added to qualify what is meant.

◆ - `length`

Obtain the length (number of characters) of the string. This is a single phrase because it is, in effect, a property of the string. It will unlikely be backed by an instance variable, but it is nevertheless still a property of the string. An example of a bad name for this method is `stringLength`. The `string` is superfluous, since the receiver of the method is known to be a string.

◆ - `lengthOfBytesUsingEncoding:`

Obtain the length of the byte array if the string is encoded using the given encoding (ASCII, UTF8, UTF16, etc.). This is similar to `length`, so the same reasons apply from that description. Additionally, a parameter is required by the method. The method name places the parameter immediately after the noun describing its type.

+ - getCharacters:range:

Obtain the individual characters within a given range of the string. This is an example of where get is used as a prefix, something that is not done for accessors, unlike in some other languages. The reason it's used here is that the characters are returned via the array that is passed in as the first argument. The full method signature is as follows:

+ - (void)getCharacters:(unichar*)buffer range:(NSRange)aRange

The first parameter, buffer, should be a pointer to an array large enough to hold the characters in the requested range. The method returns through a parameter (often referred to as an out-parameter) like this, rather than through the return value, since it makes more sense from a memory-management perspective. The caller of the method handles all memory management rather than having creation be performed by the method and requiring the caller to free it. The second parameter is prefixed by a noun describing its type, just as for any parameter. Sometimes, these parameter names are prefixed with a preposition; for example, this method could be named getCharacters:inRange:. This is usually done if extra significance is required for that parameter over any other parameters.

+ - hasPrefix:

Determine whether the string is prefixed by another string. The return type is a Boolean, so it's common here to use has to make any use of it read like a sentence. For example:

[@"Effective Objective-C" hasPrefix:@"Effective"] == YES

If the name were simply prefix:, it would not read as well as it does. Similarly, it could be named isPrefixedWith:, but that would be longer and sound more clumsy.

+ - isEqualToString:

Determine whether two strings are equal. The return type is a Boolean, so just as with hasPrefix:, the method name starts with is to ensure that the method reads like a sentence. Another place that is is used as a prefix is with Boolean properties. If the property name were enabled, for example, the accessors would usually be called setEnabled: and isEnabled.

In summary, following a few rules will help you write well-named methods.

✦ If the method returns a newly created value, the first word in the method name should be its type, unless a qualifier needs to go in front, such as with the localizedString methods. This excludes property accessors, as they do not logically create a new object, even though they may return a copy of an internal object. These accessors should be named after the property they represent.

✦ A parameter should be immediately preceded by a noun describing its type.

✦ Methods that cause an action to happen on an object should contain a verb followed by a noun (or multiple nouns) if the method requires parameters to perform the action.

✦ Avoid abbreviations, such as str, and instead use full names, such as string.

✦ Prefix Boolean properties with is. Methods that return a Boolean but are not direct properties should be prefixed by either has or is, depending on what makes sense for that method.

✦ Reserve the prefix get for use with methods that return values via an out-parameter, such as those that fill a C-style array.

Class and Protocol Naming

Classes and protocols should be given a prefix to avoid namespace clashes (see Item 15) and should be structured so that they read left to right, just like methods do. For example, in the class NSArray and its mutable counterpart subclass, NSMutableArray, mutable comes before array because it describes a specialization of the type.

To illustrate the naming conventions, consider the following, taken from the iOS UI library, UIKit:

✦ UIView (class)

This is a class from which all "views" inherit. They are the building blocks of the user interface and perform the drawing of buttons, text fields, and tables. The name of the class is self-explanatory and uses the UI prefix used throughout the UIKit framework.

✦ UIViewController (class)

A view (UIView) handles drawing views but is not responsible for controlling what is displayed within the view. That is the job of this class: a "view controller." It is named in such a way that it maintains the left-to-right readability.

✦ UITableView (class)

This is a specific type of view to display a list of items in a table. So it is named as the superclass prefixed with a qualifier to distinguish the kind of view it is. This prefixing of the superclass is a common theme throughout the naming conventions. It could be named simply UITable, but that would not be fully clear that it was a view. You would need to look up in the interface declaration to be sure what it was. If you were to create a specific table view designed to display images, you could create a subclass called EOCImageTableView, for example. You always prepend your own prefix, though, rather than use the prefix of the superclass (UIKit's UI prefix in this case). The reason is that you have no right to add something to another framework's namespace, and the other framework may decide to make an identically named class in the future.

✦ UITableViewController (class)

Just as UITableView is a specific kind of view, this is a special kind of view controller designed specifically to control a table view. It is therefore named in a similar manner.

✦ UITableViewDelegate (protocol)

This protocol defines an interface through which a table view can communicate with another object and is named after the class for which it defines the delegate interface, which ensures left-to-right readability. (See Item 23 for more information on the Delegate pattern.)

Above all, you should be consistent with your naming. Also, if you are subclassing a class within another framework, make sure to stick to its conventions. For example, if you create a custom view by subclassing UIView, make sure that the final word of the class name is View. Similarly, if you create your own delegate protocol, you should name it as the class it is a delegate for, followed by the word Delegate. Adhering to this naming structure will ensure that your code makes sense when you come back to it later or another person uses it.

Things to Remember

✦ Follow the naming that has become standard in Objective-C to create interfaces that fit in and feel right.

✦ Ensure that method names are concise but precise, and make their use read left to right just like a sentence.

✦ Avoid using abbreviations of types in method names.

✦ Most important, make sure that method names are consistent with your own code or that with which it is being integrated.

Item 20: Prefix Private Method Names

It's extremely common for a class to do much more than it appears on the outside. When writing a class implementation, it is common to write methods that are used only internally. For such methods, I suggest that you prefix their names with something. This helps with debugging by clearly separating the public methods from the private ones.

Another reason for using a marker for private methods arises when considering changing a method name or signature. If the method is public, a change such as this should be thought about more carefully, since it might not be ideal to change the public API to a class. Thus, consumers of the class would have to update their code as well. However, if the method is an internal one, only the class's own code need change, with no effect on the public-facing API. Using a marker to indicate private methods means that this distinction is easy to see when making such a change.

The prefix to use depends on your personal preference. Good choices of characters to include in a prefix are underscores and the letter p. My preference is for the prefix to be p_, since the p indicates "private," and the underscore gives a visual gap before the start of the method name. The method name then continues in the usual camel case, with a lowercase first letter. For example, a class called EOCObject with private methods might look like this:

```
#import <Foundation/Foundation.h>

@interface EOCObject : NSObject
- (void)publicMethod;
@end

@implementation EOCObject

- (void)publicMethod {
    /* … */
}

- (void)p_privateMethod {
    /* … */
```

```
}
```

@end

Unlike the public method, the private method does not appear in the interface definition. Sometimes, you will want to declare the private method in the class-continuation category (see Item 27); however, recent compiler changes mean that a method does not need to be declared before it is used. So usually, private methods will be declared only in their implementation.

If you've come from a language such as C++ or Java, you're probably wondering why you have to do this rather than simply declaring the method private. In Objective-C, there is no way to mark a method as private. All objects are able to respond to all messages (see Item 12), and it's possible to inspect an object at runtime to determine which messages it will respond to (see Item 14). Method lookup for a given message is performed at runtime (see Item 11), and there is no mechanism for limiting the scope of who, what, or when a certain method can be invoked. It is left to naming conventions to dictate semantics such as private methods. Newcomers may not feel comfortable with this, but embracing the dynamism of Objective-C unleashes its power. Taming the dynamism is crucial, though, and using naming conventions is one way to achieve this.

Apple tends to use a single underscore to prefix its private methods. So you might think that it would be a good idea to follow Apple's cue and also use an underscore. However, this would be a potentially disastrous decision; if you did this in a subclass of an Apple-provided class, you could inadvertently override one of its methods. For this reason, Apple has documented that you should avoid using an underscore as the prefix. It is possibly a downside to the language that there is no way to indicate that a method should exist only in a certain scope, but it is part of the powerful, dynamic method dispatch system (see Item 11), which has many upsides also.

This scenario is potentially not as uncommon as you may think. For example, if you are creating a view controller in an iOS application, you subclass UIViewController. The view controller may hold a lot of state. You want a method that is used to clear all that state, which will be run whenever the view controller comes on screen. So you may end up implementing that method like this:

```
#import <UIKit/UIKit.h>

@interface EOCViewController : UIViewController
```

@end

```
@implementation EOCViewController
- (void)_resetViewController {
    // Reset state and views
}
@end
```

However, it turns out that UIViewController also implements a method called _resetViewController! The version from EOCViewController will be run whenever you call it and for all times that the original version should be run. You wouldn't know that unless you went digging deep into the library, as the method name is not exposed. After all, it's a private method as denoted by the underscore. In this situation, you might end up with strange things happening to the view controller because the original implementation is never called, or you might get confused as to why your version is being called much more often than it should be.

In sum, when you subclass a class in a framework that is neither Apple's nor your own, you cannot know what private prefix, if any, the framework is using unless it is documented. In this case, you may choose to use your chosen class prefix (see Item 15) as the private method prefix to greatly reduce the risk of any potential clashes. Similarly, you should consider how other people might subclass your classes. This is why you should use a prefix for private method names. Without the implementation source code, there is no way, except using rather complicated tools, to find out what methods a class implements other than those documented in the public interface definition.

Things to Remember

✦ Prefix private method names so that they are easily distinguished from public methods.

✦ Avoid using a single underscore as the method prefix, since this is reserved by Apple.

Item 21: Understand the Objective-C Error Model

Many modern languages, including Objective-C, have exceptions. If you have come from a Java background, you'll most likely be accustomed to using exceptions to handle error cases. If you're used to using exceptions for this task, you are going to have to go back and forget everything you knew about exceptions and start again.

The first thing to note is that Automatic Reference Counting (ARC, see Item 30) is not exception safe by default. In practice, this means that any objects that should be released at the end of a scope in which an exception is thrown will not be released. It is possible to turn on a compiler flag to enable exception-safe code to be generated, but it introduces extra code that has to be run even for the scenario in which no exception is thrown. The compiler flag that turns this on is –fobjc-arc-exceptions.

Even when not using ARC, it is difficult to write code that is safe against memory leaks when exceptions are used. Suppose that a resource is created and needs to be released once it is no longer needed. If an exception is thrown before the resource has been released, that release will never be done:

```
id someResource = /* … */;
if ( /* check for error */ ) {
    @throw [NSException exceptionWithName:@"ExceptionName"
                                   reason:@"There was an error"
                                 userInfo:nil];
}
[someResource doSomething];
[someResource release];
```

Of course, the way to solve this problem is to release someResource before throwing; however, if there are many resources to release and more complicated code paths, the code easily becomes cluttered. Also, if something is added to such code, it would be easy to forget to add releases before all times an exception is thrown.

Objective-C has taken the approach recently to save exceptions for the rare scenario in which recovery should be avoided and an exception should cause an application to exit. This means that complex exception-safe code does not need to be involved.

Remembering that exceptions are to be used for fatal errors only, an example of a scenario in which you should consider throwing an exception in your own classes is when creating an abstract base class that should be subclassed before being used. Objective-C has no language construct to say that a class is abstract, unlike some other languages. So the best way to achieve a similar effect is to throw an exception in any method that must be overridden in subclasses. Anyone who then tries to create an instance of the abstract base class and use it will get an exception thrown:

```
- (void)mustOverrideMethod {
    NSString *reason = [NSString stringWithFormat:
```

```
                              @"%@ must be overridden",
                        NSStringFromSelector(_cmd)];
    @throw [NSException
          exceptionWithName:NSInternalInconsistencyException
                        reason:reason
                     userInfo:nil];
}
```

But if exceptions are to be used only for fatal errors, what about other errors? The paradigm chosen by Objective-C to indicate nonfatal errors is either to return nil / 0 from methods where an error has occurred or to use NSError. An example of returning nil / 0 is when in an initializer and an instance cannot be initialized with the parameters passed in:

```
- (id)initWithValue:(id)value {
    if ((self = [super init])) {
        if ( /* Value means instance can't be created */ ) {
            self = nil;
        } else {
            // Initialize instance
        }
    }
    return self;
}
```

In this scenario, if the if statement determines that the instance can't be created with the value passed in—maybe value needs to be non-nil itself—self is set to nil, and this is what will be returned. A caller of the initializer will understand that there has been an error, because no instance will have been created.

Using NSError provides much more flexibility because it enables a reason to be given back as to what the error is. An NSError object encapsulates three pieces of information:

✦ *Error domain (String)*

The domain in which the error occurred. This is usually a global variable that can be used to uniquely define the source of the error. The URL-handling subsystem uses the domain NSURLErrorDomain, for example, for all errors that come from parsing or obtaining data from URLs.

✦ *Error code (Integer)*

A code that uniquely defines within a certain error domain what error has occurred. Often, an enum is used to define the set of errors that can occur within a certain error domain. HTTP requests that fail might use the HTTP status code for this value, for example.

✦ *User info (Dictionary)*

Extra information about the error, such as a localized description and another error representing the error that caused this error to occur, to allow information about chains of errors to be represented.

The first way in which errors are commonly used in API design is through the use of delegate protocols. When an error occurs, an object may pass its delegate the error through one of the protocol's methods. For example, NSURLConnection includes the following method as part of its delegate protocol, NSURLConnectionDelegate:

```
- (void)connection:(NSURLConnection *)connection
    didFailWithError:(NSError *)error
```

When a connection decides that there is an error, such as the connection to the remote server times out, this method is called handing an error representing what happened. This delegate method doesn't have to be implemented, so it is up to the user of the NSURLConnection class to decide it is necessary to know about the error. This is preferable to throwing an exception, since it's left up to the user to decide whether to be told about the error.

The other common way in which NSError is used is through an out-parameter passed to a method. It looks like this:

```
- (BOOL)doSomething:(NSError**)error
```

The error variable being passed to the method is a pointer to a pointer to an NSError. Or you can think of it as a pointer to an NSError object. This enables the method to, in effect, return an NSError object in addition to its return value. It's used like this:

```
NSError *error = nil;
BOOL ret = [object doSomething:&error];
if (error) {
    // There was an error
}
```

Often, methods that return an error like this also return a Boolean to indicate success or failure so that you can check the Boolean if you don't care about what the precise error was or, if you do care, you can check the returned error. The error parameter can also be nil when you don't care what the returned error is. For instance, you might use the method like this:

```
BOOL ret = [object doSomething:nil];
if (ret) {
    // There was an error
}
```

In reality, when using ARC, the compiler translates the NSError** in the method signature to NSError*__autoreleasing*; this means that the object pointed to will be autoreleased at the end of the method. The object has to do this because the doSomething: method cannot guarantee that the caller will be able to release the NSError object it created and therefore must add in an autorelease. This gives the same semantics as return values from most methods (excluding, of course, methods that begin with new, alloc, copy, and mutableCopy).

The method passes back the error through the out-parameter like this:

```
- (BOOL)doSomething:(NSError**)error {
    // Do something that may cause an error

    if ( /* there was an error */ ) {
        if (error) {
            // Pass the 'error' through the out-parameter
            *error = [NSError errorWithDomain:domain
                                         code:code
                                     userInfo:userInfo];
        }
        return NO; ///< Indicate failure
    } else {
        return YES; ///< Indicate success
    }
}
```

The error parameter is dereferenced using the *error syntax, meaning that the value pointed to by error is set to the new NSError object. The error parameter must first be checked to see whether it is non-nil, since dereferencing the null pointer will result in a segmentation fault and cause a crash. Since it is fine for a caller to pass nil, this check must be made for the case that it doesn't care about the error,

The domain, code, and user information portions of the error object should be set to something that makes sense for the error that has happened. This enables the caller to behave differently, depending on the type of error that has occurred. The domain is best defined as a global constant NSString, and the error codes are best defined as an enumeration type. For example, you might define them like this:

```
// EOCErrors.h
extern NSString *const EOCErrorDomain;

typedef NS_ENUM(NSUInteger, EOCError) {
    EOCErrorUnknown                 = -1,
    EOCErrorInternalInconsistency = 100,
    EOCErrorGeneralFault            = 105,
    EOCErrorBadInput                = 500,
};
// EOCErrors.m
NSString *const EOCErrorDomain = @"EOCErrorDomain";
```

Creating an error domain for your library is prudent, since it allows you to create and return NSError objects that consumers can ascertain came from your library. Creating an enumeration type for the error codes is also a good idea, since it documents the errors and gives the codes a meaningful name. You may also decide to comment the header file where they are defined with even more detailed descriptions of each error type.

Things to Remember

✦ Use exceptions only for fatal errors that should bring down the entire application.

✦ For nonfatal errors, either provide a delegate method to handle errors or offer an out-parameter NSError object.

Item 22: Understand the NSCopying Protocol

A common thing to want to do with an object is to copy it. In Objective-C, this is done through the use of the copy method. The way in which you can support copying of your own classes is to implement the NSCopying protocol, which contains a single method:

```
- (id)copyWithZone:(NSZone*)zone
```

This harks back to the day when NSZone was used to segment memory into zones, and objects were created within a certain zone. Nowadays, every app has a single zone: the default zone. So even though this is the method you need to implement, you do not need to worry about what the zone parameter is.

The copy method is implemented in NSObject and simply calls copyWithZone: with the default zone. It's important to remember that even though it might be tempting to override copy, it's copyWithZone: that needs to be implemented instead.

To support copying, then, all you need to do is state that you implement the NSCopying protocol and implement the single method within it. For example, consider a class representing a person. In the interface definition, you would declare that you implement NSCopying:

```
#import <Foundation/Foundation.h>

@interface EOCPerson : NSObject <NSCopying>

@property (nonatomic, copy, readonly) NSString *firstName;
@property (nonatomic, copy, readonly) NSString *lastName;

- (id)initWithFirstName:(NSString*)firstName
            andLastName:(NSString*)lastName;

@end
```

Then, you would implement the single required method of the protocol:

```
- (id)copyWithZone:(NSZone*)zone {
    EOCPerson *copy = [[[self class] allocWithZone:zone]
                        initWithFirstName:_firstName
                              andLastName:_lastName];
    return copy;
}
```

This example simply passes all work in initializing the copy to the designated initializer. Sometimes, you might need to perform further work on the copy, such as if other data structures within the class are not set up in the initializer: for example, if EOCPerson contained an array that was manipulated using a couple of methods to befriend and unfriend another EOCPerson. In that scenario, you'd also want to copy the array of friends. Following is a full example of how this would work:

```
#import <Foundation/Foundation.h>

@interface EOCPerson : NSObject <NSCopying>

@property (nonatomic, copy, readonly) NSString *firstName;
@property (nonatomic, copy, readonly) NSString *lastName;

- (id)initWithFirstName:(NSString*)firstName
            andLastName:(NSString*)lastName;
```

```objc
- (void)addFriend:(EOCPerson*)person;
- (void)removeFriend:(EOCPerson*)person;

@end

@implementation EOCPerson {
    NSMutableSet *_friends;
}

- (id)initWithFirstName:(NSString*)firstName
             andLastName:(NSString*)lastName {
    if ((self = [super init])) {
        _firstName = [firstName copy];
        _lastName = [lastName copy];
        _friends = [NSMutableSet new];
    }
    return self;
}

- (void)addFriend:(EOCPerson*)person {
    [_friends addObject:person];
}

- (void)removeFriend:(EOCPerson*)person {
    [_friends removeObject:person];
}

- (id)copyWithZone:(NSZone*)zone {
    EOCPerson *copy = [[[self class] allocWithZone:zone]
                        initWithFirstName:_firstName
                              andLastName:_lastName];
    copy->_friends = [_friends mutableCopy];
    return copy;
}

@end
```

This time, the copying method has been changed to additionally set the _friends instance variable of the copy to a copy of its own _friends instance variable. Note that the -> syntax has been used here, since the _friends instance variable is internal. A property could have been declared for it, but since it's never used externally, there is no need to do so.

An interesting question is raised by this example: Why is a copy taken of the _friends instance variable? You could have just as easily not taken a copy, and each object would then share the same mutable set. But that would mean that if a friend were added to the original object, it would also magically become a friend of the copy. That's clearly not what you would want in this scenario. But if the set were immutable, you might have chosen to not take a copy, since the set cannot change, anyway. This would save having two identical sets lying around in memory.

You should generally use the designated initializer to initialize the copy, just as in this example. But you wouldn't want to do this when the designated initializer has a side effect that you don't want to happen to the copy, such as setting up complex internal data structures that you are immediately going to overwrite.

If you look back up to the copyWithZone: method, you will see that the friends set is copied using the mutableCopy method. This comes from another protocol, called NSMutableCopying. It is similar to NSCopying but defines the following method instead:

```
- (id)mutableCopyWithZone:(NSZone*)zone
```

The mutableCopy helper is just like the copy helper and calls the preceding method with the default zone. You should implement NSMutableCopying if you have mutable and immutable variants of your class. When using this pattern, you should not override copyWithZone: in your mutable class to return a mutable copy. Instead, if a mutable copy is required of either an immutable or a mutable instance, you should use mutableCopy. Similarly, if an immutable copy is required, you should use copy.

The following holds true in the case of NSArray and NSMutableArray:

```
-[NSMutableArray copy] => NSArray
-[NSArray mutableCopy] => NSMutableArray
```

Note the subtlety with calling copy on a mutable object and being given an instance of another class, the immutable variant. This is done so that it is easy to switch between mutable and immutable variants. Another way this could have been achieved is to have three methods: copy, immutableCopy, and mutableCopy, where copy always returns the same class, but the other two return specific variants. However, this would not be good if you don't know whether the instance you have is immutable. You may decide to call copy on something you have been returned as an NSArray but in fact it's an NSMutableArray. In that case, you would assume that you have an immutable array returned, but instead it's a mutable one.

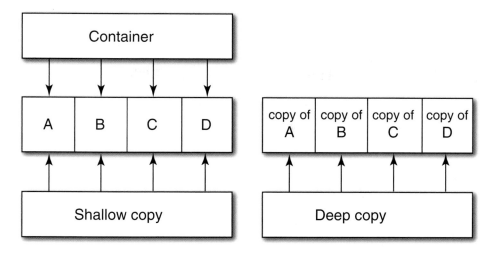

Figure 3.2 Shallow versus deep copy. The contents of a shallow copy point to the same objects as the original. The contents of a deep copy point to copies of the original contents.

You could introspect (see Item 14) to determine what type of instance you have, but that would add complexity everywhere a copy is taken. So you would end up always using immutableCopy or mutableCopy to be on the safe side, in which case, it's back to just having just two methods, which is exactly the same as having only copy and mutableCopy. The benefit of calling it copy instead of immutableCopy is that NSCopying is designed not only for classes with mutable and immutable variants but also cases in which there is not the distinction, so immutableCopy would be a badly named method.

Another decision to make with your copying method is whether to perform a deep or a shallow copy. A deep copy copies all the backing data as well. Copying by default for all the collection classes in Foundation is shallow, meaning that only the container is copied, not the data stored within the container. This is mainly because objects within the container might not be able to be copied; also, it's usually not desirable to copy every object. The difference between a deep and a shallow copy is illustrated in Figure 3.2.

Usually, you will want your own classes to follow the same pattern as used in the system frameworks, with copyWithZone: performing a shallow copy. But if required, a method can be added to perform a deep copy. In the case of NSSet, this is provided through the following initializer method:

```
- (id)initWithSet:(NSArray*)array copyItems:(BOOL)copyItems
```

If copyItems is set to YES, the items in the array are sent the copy message to create a copy to build up the new set to return.

In the example of the EOCPerson class, the set containing the friends is copied in copyWithZone:, but as discussed, this does not copy the items in the set themselves. But if such a deep copy were required, you could provide a method such as the following:

```
- (id)deepCopy {
    EOCPerson *copy = [[[self class] alloc]
                         initWithFirstName:_firstName
                             andLastName:_lastName];
    copy->_friends = [[NSMutableSet alloc] initWithSet:_friends
                                             copyItems:YES];

    return copy;
}
```

No protocol defines deep copying, so it is left up to each class to define how such a copy is made. You simply need to decide whether you need to provide a deep copy method. Also, you should never assume that an object conforming to NSCopying will be performing a deep copy. In the vast majority of cases, it will be a shallow copy. If you need a deep copy of any object, either find the relevant method, or assume that you have to create your own, unless the documentation states that its implementation of NSCopying is providing a deep copy.

Things to Remember

✦ Implement the NSCopying protocol if your object will need to be copied.

✦ If your object has mutable and immutable variants, implement both the NSCopying and NSMutableCopying protocols.

✦ Decide whether a copy will be shallow or deep, and prefer shallow, where possible, for a normal copy.

✦ Consider adding a deep-copy method if deep copies of your object will be useful.

Protocols and Categories

Protocols are a language feature similar to interfaces in Java. Objective-C does not have multiple inheritance, so protocols provide a way to define a set of methods that a class should implement. Protocols are most often used in implementing the Delegate pattern (see Item 23), but there are other uses as well. Getting to know them and using them can make code a lot more maintainable, as they are a good way of documenting an interface to your code.

Categories too are an important language feature of Objective-C. They provide a mechanism for adding methods to a class without having to subclass it as you would have to in other languages. This feature is made possible by the highly dynamic nature of the runtime but also comes with pitfalls that you should understand before using categories.

Item 23: Use Delegate and Data Source Protocols for Interobject Communication

Objects will often need to talk to each other and can do so in many ways. One such programming design pattern used extensively by Objective-C developers is known as the Delegate pattern, the essence of which is to define an interface that any object can conform to in order to become the delegate of another object. This other object then talks back to its delegate to get some information or to inform the delegate when interesting things happen.

Using this pattern enables the decoupling of data from business logic. For instance, a view in a user interface to display a list of data should be responsible only for the logic of how data is displayed, not for deciding what data should be displayed or what happens in data interaction. The view object can have properties that contain objects responsible for the data and event handling. These are known as the data source and delegate, respectively.

In Objective-C, the usual way of achieving this pattern is to use the protocol language feature, which is used throughout the frameworks that make up Cocoa. If you use this feature yourself, you'll find that your own code will fit appropriately.

As an example, consider a class that is used to fetch data from the network. A class might do so to retrieve some data from a resource on a distant server. It might take a long time for the server to respond, and it would be rather bad practice to block while the data was being retrieved. So it's common in this scenario to use the Delegate pattern, whereby the fetcher class has a delegate that it calls back once the data has been retrieved. Figure 4.1 illustrates this concept; the EOCDataModel object is the delegate of EOCNetworkFetcher. The EOCDataModel asks the EOCNetworkFetcher to perform a task asynchronously, and EOCNetworkFetcher tells its delegate, the EOCDataModel, when that task has completed.

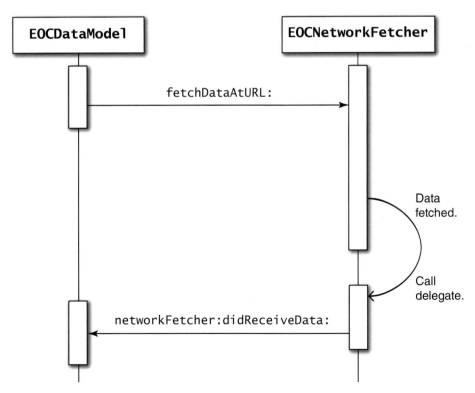

Figure 4.1 A delegate callback. Note that the EOCDataModel instance doesn't necessarily have to be the delegate but could be another object.

This pattern is easy to implement using Objective-C through the use of a protocol. In the case of Figure 4.1, the protocol might look like this:

```
@protocol EOCNetworkFetcherDelegate
- (void)networkFetcher:(EOCNetworkFetcher*)fetcher
        didReceiveData:(NSData*)data;
- (void)networkFetcher:(EOCNetworkFetcher*)fetcher
        didFailWithError:(NSError*)error;
@end
```

A delegate protocol is usually named as the class name followed by the word delegate, using camel casing for the whole name. Following this naming pattern will make your delegate protocol feel familiar to anyone using it.

The protocol provides a property on the class that has the delegate. In our example, this is the EOCNetworkFetcher class. Therefore, the interface would look like this:

```
@interface EOCNetworkFetcher : NSObject
@property (nonatomic, weak)
    id <EOCNetworkFetcherDelegate> delegate;
@end
```

It's important to make sure that the property is defined as weak and not strong, since it must be a nonowning relationship. Usually, the object that will be the delegate will also hold onto the object. An object wanting to use an EOCNetworkFetcher, for example, will keep hold of it until finished with it. If the property holding the delegate were an owning relationship using the strong attribute, a retain cycle would be introduced. For this reason, a delegate property will always be defined using either the weak attribute to benefit from autonilling (see Item 6) or unsafe_unretained if autonilling is not required. The ownership diagram shown in Figure 4.2 illustrates this.

Implementing the delegate is a matter of declaring that your class implements the delegate protocol and then implementing any methods you want from the protocol. You can declare that a class implements a protocol in either the interface or the class-continuation category (see Item 27). Declaring it in the interface is useful if you want to advertise to others that you implement that protocol; however, in the case of delegates, it's usual to care only about it internally. So it's common to declare it in the class-continuation category like so:

```
@implementation EOCDataModel () <EOCNetworkFetcherDelegate>
@end
```

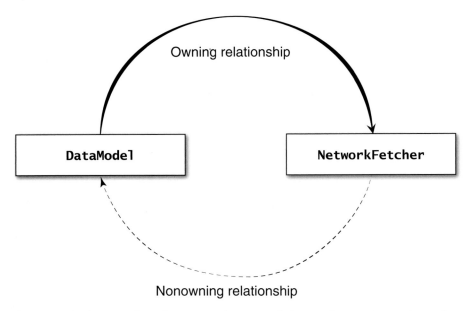

Figure 4.2 Ownership diagram showing delegate being nonretained in order to avoid retain cycle

```
@implementation EOCDataModel
- (void)networkFetcher:(EOCNetworkFetcher*)fetcher
        didReceiveData:(NSData*)data {
   /* Handle data */
}
- (void)networkFetcher:(EOCNetworkFetcher*)fetcher
        didFailWithError:(NSError*)error {
   /* Handle error */
}
@end
```

Usually, methods within a delegate protocol will be optional, since the object being the delegate may not care about all the methods. In the example, the DataModel class may not care that an error occurred, so might not implement the networkFetcher:didFailWithError: method. To indicate this, delegate protocols usually make most or all methods optional by applying the @optional keyword:

```
@protocol EOCNetworkFetcherDelegate
@optional
- (void)networkFetcher:(EOCNetworkFetcher*)fetcher
        didReceiveData:(NSData*)data;
- (void)networkFetcher:(EOCNetworkFetcher*)fetcher
```

```
        didFailWithError:(NSError*)error;
@end
```

Before any optional method is called on the delegate, introspection (see Item 14) should be used to determine whether the delegate responds to that selector. In the case of EOCNetworkFetcher, it would look like this:

```
NSData *data = /* data obtained from network */;
if ([_delegate respondsToSelector:
        @selector(networkFetcher:didReceiveData:)])
{
    [_delegate networkFetcher:self didReceiveData:data];
}
```

The respondsToSelector: method is used to determine whether the delegate has implemented that method. If yes, it's called; otherwise, nothing happens. In that way, the delegate method is truly optional, and nothing will break if it's not implemented. Even if no delegate is set, it will still function perfectly well, since sending a message to nil will make the if statement evaluate to false.

Getting the name of your delegate methods correct is also important. The name should indicate exactly what is happening and why the delegate is being told something. In the example, the delegate method reads very clearly, saying that a certain network fetcher object has just received some data. You should also always pass the instance that is delegating, just as in the example, so that the delegate method implementation can switch based on the specific instance. For example:

```
- (void)networkFetcher:(EOCNetworkFetcher*)fetcher
        didReceiveData:(NSData*)data
{
    if (fetcher == _myFetcherA) {
        /* Handle data */
    } else if (fetcher == _myFetcherB) {
        /* Handle data */
    }
}
```

Here, the object being the delegate has two network fetchers and so must be told which network fetcher is telling it that data has been received. Without being told this information, the object would be able to use only one network fetcher at a time, which would not be ideal.

The delegate methods can also be used to obtain information from the delegate. For example, the network fetcher class might want to

provide a mechanism such that if it encounters a redirect while fetching the data, it asks its delegate whether the redirect should occur.
The delegate method for this may look like the following:

```
- (BOOL)networkFetcher:(EOCNetworkFetcher*)fetcher
        shouldFollowRedirectToURL:(NSURL*)url;
```

This example should make it easy to see why it's called the Delegate
pattern, since the object is delegating responsibility for an action to
another class.

Protocols can also be used to provide an interface through which the
data that a class requires is obtained. This other use of the Delegate
pattern is referred to as the Data Source pattern because its aim is to
provide data to the class. The flow of information is toward the class;
with a normal delegate, the flow of information is away from the class.
This flow is illustrated in Figure 4.3.

For example, a list view object in a user interface framework might
use a data source protocol to provide the data to show in the list. The
list view may also have a delegate to handle user interaction with the
list. The separation of the data source and delegate protocols provides
a cleaner interface by separating distinct portions of logic. In addition, you could have one object be the data source and another be the
delegate. However, the same object usually ends up being both.

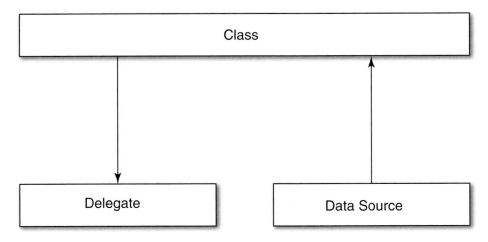

Figure 4.3 Flow of information is out of the class for a delegate and
into the class for a data source.

With the Delegate and Data Source patterns where implementing any of the methods is optional, you will have a lot of code that looks like the following:

```
if ([_delegate respondsToSelector:
        @selector(someClassDidSomething:)])
{
    [_delegate someClassDidSomething];
}
```

Checking whether the delegate responds to a certain selector is pretty quick, but if you do this repeatedly, responses after the first one are potentially redundant. If the delegate hasn't changed, it's extremely unlikely that it has suddenly started or stopped responding to the given selector. For this reason, it is common to make the optimization of caching whether the delegate responds to the methods in the protocol. For example, the network fetcher in the example has a delegate method that is called back as a progress indicator, telling the delegate every so often how far the network fetch has progressed. This method may get called many times during the life cycle of the fetcher, and checking each time whether the delegate responds to the selector is redundant.

Consider the expanded delegate protocol for the selector defined like so:

```
@protocol EOCNetworkFetcherDelegate
@optional
- (void)networkFetcher:(EOCNetworkFetcher*)fetcher
        didReceiveData:(NSData*)data;
- (void)networkFetcher:(EOCNetworkFetcher*)fetcher
        didFailWithError:(NSError*)error;
- (void)networkFetcher:(EOCNetworkFetcher*)fetcher
        didUpdateProgressTo:(float)progress;
@end
```

The single, optional method networkFetcher:didUpdateProgressTo: has been called in here. The best way for the caching to be done is to use the bitfield data type. This feature from C is often overlooked but is excellent for this purpose. It allows you to define that a certain field of a structure should be sized a certain number of bits. It looks like this:

```
struct data {
    unsigned int fieldA : 8;
    unsigned int fieldB : 4;
    unsigned int fieldC : 2;
    unsigned int fieldD : 1;
};
```

In this structure, fieldA will use exactly 8 bits, fieldB will use 4 bits, fieldC will use 2 bits, and fieldD will use 1 bit. So fieldA will be able to hold values from 0 to 255, and fieldD will be able to hold either 0 or 1. The latter is of interest for caching what methods a delegate implements. If you create a structure that uses only 1-bit bitfields, you can pack in a lot of Booleans into a small amount of data. For the example of the network fetcher, you would make the instance have a structure as one of its instance variables containing the bitfield, one variable for each delegate method. The structure would look like this:

```
@interface EOCNetworkFetcher () {
    struct {
        unsigned int didReceiveData       : 1;
        unsigned int didFailWithError     : 1;
        unsigned int didUpdateProgressTo  : 1;
    } _delegateFlags;
}
@end
```

Here, I have used the class-continuation category to add the instance variable, as explained in Item 27: The instance variable that has been added is a structure containing three fields, one for each of the optional delegate methods. The structure can be queried and set by using the following from within the EOCNetworkFetcher class:

```
// Set flag
_delegateFlags.didReceiveData = 1;

// Check flag
if (_delegateFlags.didReceiveData) {
    // Yes, flag set
}
```

This structure is used to cache whether the delegate responds to the given selectors. This can be done from within the setter accessor method for the delegate property:

```
- (void)setDelegate:(id<EOCNetworkFetcher>)delegate {
    _delegate = delegate;
    _delegateFlags.didReceiveData =
        [delegate respondsToSelector:
                @selector(networkFetcher:didReceiveData:)];
    _delegateFlags.didFailWithError =
        [delegate respondsToSelector:
                @selector(networkFetcher:didFailWithError:)];
    _delegateFlags.didUpdateProgressTo =
```

```
    [delegate respondsToSelector:
            @selector(networkFetcher:didUpdateProgressTo:)];
}
```

Then, instead of checking whether the delegate responds to the given selector each time a delegate method is called, the flags are checked instead:

```
if (_delegateFlags.didUpdateProgressTo) {
    [_delegate networkFetcher:self
            didUpdateProgressTo:currentProgress];
}
```

If this is called many times, it's a worthwhile optimization to make. The need to make this optimization depends on your code. You should instrument your code and determine where the hot spots are and keep this under your belt as a potential for a speed improvement. It's most likely to make an impact in data source protocols in which the data source is asked repeatedly for each individual piece of data.

Things to Remember

✦ Use the Delegate pattern to provide an interface to your objects that need to tell other objects about pertinent events.

✦ Define a protocol with potentially optional methods to define the interface that your delegate should support.

✦ Use the Delegate pattern when an object needs to obtain data from another object. In this case, it is often referred to as a "data source protocol."

✦ If required, implement the bitfield structure approach to cache which methods a delegate responds to from the protocol.

Item 24: Use Categories to Break Class Implementations into Manageable Segments

A class can easily become bloated with many methods all interspersed throughout a huge implementation file. Sometimes, that's just the way it is, and no amount of refactoring to split up the class can make the situation better. In that case, Objective-C categories can be used to great effect to split up a class into logical subsections that aid not only development but also debugging.

Consider a class that models a person. The person might have a few methods available on it:

```
#import <Foundation/Foundation.h>

@interface EOCPerson : NSObject
@property (nonatomic, copy, readonly) NSString *firstName;
@property (nonatomic, copy, readonly) NSString *lastName;
@property (nonatomic, strong, readonly) NSArray *friends;

- (id)initWithFirstName:(NSString*)firstName
            andLastName:(NSString*)lastName;

/* Friendship methods */
- (void)addFriend:(EOCPerson*)person;
- (void)removeFriend:(EOCPerson*)person;
- (BOOL)isFriendsWith:(EOCPerson*)person;

/* Work methods */
- (void)performDaysWork;
- (void)takeVacationFromWork;

/* Play methods */
- (void)goToTheCinema;
- (void)goToSportsGame;

@end
```

The implementation for such a class would contain all methods in a long list in one big file. As more methods are added to the class, the file will only get longer and more unmanageable. So it is often useful to split up such a class into separate, distinct portions. For example, the preceding could be rewritten to make use of categories:

```
#import <Foundation/Foundation.h>

@interface EOCPerson : NSObject
@property (nonatomic, copy, readonly) NSString *firstName;
@property (nonatomic, copy, readonly) NSString *lastName;
@property (nonatomic, strong, readonly) NSArray *friends;

- (id)initWithFirstName:(NSString*)firstName
            andLastName:(NSString*)lastName;
@end

@interface EOCPerson (Friendship)
- (void)addFriend:(EOCPerson*)person;
- (void)removeFriend:(EOCPerson*)person;
```

```
- (BOOL)isFriendsWith:(EOCPerson*)person;
@end

@interface EOCPerson (Work)
- (void)performDaysWork;
- (void)takeVacationFromWork;
@end

@interface EOCPerson (Play)
- (void)goToTheCinema;
- (void)goToSportsGame;
@end
```

Now, each distinct part of the class is split into separate categories of methods. Not surprisingly, this language feature is called categories! In the example, the bases of the class, including the properties and initializer, are declared within the main implementation. Additional sets of methods, relating to different types of actions, are split into categories.

The entire class could still be defined within one interface file and one implementation file, but as the categories grow, the single implementation file could easily become unmanageable. In that case, categories could be extracted into their own files. For example, the categories in EOCPerson could be extracted into separate files:

✦ EOCPerson+Friendship(.h/.m)

✦ EOCPerson+Work(.h/.m)

✦ EOCPerson+Play(.h/.m)

For example, the friendship category would look like this:

```
// EOCPerson+Friendship.h
#import "EOCPerson.h"

@interface EOCPerson (Friendship)
- (void)addFriend:(EOCPerson*)person;
- (void)removeFriend:(EOCPerson*)person;
- (BOOL)isFriendsWith:(EOCPerson*)person;
@end

// EOCPerson+Friendship.m
#import "EOCPerson+Friendship.h"

@implementation EOCPerson (Friendship)
- (void)addFriend:(EOCPerson*)person {
```

```
        /* … */
}
-  (void)removeFriend:(EOCPerson*)person {
        /* … */
}
-  (BOOL)isFriendsWith:(EOCPerson*)person {
        /* … */
}
@end
```

The class has been split up into much more manageable chunks of code that can be inspected individually. You must then remember to import the EOCPerson.h header along with any category headers anywhere that the category methods are required. But this is a good way of making your code more manageable.

Even if a class is not too large, using categories to split it into subsections can be a useful way to segment code into functional areas. An example of such a class that does this within Cocoa is NSURLRequest and its mutable counterpart, NSMutableURLRequest. This class performs requests to obtain data from a URL and is used mostly with HTTP to obtain data from a server on the Internet somewhere, but the class is generic and can be used with other protocols as well. However, HTTP requests require additional information to be set on them beyond what standard URL requests require, such as the HTTP methods (GET, POST, etc.) or HTTP headers.

But NSURLRequest is not easily subclassed, since it wraps a set of C functions that act on a CFURLRequest data structure, including all the HTTP methods. So the HTTP-specific methods are simply added to NSURLRequest as a category called NSHTTPURLRequest, and the mutation methods are added to NSMutableURLRequest as a category called NSMutableHTTPURLRequest. This way, all the underlying CFURLRequest functions are wrapped within the same Objective-C class, but the HTTP-specific methods are split into a separate area to avoid confusion such that users might wonder why they are able to set the HTTP method on a request object that uses the protocol FTP.

Another useful reason to split up a class into categories is for debugging purposes; the category name is added to the symbol for all methods within that category. For example, the addFriend: method has the following symbol name:

```
-[EOCPerson(Friendship) addFriend:]
```

When it appears in backtraces in a debugger, it will look something like this:

```
frame #2: 0x00001c50 Test'-[EOCPerson(Friendship) addFriend:]
+ 32 at main.m:46
```

The category name within the backtrace can be extremely useful for pinpointing exactly which functional area of the class the method relates to, which is particularly useful when certain methods should be regarded as private. In that case, it might be useful to create a category called Private that contains all these methods. Such categories' methods are generally used only internally to a class or framework and not exposed. If a user finds such a method—perhaps by reading a backtrace—the private in the name should help to indicate that the method should not be used directly. In a way, it is a method of self-documenting code.

The idea of a Private category is useful when creating a library that will be shared by other developers. Often, some methods should not form part of the public API but are quite nice to use within the library itself. In this scenario, creating a Private category is a good option, since its header can be imported wherever the methods need to be used within the library. If that category header is not released as part of the library's release, consumers of the library would have no idea that those private methods exist.

Things to Remember

✦ Use categories to split a class implementation into more manageable fragments.

✦ Create a category called Private to hide implementation detail of methods that should be considered as private.

Item 25: Always Prefix Category Names on Third-Party Classes

Categories are commonly used to add functionality to an existing class for which you don't own the source code. This is an extremely powerful feature, but it is also very easy to overlook a problem that can arise when doing so. The problem stems from the fact that methods in a category are added to the class as if they were part of the class itself. This happens at runtime when the category is loaded. The runtime goes through each method implemented by a category and adds it to the class's method list. If a method in a category already exists, the category method wins and becomes the implementation of that method. This overriding can happen over and over again in fact, so a method in one category can override a method in another category that overrides a method in the main class implementation. The last category to be loaded wins.

For example, suppose that you decide to add a category on NSString to provide some helper methods for dealing with strings related to HTTP URLs. You may decide to define the category like this:

```
@interface NSString (HTTP)

// Encode a string with URL encoding
- (NSString*)urlEncodedString;

// Decode a URL encoded string
- (NSString*)urlDecodedString;

@end
```

This reads absolutely fine here, but consider what might happen if another category is added that also adds methods to NSString. The second category might also add a method called urlEncodedString but might implement it slightly differently and incorrectly for your purposes. If loaded after your category, the second category will win, and your code will be calling the implementation defined in that category. This may cause your own code to not work properly, as it will get unexpected results. This bug may be hard to track down, as you may not know that your implementation of urlEncodedString is not the code being run.

A typical way to overcome this problem is to namespace the category name and the methods it defines. The only way within Objective-C to namespace is to prepend names with a common prefix. Just as you should do with classes (see Item 15), you should choose a prefix that suits the situation. Often, the prefix will be the same one used with the rest of your application or library. Thus, the NSString category might become the following for a prefix of ABC:

```
@interface NSString (ABC_HTTP)

// Encode a string with URL encoding
- (NSString*)abc_urlEncodedString;

// Decode a URL encoded string
- (NSString*)abc_urlDecodedString;

@end
```

Technically, you don't have to namespace the name of the category itself. Nothing goes wrong if you have two categories named the same. But it's not good practice, and you will get a compiler warning that looks like this:

```
warning: duplicate definition of category 'HTTP' on interface
'NSString'
```

It is not impossible for another category to override your method, but it's now much less likely, since another library is unlikely to use the same prefix. It also avoids the potential for the developer of the class to add in an update a method that clashes with your added method. For instance, if Apple were to add the method urlEncodedString to NSString, your method of the same name would override Apple's, which is undesirable, since other users of NSString may be expecting the output from Apple's implementation. Or Apple's implementation may include side effects that your method does not provide and potentially produce inconsistencies internally, producing bugs that are hard to find.

You also need to remember that methods added to a class in a category are available to every single instance of that class within your application. If you add methods to a system-supplied class, such as NSString, NSArray or NSNumber, for example, every instance of those classes will be able to call your added methods even if they are not created from your own code. If you accidentally override a method by using the category or clash with a category added by a third-party library, strange bugs can occur because you think it's your code being executed when it's not. Similarly, purposefully overriding methods in a category is bad practice, especially if your code will form a library used by other developers who might rely on the existing functionality, for instance. Worse still, another developer may override the same method, in which case the method winning in the overriding process is undefined. This is another example of why you should namespace method names in categories.

Things to Remember

✦ Always prepend your naming prefix to the names of categories you add to classes that are not your own.

✦ Always prepend your naming prefix to the method names within categories you add to classes that are not your own.

Item 26: Avoid Properties in Categories

A property is a way of encapsulating data (see Item 6). Although it is technically possible to declare a property in a category, you should avoid doing so if possible. The reason is that it is impossible for a category, except the class-continuation category (see Item 27), to add instance variables to a class. Therefore, it is also impossible for the category to synthesize an instance variable to back the property.

Suppose that after reading Item 24, you have decided to use categories to split up into distinct fragments your implementation of a class representing a person. You might decide to have a friendship category for all the methods relating to manipulating the list of friends associated with a person. Without knowing about the problem described earlier, you may also put the property for the list of friends within the friendship category, like so:

```
#import <Foundation/Foundation.h>

@interface EOCPerson : NSObject
@property (nonatomic, copy, readonly) NSString *firstName;
@property (nonatomic, copy, readonly) NSString *lastName;

- (id)initWithFirstName:(NSString*)firstName
          andLastName:(NSString*)lastName;
@end

@implementation EOCPerson
// Methods
@end

@interface EOCPerson (Friendship)
@property (nonatomic, strong) NSArray *friends;
- (BOOL)isFriendsWith:(EOCPerson*)person;
@end

@implementation EOCPerson (Friendship)
// Methods
@end
```

If you compile this, however, you would end up with compiler warnings:

```
warning: property 'friends' requires method 'friends' to be
defined - use @dynamic or provide a method implementation in
this category [-Wobjc-property-implementation]
```

warning: property 'friends' requires method 'setFriends:' to be defined - use @dynamic or provide a method implementation in this category [-Wobjc-property-implementation]

This slightly cryptic warning means that instance variables cannot be synthesized by a category and, therefore, that the property needs to have the accessor methods implemented in the category. Alternatively, the accessor methods can be declared @dynamic, meaning that you are declaring that they will be available at runtime but cannot be seen by the compiler. This might be the case if you are using the message-forwarding mechanism (see Item 12) to intercept the methods and provide the implementation at runtime.

To get around the problem of categories not being able to synthesize instance variables, you can use associated objects (see Item 10). For the example, you would need to implement the accessors within the category as follows:

```
#import <objc/runtime.h>

static const char *kFriendsPropertyKey = "kFriendsPropertyKey";

@implementation EOCPerson (Friendship)

- (NSArray*)friends {
    return objc_getAssociatedObject(self, kFriendsPropertyKey);
}

- (void)setFriends:(NSArray*)friends {
    objc_setAssociatedObject(self,
                             kFriendsPropertyKey,
                             friends,
                             OBJC_ASSOCIATION_RETAIN_NONATOMIC);
}

@end
```

This works, but it's less than ideal. It's a fair amount of boilerplate and is prone to errors with memory management because it's easy to forget that the property is implemented like this. For example, you may change the memory-management semantics by changing the property attributes. However, you would also need to remember to change the memory-management semantics of the associated object in the setter. So although this is not a bad solution, it is not one that I recommend.

Also, you may want the instance variable backing the `friends` array to be a mutable array. You could take a mutable copy, but it's yet another vector for confusion to enter your code base. It is therefore much cleaner to define properties in the main interface definition rather than to define them in categories.

In this example, the correct solution is to keep all the property definitions in the main interface declaration. All the data encapsulated by a class should be defined in the main interface, the only place where instance variables (the data) can be defined. Since they are just syntactic sugar for defining an instance variable and associated accessor methods, properties fall under the same rule. Categories should be thought of as a way to extend functionality of the class, not the data that it encapsulates.

That being said, sometimes read-only properties can be successfully used within categories. For example, you might want to create a category on NSCalendar to return an array containing the months as strings. Since the method is not accessing any data and the property is not backed by an instance variable, you could implement the category like this:

```objc
@interface NSCalendar (EOC_Additions)
@property (nonatomic, strong, readonly) NSArray *eoc_allMonths;
@end

@implementation NSCalendar (EOC_Additions)
- (NSArray*)eoc_allMonths {
    if ([self.calendarIdentifier
            isEqualToString:NSGregorianCalendar])
    {
        return @[@"January", @"February",
                 @"March", @"April",
                 @"May", @"June",
                 @"July", @"August",
                 @"September", @"October",
                 @"November", @"December"];
    } else if ( /* other calendar identifiers */ ) {
        /* return months for other calendars */
    }
}
@end
```

Autosynthesis of an instance variable to back the property will not kick in, because all the required methods (only one in this read-only case) have been implemented. Therefore, no warnings will be emitted by the compiler. Even in this situation, however, it is generally better to avoid using a property. A property is meant to be backed by data held by the class. A property is for encapsulating data. In this example, you would instead declare the method to retrieve the list of months within the category:

```
@interface NSCalendar (EOC_Additions)
- (NSArray*)eoc_allMonths;
@end
```

Things to Remember

- ✦ Keep all property declarations for encapsulated data in the main interface definition.

- ✦ Prefer accessor methods to property declarations in categories, unless it is a class-continuation category.

Item 27: Use the Class-Continuation Category to Hide Implementation Detail

Often, you will want a class to contain more methods and instance variables than are exposed externally. You could expose them externally and document that they are private and shouldn't be relied on. After all, no method or instance variable is truly private in Objective-C, owing to the way the dynamic messaging system works (see Item 11). However, it is good practice to expose publicly only what needs to be exposed. So what do you do about methods and instance variables that should not be exposed publicly but whose existence you still want to document? That's where a special category—the "class-continuation category"—can come in handy.

The class-continuation category, unlike normal categories, must be defined in the implementation file of the class for which it is a continuation. Importantly, it is the only category that is allowed to declare extra instance variables. Also, this category doesn't have a specific implementation. Any method defined within it is expected to appear in the main implementation of the class. Unlike other categories, a class-continuation category has no name. A class-continuation category for a class named EOCPerson would look like this:

```
@interface EOCPerson ()
// Methods here
@end
```

Why is such a category useful? It's useful because both methods and instance variables can be defined there. This is possible only because of the nonfragile ABI (see Item 6 for more detail about this), which means that the size of an object does not have to be known in order to use it. Therefore, instance variables do not have to be defined in the public interface, since consumers of the class do not have to know their layout. For this reason, adding instance variables to a class was made possible in the class-continuation category, as well as in the implementation of a class. To do this, you simply need to add some braces in the right place and put the instance variables in there:

```
@interface EOCPerson () {
    NSString *_anInstanceVariable;
}
// Method declarations here
@end

@implementation EOCPerson {
    int _anotherInstanceVariable;
}
// Method implementations here
@end
```

What is the point of doing this? You could define instance variables in the public interface. But a benefit to hiding them away in the class-continuation category or implementation block is that they are known about only internally. Even if you mark them as private in the public interface, you are still leaking implementation detail. For example, suppose that you don't want others to know about the existence of a supersecret class used only internally. If one of your classes owns an instance of this class and you were to declare the instance variable in the public interface, it would look like this:

```
#import <Foundation/Foundation.h>

@class EOCSuperSecretClass;

@interface EOCClass : NSObject {
@private
    EOCSuperSecretClass *_secretInstance;
}
@end
```

The fact that a class named EOCSuperSecretClass exists has been leaked. You could get around this by not strongly typing the instance variable and declaring it of id type instead of EOCSuperSecretClass*. However, this would be less than ideal because you would lose any help from the compiler when using it internally. And why should you miss out on help like that just because you don't want to expose something? This is where the class-continuation category can help. Now it can be declared like so:

```
// EOCClass.h
#import <Foundation/Foundation.h>

@interface EOCClass : NSObject
@end


// EOCClass.m
#import "EOCClass.h"
#import "EOCSuperSecretClass.h"

@interface EOCClass () {
    EOCSuperSecretClass *_secretInstance;
}
@end

@implementation EOCClass
// Methods here
@end
```

Similarly, the instance variable could have been added to the implementation block, semantically equivalent to adding it to the class-continuation category and more a matter of preference. I prefer adding it to the category because it keeps all data definitions in the same place. You may also have properties defined in the class-continuation category, so it's good to declare extra instance variables here also. This instance variable is not truly private, since it is always possible to hack around using methods from the runtime, but to all intents and purposes, it is private. Also, since it is not declared in the public header, it is much more hidden if you were to ship this code as part of a library.

Another place where this is particularly useful is with Objective-C++ code. In this hybrid of Objective-C and C++, code written in both languages can be used. Often, back ends to games are written in C++ for portability reasons. Other times, you may need to use C++ because you're interfacing with a third-party library that has only C++ bindings. For these times, the class-continuation category can come in handy as well. Suppose that previously, you would have written the class like so:

```
#import <Foundation/Foundation.h>
#include "SomeCppClass.h"
```

```
@interface EOCClass : NSObject {
@private
    SomeCppClass _cppClass;
}
@end
```

The implementation file for this class would be called EOCClass.
mm, where the .mm extension indicates to the compiler that the file
should be compiled as Objective-C++. Without this, the inclusion of
SomeCppClass.h would be impossible. However, note that the C++ class
SomeCppClass has had to be imported fully because the definition
needs to be fully resolved such that the compiler knows how big the
_cppClass instance variable is. So any file that includes EOCClass.h to
use the class also needs to be compiled as Objective-C++, since it will
also be including the SomeCppClass header file. This can easily spiral
out of control and end up with your entire application being compiled as Objective-C++. This is perfectly fine, but I consider this to be
fairly ugly, especially if the code is being shipped as a library for use
in other applications. It's not very nice for a third-party developer to
have to rename all files to have the .mm extension.

You may think that one way to get around the problem described is
to forward declare the C++ class instead of importing its header and
then make the instance variable a pointer to an instance, as follows:

```
#import <Foundation/Foundation.h>

class SomeCppClass;

@interface EOCClass : NSObject {
@private
    SomeCppClass *_cppClass;
}
@end
```

The instance variable needs to be a pointer now, since if it were a
nonpointer, the compiler wouldn't be able to work out the size the
instance variable needed to be and would cause an error. Pointers
are all of fixed size, so the compiler simply needs to know the type to
which the pointer is pointing. But this exhibits the same problem in
that any class importing the EOCClass header will meet the class keyword, which is a C++ keyword and therefore will need to be compiled
as Objective-C++. This is ugly and unnecessary, since the instance
variable is private anyway, so why should other classes even care
that it exists? Well, class-continuation category to the rescue once
again. Using it makes the class look like so:

```
// EOCClass.h
#import <Foundation/Foundation.h>

@interface EOCClass : NSObject
@end
```

```
// EOCClass.mm
#import "EOCClass.h"
#include "SomeCppClass.h"

@interface EOCClass () {
    SomeCppClass _cppClass;
}
@end


@implementation EOCClass
@end
```

Now the EOCClass header is free from any C++, and consumers of that header will not even be aware that underneath, it is riddled with C++. This pattern is seen in some of the system libraries, such as where WebKit, the web browser framework, is written largely in C++ and exposed through a clean Objective-C interface. This pattern is also seen in CoreAnimation, where a lot of the back-end code is written in C++ but exposed through a pure Objective-C interface.

Another good use of the class-continuation category is to expand properties that are read-only in the public interface but need to be set internally. Usually, you will want to set via the setter accessor method rather than direct access to the instance variable (see Item 7) because it will trigger Key-Value Observing (KVO) notifications, to which another object may be listening. A property that appears in the class-continuation or any other category and in the class interface must have the exact same attributes, with the exception that the read-only status can be expanded to read-write. For example, consider a class representing a person with a public interface like this:

```
#import <Foundation/Foundation.h>

@interface EOCPerson : NSObject
@property (nonatomic, copy, readonly) NSString *firstName;
@property (nonatomic, copy, readonly) NSString *lastName;

- (id)initWithFirstName:(NSString*)firstName
               lastName:(NSString*)lastName;
@end
```

Usually, a class-continuation category would be defined to expand the status of the two properties to read-write:

```
@interface EOCPerson ()
@property (nonatomic, copy, readwrite) NSString *firstName;
@property (nonatomic, copy, readwrite) NSString *lastName;
@end
```

That is all that needs to be done. Now the implementation of EOCPerson is free to use the setter accessor either by calling setFirstName: or setLastName: or by using the property dot syntax. Doing so can be a very useful way to keep your objects immutable publicly but still be able to manage the data internally as required. Therefore, the data encapsulated by the class is controlled by the instance itself rather than being able to be changed externally. See Item 18 for more about this topic. Note that there is a potential for race conditions to be introduced with this approach if an observer reads a property at the same time as the property is written internally. Sensible use of synchronization (see Item 41) will mitigate this problem.

Another good use of the class-continuation category is to declare private methods that are going to be used only inside the implementation of the class. This is useful because it documents the methods available inside the class implementation. It looks like this:

```
@interface EOCPerson ()
- (void)p_privateMethod;
@end
```

Here, the prefix idea from Item 20 is used to indicate a private method. You don't strictly need to declare methods before using them in recent compiler versions. However, it is still often a good idea to do so in a class-continuation category like this, as it is a way to document what methods exist in one place. I often like to write the method prototypes like this first, before implementing the class. Then I go through and implement the methods. It is a great way to improve readability of a class.

Finally, the class-continuation category is a good place to state that your object conforms to protocols that should be considered private. Often, you don't want to leak information that you conform to a certain protocol in the public interface, maybe because the protocol is part of your private API. For example, consider that EOCPerson conformed to a protocol called EOCSecretDelegate. Using the public interface, it would look like this:

```
#import <Foundation/Foundation.h>
#import "EOCSecretDelegate.h"
```

```
@interface EOCPerson : NSObject <EOCSecretDelegate>
@property (nonatomic, copy, readonly) NSString *firstName;
@property (nonatomic, copy, readonly) NSString *lastName;

- (id)initWithFirstName:(NSString*)firstName
                lastName:(NSString*)lastName;
@end
```

You may think that you could just forward declare the EOCSecretDelegate protocol rather than importing it (or rather, the header file in which it is defined). You would forward declare it like this, instead of the import:

```
@protocol EOCSecretDelegate;
```

However, any place that the EOCPerson header would be imported, the compiler would emit the following warning:

```
warning: cannot find protocol definition for 'EOCSecretDelegate'
```

It's warning you because it knows that it will never be able to know what methods are included in the protocol without being able to see its definition. But since this is a private internal protocol, you don't even want to leak its name. Class-continuation category to the rescue again! Instead of declaring that EOCPerson conforms to EOCSecretDelegate in the public interface, you simply do it in the class-continuation category:

```
#import "EOCPerson.h"
#import "EOCSecretDelegate.h"

@interface EOCPerson () <EOCSecretDelegate>
@end

@implementation EOCPerson
/* … */
@end
```

The public interface can have all references to EOCSecretDelegate removed. The private protocol is no longer exposed, and consumers would have to do deep introspection to find out that it exists.

Things to Remember

✦ Use the class-continuation category to add instance variables to a class.

✦ Redeclare properties in the class-continuation category as read-write if they are read-only in the main interface, if the setter accessor is required internally within the class.

+ Declare method prototypes for private methods within the class-continuation category.

+ Use the class-continuation category to declare protocols that your class conforms to that you want to keep private.

Item 28: Use a Protocol to Provide Anonymous Objects

Protocols define a set of methods that a conforming object should (or must if not optional) implement. They can therefore be used to hide implementation detail in your code's API by returning objects that are typed as a plain id that conforms to a protocol. This way, the specific class name is not leaked in the API. This can be useful when you want to have many different classes behind the interface and don't want to specify the full class. It might change, for example, or many different classes can be returned that don't fit into a standard class hierarchy where you can supply the common base class as the type.

This concept is often referred to as anonymous objects, which is not like the concept of anonymous objects in other languages, where it refers to the ability to create a class inline with no name. In Objective-C, this is not the case. In Item 23, where delegates and data sources are explained, the use of these anonymous objects can be seen. For example, a property definition for a delegate might look like this:

```
@property (nonatomic, weak) id <EOCDelegate> delegate;
```

The type is id<EOCDelegate>, and the class of the object can therefore be absolutely anything; it doesn't even have to derive from NSObject. It's fine so long as it conforms to EOCDelegate. To the class that has this property, the delegate is anonymous. It could, if it so desired, work out the class of the object at runtime (see Item 14). However, doing so would be seen as bad practice, since the contract dictated by the property type indicates that the class doesn't matter.

Another example of this concept in action is with NSDictionary. The standard memory-management semantics of the keys in a dictionary is that they are copied while the values are retained. In a mutable dictionary, therefore, the method signature to set a key-value pair is this:

```
- (void)setObject:(id)object forKey:(id<NSCopying>)key
```

The key parameter is typed as id<NSCopying>, since it just needs to be any object type that conforms to NSCopying so that the copy message can be sent to it successfully (see Item 22). The key can be thought of as being anonymous. Just as with the delegate property, the dictionary doesn't care about the class, and it should never need to. It simply needs to know that it can send the instance the copy message.

An example of using this idea of anonymous objects being used for objects returned from a library is where the library handles database connections. You may not want to leak the class that handles the connection, since it might be a different one for different databases. Without a sane way for them to inherit from the same base class, you would be forced to return something of type id. However, you could create a protocol to define the common methods that all database connections have and declare that the object conforms to it. Such a protocol may look like this:

```
@protocol EOCDatabaseConnection
- (void)connect;
- (void)disconnect;
- (BOOL)isConnected;
- (NSArray*)performQuery:(NSString*)query;
@end
```

Then you may have a database handler singleton that is used to provide database connections. Its interface may look like this:

```
#import <Foundation/Foundation.h>

@protocol EOCDatabaseConnection;

@interface EOCDatabaseManager : NSObject
+ (id)sharedInstance;
- (id<EOCDatabaseConnection>)connectionWithIdentifier:
                             (NSString*)identifier;
@end
```

This way, the class that handles the database connections is not leaked, and different classes from potentially different frameworks can be returned by the same method. All the consumer of this API cares about is that the object returned can be connected and disconnected and queries performed. That last point is particularly important. In this example, the back-end code to handle database connections could be using many different third-party libraries to connect to each different database type (e.g., MySQL, PostgreSQL). It may therefore be impossible to make all the connection classes inherit from the same base class as they are in these third-party libraries. So the anonymous-object approach could be used where simple wrappers are created as subclasses of each of these third-party classes, to make them conform to the EOCDatabaseConnection protocol. Then these classes can be returned by the connectionWithIdentifier: method. In future versions, the back-end classes can be swapped out without any change to the public API.

These anonymous types can also be useful when you want to convey that it is unimportant what the type of the object is but rather that it's more important that the object implements certain methods. Even if the type is always a certain class in your implementation, you might still want to use an anonymous type with a protocol to indicate that the type is not important.

An example of this approach is seen in the CoreData framework. The class called NSFetchedResultsController handles the results of a query to a CoreData database and splits the data into sections, if required. The sections can be accessed through a property on the results controller called sections. Rather than being an array of fully typed objects, this is an array of objects that conform to the NSFetchedResultsSectionInfo protocol. Using the controller to obtain section information looks like this:

```
NSFetchedResultsController *controller = /* some controller */;
NSUInteger section = /* section index to query */;

NSArray *sections = controller.sections;
id <NSFetchedResultsSectionInfo> sectionInfo = sections[section];
NSUInteger numberOfObjects = sectionInfo.numberOfObjects;
```

The sectionInfo object is anonymous. In making the API like this, the object is making it clear that it is an object providing access to the section information. Behind the scenes, the object is likely to be an internal state object created by the results controller. Exposing a public class that represents this data is not necessary, since the consumer of the results controller never needs to be concerned with how the section data is stored. All it needs to be able to do is query the data. Using a protocol to form an anonymous object like this means that the internal state object can be returned in the sections array. The consumer then knows only that it implements certain methods, and the rest of the implementation of the object is hidden.

Things to Remember

✦ Protocols can be used to provide some level of anonymity to types. The type can be reduced to an id type that implements a protocol's methods.

✦ Use anonymous objects when the type (class name) should be hidden.

✦ Use anonymous objects when the type is irrelevant, and the fact that the object responds to certain methods (the ones defined in the protocol) is more important.

Memory Management

Memory management is an important concept in any object-oriented language, such as Objective-C. Understanding the specifics of any language's memory-management model is vital to being able to write memory-efficient, bug-free code.

Once you understand the rules, memory management in Objective-C is not complicated and was made easier when Automatic Reference Counting (ARC) came along. ARC diverts nearly all the memory-management decisions to the compiler, leaving you to concentrate on the business logic.

Item 29: Understand Reference Counting

Objective-C uses reference counting for memory management, meaning that every object has a counter that is incremented and decremented. You increment the counter when you want to register your interest in keeping an object alive, and you decrement the counter when you have finished with it. When an object's counter reaches zero, the object no longer has anything interested in it and is free to be destroyed. That is a brief overview; understanding the topic fully is crucial to writing good Objective-C code, even if you are going to be using ARC (see Item 30).

The garbage collector for use with Objective-C code written for Mac OS X is officially deprecated as of Mac OS X 10.8 and has never been available for iOS. Understanding reference counting is very important going forward because you can no longer rely on the garbage collector on Mac OS X and you never have, nor will you be able to, on iOS.

If you already use ARC, you should switch off the part of your brain that tells you that most of the code presented won't compile. That's true, in an ARC world. But this item is explaining reference counting from an Objective-C perspective, which is still going on with ARC, and to do so requires showing code that uses methods that are explicitly illegal under ARC.

How Reference Counting Works

Under reference-counting architectures, an object is assigned a counter to indicate how many things have an interest in keeping that object alive. This is referred to as the retain count in Objective-C but can also be referred to as the reference count. The following three methods declared on the NSObject protocol can manipulate that counter to either increment it or decrement it:

+ **retain** Increment the retain count.

+ **release** Decrement the retain count.

+ **autorelease** Decrement the retain count later, when the autorelease pool is drained. (The autorelease pool is discussed further on page 150 and in Item 34.)

A method to inspect the retain count, called retainCount, is generally not very useful, even when debugging, so I (and Apple) encourage you not to use it. See Item 36 for more information.

An object is always created with a retain count of at least 1. Interest in keeping the object alive is indicated by invoking the retain method. When that interest has gone because the object is no longer required by a certain portion of code, release or autorelease is called. When the retain count finally reaches 0, the object is deallocated, meaning that its memory is marked for reuse. Once this has happened, any references to that object are no longer valid.

Figure 5.1 illustrates an object going through creation, a retain, and then two releases.

Many objects will be created throughout an application's life cycle. These objects all become related to one another. For example, an object representing a person has a reference to string objects for the person's names and might also have references to other person objects, such as in a set representing the friends of the person, thereby forming what is known as an object graph. Objects are said to own other objects if they hold a strong reference to them. This means that they have registered their interest in keeping them alive by retaining them. When they are finished with them, they release them.

In the Figure 5.2 object graph, ObjectA is being referenced by both ObjectB and ObjectC. When both ObjectB and ObjectC have finished with ObjectA, its retain count drops to 0 and it can be destroyed. Both ObjectB and ObjectC are being kept alive by other objects, which in

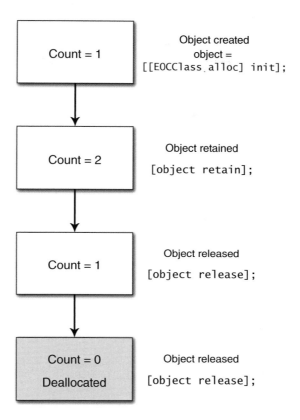

Figure 5.1 An object's retain count incrementing and decrementing as it goes through its life cycle

turn are being kept alive by other objects. Eventually, if you went up the tree of what is referencing what, you would come to a root object. In the case of Mac OS X applications, this could be the NSApplication object; in the case of iOS applications, the UIApplication object. Both are singletons created when an application launches.

The following code will help you to understand this in practice:

```
NSMutableArray *array = [[NSMutableArray alloc] init];

NSNumber *number = [[NSNumber alloc] initWithInt:1337];
[array addObject:number];
[number release];

// do something with 'array'

[array release];
```

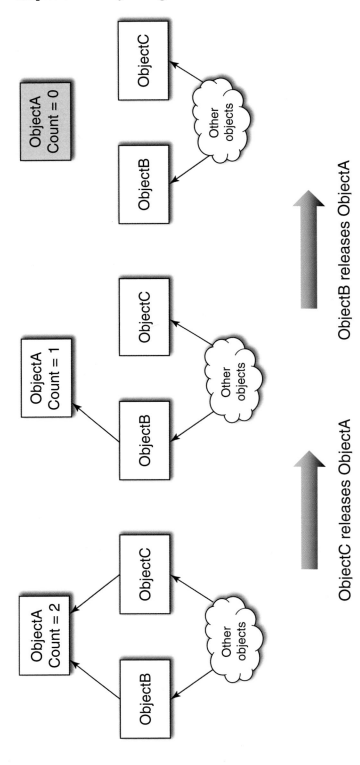

Figure 5.2 An object graph showing an object eventually being deallocated after all references to it are released

As explained previously, this code won't compile under ARC, owing to the explicit calls to release. In Objective-C, a call to alloc will result in the return of an object that is said to be owned by the caller. That is to say, the caller's interest has already been registered because it used alloc. However, it is important to note that this does not necessarily mean that the retain count is exactly 1. It might be more, since the implementation of either alloc or initWithInt: may mean that other retains have been made on the object. What is guaranteed, though, is that the retain count is at least 1. You should always think about retain counts in this way. You should never guarantee what a retain count is, only what effect your actions have had on the retain count: whether that is incremented or decremented.

The number object is then added to the array. In doing this, the array also registers its interest by calling retain on the number object within the addObject: method. At this point, the retain count is at least 2. Then, the number object is no longer required by this code, so it is released. Its retain count is now back down to at least 1. At this point, the number variable can no longer be safely used. The call to release means that the object pointed to is no longer guaranteed to be alive. Of course, the code in this scenario makes it obvious that it will be alive after the call to release, since the array is also still referencing it. However, that should never be assumed, which means that you should not do something like this:

```
NSNumber *number = [[NSNumber alloc] initWithInt:1337];
[array addObject:number];
[number release];
NSLog(@"number = %@", number);
```

Even though the code will work in this scenario, it is not good practice. If for any reason the number object were deallocated while calling release as its retain count dropped to zero, the call to NSLog would potentially crash. The reason I qualify that with "potentially" is that when an object is deallocated, its memory is simply returned to the available pool. If the memory has not been overwritten by the time the NSLog runs, the object will still exist, and there won't be a crash. For this reason, bugs where objects have been released too early are often difficult to debug.

To mitigate accidentally using an object that is no longer valid, you will often see a release followed by nilling out the pointer. This ensures that nothing can access a pointer to a potentially invalid object, often referred to as a dangling pointer. For example, it can be done like this:

```
NSNumber *number = [[NSNumber alloc] initWithInt:1337];
[array addObject:number];
[number release];
number = nil;
```

Memory Management in Property Accessors

As described earlier, objects form an object graph by being linked together. The array in the example holds onto the objects it contains by retaining them. In the same way, other objects will hold onto other objects, often through the use of properties (see Item 6), which use accessors to get and set instance variables. If the property is a strong relationship, the value of the property is retained. A setter accessor for such a property called foo, backed by an instance variable called _foo, would look like this:

```
- (void)setFoo:(id)foo {
    [foo retain];
    [_foo release];
    _foo = foo;
}
```

The new value is retained, and the old value is released. Then the instance variable is updated to point to the new value. The order is important. If the old value was released before the new value was retained and the two values are exactly the same, the release would mean that the object could potentially be deallocated prematurely. The subsequent retain could not resurrect the deallocated object, and the instance variable would be a dangling pointer.

Autorelease Pools

A feature that is important to Objective-C's reference-counting architecture is what is known as autorelease pools. Instead of calling release to immediately decrement an object's retain count (and potentially deallocate it), you can also call autorelease, which performs the release sometime later, usually the next time around the event loop, but it can also happen sooner (see Item 34).

This feature is very useful, especially when returning an object from a method. In this case, you don't always want to return it as owned by the caller. For example, consider the following method:

```
- (NSString*)stringValue {
    NSString *str = [[NSString alloc]
                        initWithFormat:@"I am this: %@", self];
    return str;
}
```

In this case, str is returned with a +1 retain count, since the call to alloc returns with a +1 count, and there is no balancing release. The meaning of +1 here is that you as the caller are responsible for one retain. You must somehow balance that one retain. This does not mean that the retain count is exactly 1, however. It might be more, but that is implementation detail within the method initWithFormat:. All you need to worry about is balancing that one retain.

However, you cannot release str inside the method, because it would then immediately be deallocated before being returned. So an autorelease is used to indicate that the object should be released sometime later but guaranteed to be long enough in the future that the returned value can be retained by the caller if it needs to hold onto it. In other words, the object is guaranteed to be alive across the method call boundary. In fact, the release will happen when the outermost autorelease pool is drained (see Item 34), which, unless you have your own autorelease pools, will be next time around the current thread's event loop. Applying this to the stringValue method gives the following:

```
- (NSString*)stringValue {
    NSString *str = [[NSString alloc]
                    initWithFormat:@"I am this: %@", self];
    return [str autorelease];
}
```

Now the returned NSString object will definitely be alive when it is returned to the caller. So the object can be used like this:

```
NSString *str = [self stringValue];
NSLog(@"The string is: %@", str);
```

No extra memory management is required here, since the str object is returned autoreleased and therefore is balanced. Since the release from being in the autorelease pool won't happen until next time around the event loop, the object does not need to be explicitly retained to be used in the log statement. However, if the object needs to be held onto, such as being set to an instance variable, the object needs to be retained and subsequently released:

```
_instanceVariable = [[self stringValue] retain];
// …
[_instanceVariable release];
```

So autorelease is a way of extending the lifetime of an object just enough so that it can survive across method call boundaries.

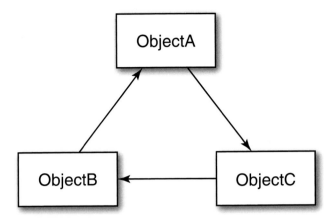

Figure 5.3 A retain cycle in an object graph

Retain Cycles

A common scenario to be aware of with reference counting is what is known as a retain cycle, which occurs when multiple objects reference one another cyclically. This leads to memory leaks because no object in the cycle will ever see its retain count drop to 0. Each object has at least one other object in the cycle maintaining a reference to it. In Figure 5.3, three objects all have a single reference to one of the other two objects. In this cycle, all retain counts are 1.

In a garbage-collected environment, this situation would usually be picked up as a so-called island of isolation. In such a scenario, the collector would deallocate all three objects. This luxury is not available under the reference-counting architecture of Objective-C. The problem is usually solved by using weak references (see Item 33) or an external influence causing one of the objects to relinquish its retain of another object. In either case, the retain cycle is broken, and memory is no longer leaked.

Things to Remember

- Reference-counting memory management is based on a counter that is incremented and decremented. An object is created with a count of at least 1. An object with a positive retain count is alive. When the retain count drops to 0, the object is destroyed.

- As it goes through its life cycle, an object is retained and released by other objects holding references to it. Retaining and releasing increments and decrements the retain count, respectively.

Item 30: Use ARC to Make Reference Counting Easier

Reference counting is a fairly easy concept to understand (see Item 29). The semantics of where retains and releases need to appear are easily expressed. So with the Clang compiler project came a static analyzer that is able to indicate the location of problems with the reference counting. For example, consider the following snippet written with manual reference counting:

```
if ([self shouldLogMessage]) {
    NSString *message = [[NSString alloc] initWithFormat:
                        @"I am object, %p", self];
    NSLog(@"message = %@", message);
}
```

This code has a memory leak because the message object is not released at the end of the `if` statement. Since it cannot be referenced outside the `if` statement, the object is leaked. The rules governing why this is a leak are straightforward. The call to `NSString's alloc` method returns an object with a +1 retain count. But there is no balancing release. These rules are easy to express, and a computer could easily apply these rules and tell us that the object has been leaked. That's exactly what the static analyzer does.

The static analyzer was taken one step further. Since it is able to tell you where there are memory-management problems, it should easily be able to go ahead and fix them by adding in the required retain or release, right? That is the idea from which Automatic Reference Counting (ARC) was born. ARC does exactly what it says in the name: makes reference counting automatic. So in the preceding code snippet, the `message` object would automatically have a `release` added in just before the end of the `if` statement scope, automatically turning the code into the following:

```
if ([self shouldLogMessage]) {
    NSString *message = [[NSString alloc] initWithFormat:
                        @"I am object, %p", self];
    NSLog(@"message = %@", message);
    [message release]; ///< Added by ARC
}
```

The important thing to remember with ARC is that reference counting is still being performed. But ARC adds in the retains and releases for you. ARC does more than apply memory-management semantics to methods that return objects, as you will see. But it is these core semantics, which have become standard throughout Objective-C, on which ARC is built.

Because ARC adds retains, releases, and autoreleases for you, calling memory-management methods directly under ARC is illegal. Specifically, you cannot call the following methods:

✦ `retain`

✦ `release`

✦ `autorelease`

✦ `dealloc`

Calling any of these methods directly will result in a compiler error because doing so would interfere with ARC's being able to work out what memory-management calls are required. You have to put your trust in ARC to do the right thing, which can be daunting for developers used to manual reference counting.

In fact, ARC does not call these methods through the normal Objective-C message dispatch but instead calls lower-level C variants. This is optimal, since retains and releases are performed frequently, and so saving CPU cycles here is a big win. For example, the equivalent for `retain` is `objc_retain`. This is also why it is illegal to override `retain`, `release`, or `autorelease`, as these methods are never called directly. For the rest of this item, I will usually talk about the equivalent Objective-C method rather than the lower-level C variants. This should help if your background is with manual reference counting.

Method-Naming Rules Applied by ARC

The memory-management semantics dictated through method names have long been convention in Objective-C, but ARC has cemented them as hard rules. The rules are simple and relate to the method name. A method returning an object returns it owned by the caller if its method name begins with one of the following:

✦ `alloc`

✦ `new`

✦ `copy`

✦ `mutableCopy`

"Owned by the caller" means that the code calling any of the four methods listed is responsible for releasing the returned object. That is to say, the object will have a positive retain count, where exactly 1 needs to be balanced by the calling code. The retain count may be greater than 1 if the object has been retained additionally and autoreleased, which is one reason why the `retainCount` method is not useful (see Item 36).

Any other method name indicates that any returned object will be returned not owned by the calling code. In these cases, the object will be returned autoreleased, so that the value is alive across the method call boundary. If it wants to ensure that the object stays alive longer, the calling code must retain it.

ARC automatically handles all memory management required to maintain these rules, including the code for returning objects autoreleased, as illustrated in the following code:

```
+ (EOCPerson*)newPerson {
    EOCPerson *person = [[EOCPerson alloc] init];
    return person;
    /**
     * The method name begins with 'new', and since 'person'
     * already has an unbalanced +1 retain count from the
     * 'alloc', no retains, releases, or autoreleases are
     * required when returning.
     */
}


+ (EOCPerson*)somePerson {
    EOCPerson *person = [[EOCPerson alloc] init];
    return person;
    /**
     * The method name does not begin with one of the "owning"
     * prefixes, therefore ARC will add an autorelease when
     * returning 'person'.
     * The equivalent manual reference counting statement is:
     *    return [person autorelease];
     */
}


- (void)doSomething {
    EOCPerson *personOne = [EOCPerson newPerson];
    // …

    EOCPerson *personTwo = [EOCPerson somePerson];
    // …

    /**
     * At this point, 'personOne' and 'personTwo' go out of
     * scope, therefore ARC needs to clean them up as required.
     * - 'personOne' was returned as owned by this block of
     *    code, so it needs to be released.
```

```
 *   - 'personTwo' was returned not owned by this block of
 *     code, so it does not need to be released.
 * The equivalent manual reference counting cleanup code
 * is:
 *     [personOne release];
 */
}
```

ARC standardizes the memory-management rules through naming conventions, something that newcomers to the language often see as unusual. Very few other languages put as much emphasis on naming as Objective-C does. Becoming comfortable with this concept is crucial to being a good Objective-C developer. ARC helps with the process because it does a lot of the work for you.

In addition to adding in retains and releases, ARC has other benefits. It is also able to perform optimizations that would be difficult or impossible to do by hand. For example, at compile time, ARC can collapse retains, releases, and autoreleases to cancel them out, if possible. If it sees that the same object is being retained multiple times and released multiple times, ARC can sometimes remove pairs of retains and releases.

ARC also includes a runtime component. The optimizations that occur here are even more interesting and should help prove why all future code should be written under ARC. Recall that some objects are returned from methods autoreleased. Sometimes, the calling code needs to retain the object straightaway, as in this scenario:

```
// From a class where _myPerson is a strong instance variable
_myPerson = [EOCPerson personWithName:@"Bob Smith"];
```

The call to personWithName: returns a new EOCPerson autoreleased. But the compiler also needs to add a retain when setting the instance variable, since it holds a strong reference. Therefore, the preceding code is equivalent to the following in a world of manual reference counting:

```
EOCPerson *tmp = [EOCPerson personWithName:@"Bob Smith"];
_myPerson = [tmp retain];
```

You would be correct to note here that the autorelease from the personWithName: method and the retain are extraneous. It would be beneficial for performance to remove both. But code compiled under ARC needs to be compatible with non-ARC code, for backward compatibility. ARC could have removed the concept of autorelease and dictated that all objects returned from methods be returned with a +1 retain count. However, that would break backward compatibility.

But ARC does in fact contain runtime behavior to detect the situation of extraneous autorelease plus immediate retain. It does this through a special function that is run when an object is returned autoreleased. Instead of a plain call to the object's autorelease method, it calls objc_autoreleaseReturnValue. This function inspects the code that is going to be run immediately after returning from the current method. If it is detected that this is going to be a retain of the returned object, a flag is set within a global data structure (processor dependent) instead of performing the autorelease. Similarly, the calling code that retains an autoreleased object returned from a method uses a function called objc_retainAutoreleasedReturnValue instead of calling retain directly. This function checks the flag and, if set, doesn't perform retain. This extra work to set and check flags is faster than performing autorelease and retain.

The following code illustrates this optimization by showing how ARC uses these special functions:

```
// Within EOCPerson class
+ (EOCPerson*)personWithName:(NSString*)name {
    EOCPerson *person = [[EOCPerson alloc] init];
    person.name = name;
    objc_autoreleaseReturnValue(person);
}
```

```
// Code using EOCPerson class
EOCPerson *tmp = [EOCPerson personWithName:@"Matt Galloway"];
_myPerson = objc_retainAutoreleasedReturnValue(tmp);
```

These special functions have processor-specific implementations to make use of the most optimal solution. The following pseudocode implementations explain what happens:

```
id objc_autoreleaseReturnValue(id object) {
    if ( /* caller will retain object */ ) {
        set_flag(object);
        return object; //< No autorelease
    } else {
        return [object autorelease];
    }
}
```

```
id objc_retainAutoreleasedReturnValue(id object) {
    if (get_flag(object)) {
        clear_flag(object);
        return object; //< No retain
```

```
    } else {
        return [object retain];
    }
}
```

The way in which objc_autoreleaseReturnValue detects whether the calling code is going to immediately retain the object is processor specific. Only the author of the compiler can implement this, since it uses inspection of the raw machine-code instructions. The author of the compiler is the only person who can ensure that the code in the calling method is arranged in such a way that detection like this is possible.

This is just one such optimization that is made possible by putting memory management in the hands of the compiler and the runtime. It should help to illustrate why using ARC is such a good idea. As the compiler and runtime mature, I'm sure that other optimizations will be making an appearance.

Memory-Management Semantics of Variables

ARC also handles memory management of local variables and instance variables. By default, every variable is said to hold a strong reference to the object. This is important to understand, particularly with instance variables, since for certain code, the semantics can be different from manual reference counting. For example, consider the following code:

```
@interface EOCClass : NSObject {
    id _object;
}
```

```
@implementation EOCClass
- (void)setup {
    _object = [EOCOtherClass new];
}
@end
```

The _object instance variable does not automatically retain its value under manual reference counting but does under ARC. Therefore, when the setup method is compiled under ARC, the method transforms into this:

```
- (void)setup {
    id tmp = [EOCOtherClass new];
    _object = [tmp retain];
    [tmp release];
}
```

Of course, in this situation, retain and release can be cancelled out. So ARC does this, leaving the same code as before. But this comes in handy when writing a setter. Before ARC, you may have written a setter like this:

```
- (void)setObject:(id)object {
    [_object release];
    _object = [object retain];
}
```

But this reveals a problem. What if the new value being set is the same as the one already held by the instance variable? If this object was the only thing holding a reference to it, the release in the setter would cause the retain count to drop to 0, and the object would be deallocated. The subsequent retain would cause the application to crash. ARC makes this sort of mistake impossible. The equivalent setter under ARC is this:

```
- (void)setObject:(id)object {
    _object = object;
}
```

ARC performs a safe setting of the instance variable by retaining the new value, then releasing the old one before finally setting the instance variable. You may have understood this under manual reference counting and written your setters correctly, but with ARC, you don't have to worry about such edge cases.

The semantics of local and instance variables can be altered through the application of the following qualifiers:

✦ **__strong** The default; the value is retained.

✦ **__unsafe_unretained** The value is not retained and is potentially unsafe, as the object may have been deallocated already by the time the variable is used again.

✦ **__weak** The value is not retained but is safe because it is automatically set to nil if the current object is ever deallocated.

✦ **__autoreleasing** This special qualifier is used when an object is passed by reference to a method. The value is autoreleased on return.

For example, to make an instance variable behave the same as it does without ARC, you would apply the __weak or __unsafe_unretained attribute:

```
@interface EOCClass : NSObject {
    id __weak _weakObject;
    id __unsafe_unretained _unsafeUnretainedObject;
}
```

In either case, when setting the instance variable, the object will not be retained. Automatically nilling weak references with the __weak qualifier is available only in the latest versions of the runtime (Mac OS X 10.7 and iOS 5.0) because they rely on features that have been added.

When applied to local variables, the qualifiers are often used to break retain cycles that can be introduced with blocks (see Item 40). A block automatically retains all objects it captures, which can sometimes lead to a retain cycle if an object retaining a block is retained by the block. A __weak local variable can be used to break the retain cycle:

```
NSURL *url = [NSURL URLWithString:@"http://www.example.com/"];
EOCNetworkFetcher *fetcher =
    [[EOCNetworkFetcher alloc] initWithURL:url];
EOCNetworkFetcher * __weak weakFetcher = fetcher;
[fetcher startWithCompletion:^(BOOL success){
    NSLog(@"Finished fetching from %@", weakFetcher.url);
}];
```

ARC Handling of Instance Variables

As explained, ARC also handles the memory management of instance variables. Doing so requires ARC to automatically generate the required cleanup code during deallocation. Any variables holding a strong reference need releasing, which ARC does by hooking into the dealloc method. With manual reference counting, you would have found yourself writing dealloc methods that look like this:

```
- (void)dealloc {
    [_foo release];
    [_bar release];
    [super dealloc];
}
```

With ARC, this sort of dealloc method is not required; the generated cleanup routine will perform these two releases for you by stealing a feature from Objective-C++. An Objective-C++ object has to call the destructors for all C++ objects held by the object during deallocation. When the compiler saw that an object contained C++ objects, it would generate a method called .cxx_destruct. ARC piggybacks on this method and emits the required cleanup code within it.

However, you still need to clean up any non-Objective-C objects if you have any, such as CoreFoundation objects or heap-allocated memory, with malloc(). But you do not need to call the superclass implementation of dealloc as you did before. Recall that calling dealloc under

ARC explicitly is illegal. So ARC, along with generating and running the .cxx_destruct method for you, also automatically calls the superclass's dealloc method. Under ARC, a dealloc method may end up looking like this:

```
- (void)dealloc {
    CFRelease(_coreFoundationObject);
    free(_heapAllocatedMemoryBlob);
}
```

The fact that ARC generates deallocation code means that usually, a dealloc method is not required. This often considerably reduces the size of a project's source code and helps to reduce boilerplate code.

Overriding the Memory-Management Methods

Before ARC, it was possible to override the memory-management methods. For example, a singleton implementation often overrode release to be a no-op, as a singleton cannot be released. This is now illegal under ARC because doing so could interfere with ARC's understanding of an object's lifetime. Also, because the methods are illegal to call and override, ARC makes the optimization of not going through an Objective-C message dispatch (see Item 11) when it needs to perform a retain, release, or autorelease. Instead, the optimization is implemented with C functions deep in the runtime. This means that ARC is able to do optimizations such as the one described earlier when returning an autoreleased object that is immediately retained.

Things to Remember

✦ Automatic Reference Counting (ARC) frees the developer from having to worry about most memory management. Using ARC reduces boilerplate code from classes.

✦ ARC handles the object life cycle almost entirely by adding in retains and releases as it sees appropriate. Variable qualifiers can be used to indicate memory-management semantics; previously, retains and releases were manually arranged.

✦ Method names have always been used to indicate memory-management semantics of returned objects. ARC has solidified these and made it impossible not to follow them.

✦ ARC handles only Objective-C objects. In particular, this means that CoreFoundation objects are not handled, and the appropriate CFRetain/CFRelease calls must be applied.

Item 31: Release References and Clean Up Observation State Only in dealloc

An object going through its life cycle eventually ends up being deal-located, which is where the dealloc method enters. It is called exactly once during the life cycle of an object: when its retain count drops to zero. When exactly it gets called is not guaranteed, though. Also, you may think that you know when it's going to be called from manually seeing where retains and releases are. But in practice, any library could be manipulating the object without your knowing, causing deallocation to happen at another time. You should never call dealloc yourself. The runtime will call it at exactly the right time for you. Also, after dealloc has been called on an object, that object is no longer valid, and subsequent method calls are invalid.

So what should you do in dealloc then? The main thing to do is to release any references that the object owns. This means releasing any Objective-C objects, something that ARC automatically adds for you into the dealloc method, through the .cxx_destruct automatic method (see Item 30). Any other non-Objective-C objects that the object owns also need releasing. For instance, CoreFoundation objects need to be explicitly released, since they are pure C APIs.

Another usual thing to do in a dealloc method is to clean up any observation behavior that has been set up. If NSNotificationCenter has been used to register the object for certain notifications, this is often a good place to unregister for notifications so that they are not attempted to be sent to a deallocated object, which would certainly cause an application to crash.

A dealloc method looks like this:

```
- (void)dealloc {
    CFRelease(coreFoundationObject);
    [[NSNotificationCenter defaultCenter] removeObserver:self];
}
```

Note that when using manual reference counting rather than ARC, [super dealloc] should be the last thing done. ARC automatically enforces this, which is another reason why it is a lot easier and safer to use than manual reference counting. With manual reference counting, this method would also have to manually release every Objective-C object owned by the object.

That said, you should certainly not free resources that are potentially expensive or scarce within the system. Such resources are file descriptors, sockets, or large blocks of memory. The dealloc method should not be relied on to be called at any specific time, since something you hadn't realized might be holding onto the object. In such a situation, you are keeping hold of scarce system resources longer than you need to, which is undesirable. It is usual in these scenarios to implement another method that should be called when the application has finished with the object. The resources' life cycles are then made deterministic.

An example of an object that might need a cleanup method is one that manages a socket connection to a server. Perhaps it is a connection to a database. Such a class's interface may look like this:

```
#import <Foundation/Foundation.h>

@interface EOCServerConnection : NSObject
- (void)open:(NSString*)address;
- (void)close;
@end
```

The contract for this class would be that the open: method is called to open the connection; then, when finished with the connection, the application calls close. The close must happen before the connection object is deallocated; otherwise, it is deemed to be a programmer error, just as you have to balance retains and releases with reference counting.

Another reason for cleaning up resources in another cleanup method is that the dealloc method is in fact not guaranteed to be run for every created object. There is the edge case of objects that are still around when an application terminates. These objects do not receive the dealloc message. Instead, they are destroyed by the fact that a terminated application's resources are returned to the operating system. It is an optimization not to call the dealloc method. But this means that you cannot guarantee that it is always called for every object. Mac OS X and iOS applications both have within their application delegates a method that is called on application termination. This method can be used to run any cleanup methods on objects that need to be guaranteed to be cleaned up.

In the case of Mac OS X, the method called at application termination is on NSApplicationDelegate:

```
- (void)applicationWillTerminate:(NSNotification *)notification
```

In the case of iOS, the method is on UIApplicationDelegate:

```
- (void)applicationWillTerminate:(UIApplication *)application
```

With regard to the cleanup method for objects that manage resources, this should also be called in dealloc to mitigate the case in which the cleanup method was not called. If this does happen, it is often a good idea to output a log line to indicate that a programmer error has occurred. It is a programmer error because close should have been called before the object was deallocated; otherwise, the close method is irrelevant. This log line will alert the programmer to rectify the problem. It's still good practice to close the resources in dealloc in order to avoid leaks. An example of such a close and dealloc method is as follows:

```
- (void)close {
    /* clean up resources */
    _closed = YES;
}

- (void)dealloc {
    if (!_closed) {
        NSLog(@"ERROR: close was not called before dealloc!");
        [self close];
    }
}
```

Instead of simply logging an error if the close method is not called, you might decide to throw an exception to indicate that a serious programmer error has occurred.

Another thing to be aware of and avoid in dealloc methods is calling other methods. In the preceding example, of course, a method is called in dealloc. But this is a special case: to detect programmer error. It is not ideal to have to call any other methods at all, because the object being deallocated is in a winding-down state. If the other method happens to perform work asynchronously or calls methods that themselves do, the object being deallocated could be completely dead by the time those methods finish doing their work. This can cause all sorts of problems and often results in an application crash because it calls back to tell the object that it has finished. If the object is dead, this call will fail.

Also, the dealloc method is called on the thread in which the final release that caused the retain count to zero occurred. Some methods are required to be run in a certain thread, such as the main thread. If these methods are called from dealloc, there is no safe way to ensure that it is run on the correct thread. Any usual code to force it to be run on the correct thread is not at all safe, because the object is in a deallocating state, and the runtime has already started altering its internal data structures to indicate this.

The avoidance of method calls in dealloc should also go for property accessors, which can be overridden and therefore themselves try to perform work that is unsafe to do during deallocation. Alternatively, the property may be being observed through Key-Value Observation (KVO), and the observer may try to do some work, such as attempting to retain the object, using the object that is being deallocated. Doing so would cause the runtime to get in a completely inconsistent state, and strange crashes would likely result.

Things to Remember

+ The dealloc method should be used only to release references to other objects and to unregister anything that needs to be, such as Key-Value Observing (KVO) or NSNotificationCenter notifications.

+ If an object holds onto system resources, such as file descriptors, there should be a method for releasing these resources. It should be the contract with the consumer of such a class to call this close method when finished using the resources.

+ Method calls should be avoided in dealloc methods in case those methods try to perform asynchronous work or end up assuming that the object is in a normal state, which it won't be.

Item 32: Beware of Memory Management with Exception-Safe Code

Exceptions are a language feature offered by many modern languages. Exceptions do not exist in pure C but do in both C++ and Objective-C. In fact, in the modern runtime, C++ and Objective-C exceptions are compatible, meaning that an exception thrown from one language can be caught using a handler from the other language.

Even though the error model of Objective-C (see Item 21) states that you should use exceptions only for fatal errors, you may still need code that catches and handles them. Examples are Objective-C++ code or code that interfaces with a third-party library such that you have no control over the exceptions being thrown. Also, some system libraries still make use of exceptions, harking back to the days when exceptions were in common use. For example, Key-Value Observing (KVO) will throw an exception if you attempt to unregister an observer that was not already registered.

When it comes to memory management, exceptions introduce an interesting problem. Inside a try block, if an object is retained and then an exception is thrown before the object has been released, the object will leak unless this case is handled in the catch block. C++ destructors are run by the Objective-C exception-handling routines. This is important for C++ because any object whose lifetime has been cut short by a thrown exception needs to be destructed; otherwise, the memory it uses will be leaked, not to mention all the other system resources, such as file handles, that may not be cleaned up properly.

The destruction of objects automatically by the exception-handling routines is something that is trickier to do in an environment of manual reference counting. Consider the following Objective-C code, which uses manual reference counting:

```
@try {
    EOCSomeClass *object = [[EOCSomeClass alloc] init];
    [object doSomethingThatMayThrow];
    [object release];
}
@catch (...) {
    NSLog(@"Whoops, there was an error. Oh well...");
}
```

At first glance, this may seem correct. But what happens if doSomethingThatMayThrow throws an exception? The release on the following line would not be run, because the exception would halt the execution and jump to the catch block. So in this scenario, the object would be leaked if an exception were thrown. That's not ideal. The way this is solved is to use the @finally block, which is guaranteed to be run once and only once, whether or not an exception is thrown. For example, the code could be transformed into this:

```
EOCSomeClass *object;
@try {
    object = [[EOCSomeClass alloc] init];
    [object doSomethingThatMayThrow];
}
@catch (...) {
    NSLog(@"Whoops, there was an error. Oh well...");
}
@finally {
    [object release];
}
```

Note how the object has had to be pulled out of the @try block because it needs to be referenced in the @finally block. This can get very tedious if you have to do this for all objects that need releasing. Also, if the logic is more complex than this, with multiple statements within the @try block, it can be easy to overlook the scenario in which an object might potentially leak. If the object that is leaked is a scarce resource (or manages one), such as a file descriptor or database connection, the leak is potentially disastrous because eventually, the application could end up unnecessarily holding onto all of a system's resources.

With ARC, the situation is even more serious. The equivalent ARC code for the original code is this:

```
@try {
    EOCSomeClass *object = [[EOCSomeClass alloc] init];
    [object doSomethingThatMayThrow];
}
@catch (...) {
    NSLog(@"Whoops, there was an error. Oh well…");
}
```

Now it is even more of a problem; you can't use the trick of putting the release in the @finally block, as it is illegal to call release. But surely ARC handles this situation, you are probably thinking. Well, by default, it does not; to do so requires a large amount of boilerplate code to be added to track the objects that potentially need cleaning up if an exception is thrown. This code can severely decrease performance at runtime even when no exceptions are thrown. This code also increases the size of an application significantly with all the extra code that has to be added. These side effects are not ideal.

Although it is not turned on by default, ARC does support emitting this extra code to handle exceptions safely. The code can be turned on by using the compiler flag -fobjc-arc-exceptions. The rationale behind not turning it on by default is that in Objective-C programming, exceptions should be used only when the application will terminate as a result of that exception being thrown (see Item 21). Therefore, if the application is going to terminate anyway, the potential memory leak is irrelevant. There is no point adding the required code to become exception safe if the application is going to terminate.

The one scenario in which the -fobjc-arc-exceptions flag is turned on by default occurs when the compiler is in Objective-C++ mode. C++ already needs to have code similar to the code that ARC would implement, so the performance hit is not as great if ARC adds in its own code to ensure exception safety. Also, C++ makes heavy use of exceptions, so it's likely that a developer using Objective-C++ would want to use exceptions.

If you are using manual reference counting and must catch exceptions, remember to ensure that code is written in such a way to clean up correctly. If you are using ARC and must catch exceptions, you will need to turn on the -fobjc-arc-exceptions flag. But above all, if you find yourself catching a lot of exceptions, consider refactoring to make use of NSError-style error passing instead, as explained in Item 21.

Things to Remember

✦ When exceptions are caught, care should be taken to ensure that any required cleanup is done for objects created within the try block.

✦ By default, ARC does not emit code that handles cleanup when exceptions are thrown. This can be enabled with a compiler flag but produces code that is larger and comes with a runtime cost.

Item 33: Use Weak References to Avoid Retain Cycles

A typical situation in an object graph is that a cycle of objects all reference each other in some way. When this happens in a reference-counting architecture such as the Objective-C memory-management model, a memory leak will usually occur at some point because eventually, no object in the cycle of objects will be referenced by anything else. Therefore, none of the objects in the cycle can be accessed, but they won't be deallocated either, since they are all keeping each other alive.

In the most simple of all retain cycles, two objects reference each other. Figure 5.4 shows an example.

This sort of retain cycle is easy to understand and detect by looking at code:

```
#import <Foundation/Foundation.h>

@class EOCClassA;
@class EOCClassB;

@interface EOCClassA : NSObject
@property (nonatomic, strong) EOCClassB *other;
@end

@interface EOCClassB : NSObject
@property (nonatomic, strong) EOCClassA *other;
@end
```

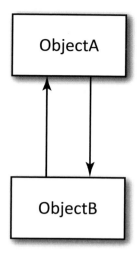

Figure 5.4 Retain cycle in which two objects have a strong reference to each other

It is easy to see from this code that there is a potential retain cycle; if the other property of an instance of EOCClassA is set to an instance of EOCClassB and vice versa with the same instances, the retain cycle as shown in Figure 5.4 would occur.

The result of a retain cycle can be a memory leak. When the last remaining reference to any member of the retain cycle is removed, the entire retain cycle is leaked. This means that none of the objects can be accessed any more. In Figure 5.5, a more complex retain cycle involving four objects is leaked when the last remaining reference to ObjectB is removed.

Objective-C applications on Mac OS X have the option to use a garbage collector, which will detect cycles and deallocate any objects when they cannot be referenced any more. However, the garbage-collected environment was officially deprecated in Mac OS X 10.8 and has never existed on iOS. Therefore, when writing code, it is important to remember the retain-cycle problem and ensure that it doesn't occur in the first place.

The best way to avoid retain cycles is to make use of weak references. Such references are also referred to as representing nonowning relationships. This can be achieved by using the unsafe_unretained property attribute. Applying this attribute to the previous example would look like this:

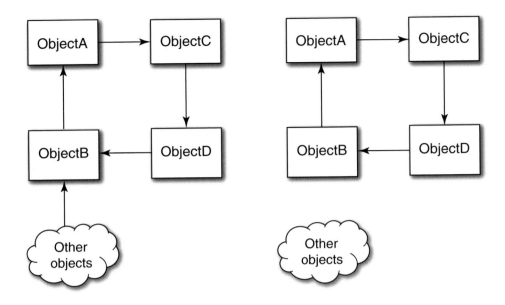

Figure 5.5 Retain cycle being leaked when the remaining reference from the rest of the object graph to any member of the cycle is removed

```
#import <Foundation/Foundation.h>

@class EOCClassA;
@class EOCClassB;

@interface EOCClassA : NSObject
@property (nonatomic, strong) EOCClassB *other;
@end

@interface EOCClassB : NSObject
@property (nonatomic, unsafe_unretained) EOCClassA *other;
@end
```

In this case, EOCClassB instances do not own the EOCClassA instance in the other property. The attribute is called unsafe_unretained to indicate that the value in that property is potentially unsafe and is unretained by the instance. If that object has been deallocated, calling a method on it would likely cause the application to crash. Since this object is not retaining it, it could possibly have been deallocated.

The unsafe_unretained property attribute is semantically equivalent to the assign attribute (see Item 6). However, assign is usually used only for integral types (int, float, structs, etc.), favoring unsafe_unretained for object types. This is a form of self-documentation to make it clear that the property value is potentially unsafe.

Along with ARC came an Objective-C runtime feature that allows safe weak references: a new property attribute named weak, which works in exactly the same way as unsafe_unretained. However, it also automatically sets the property value to nil as soon as the value in the property is deallocated. In the example, the other property of EOCClassB could be changed to this:

@property (nonatomic, weak) EOCClassA *other;

The difference between unsafe_unretained and weak properties is illustrated in Figure 5.6.

When the reference to the instance of EOCClassA is removed, the property unsafe_unretained still points to the instance that is now deallocated. With the weak property, the property points to nil.

However, using weak properties is not an excuse to be lazy. In the preceding example, it should be seen as an error that the instance of EOCClassB is still alive when the referenced EOCClassA object is deallocated. If this ever does happen, it is a bug. You should still aim to ensure that such a situation does not arise. But using weak rather than unsafe_unretained references makes code safe. Rather than crashing, an application may instead display incorrect data. The latter is certainly more desirable should the problem be exhibited for end users. However, it's still a bug that the weak-referenced object was prematurely destroyed in the first place. An example of this would be a user interface element having a data source property that it queries to get the data to display. Such a property would usually need to be a weak reference (see Item 23). If the data source object was deallocated before the element had finished with it, a weak reference means that it will not crash but won't display any data.

The general rule is that if you don't own an object, you should not retain it. One exception to that rule is collections, which often don't directly own their contents but are retaining them on behalf of the object that owns the collection. An example of an object having a reference to something it doesn't own is the Delegate pattern (see Item 23).

Things to Remember

✦ Retain cycles can be avoided by making certain references weak.

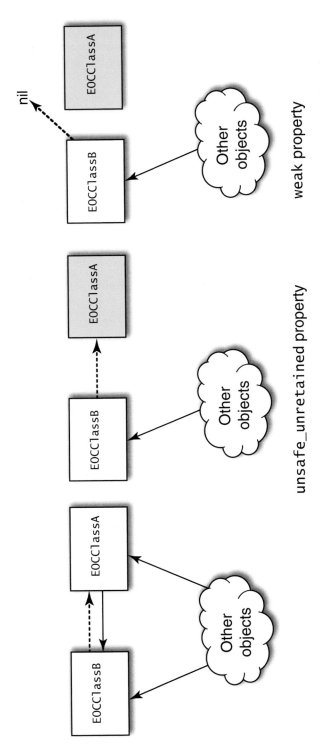

Figure 5.6 Difference between unsafe_unretained and weak attributes when the object pointed to by the property is deallocated

✦ Weak references may or may not be autonilling. Autonilling is a new feature introduced with ARC and is implemented in the runtime. Autonilling weak references are always safe to read, as they will never contain a reference to a deallocated object.

Item 34: Use Autorelease Pool Blocks to Reduce High-Memory Waterline

Objective-C objects going through their lives are subjected to reference counting (see Item 29). One of the features of Objective-C's reference-counted architecture is a concept known as autorelease pools. Releasing an object means that its retain count either is decremented immediately through a call to release or is added to an autorelease pool through a call to autorelease. An autorelease pool is used as a collection of objects that will need releasing at some point in the future. When a pool is drained, all the objects in the pool at that time are sent the release message.

The syntax for creating an autorelease pool is as follows:

```
@autoreleasepool {
    // …
}
```

If no autorelease pool is in place when an object is sent the autorelease message, you will see a message like this in the console:

```
Object 0xabcd0123 of class __NSCFString autoreleased
with no pool in place - just leaking - break on objc_
autoreleaseNoPool() to debug
```

However, you generally do not need to worry about autorelease pools. An application running on either Mac OS X or iOS is running in a Cocoa (or Cocoa Touch for iOS) environment. Threads that the system creates for you, such as the main thread or threads created as part of Grand Central Dispatch (GCD), have an implicit autorelease pool that is drained each time the thread goes through its event loop. Therefore, you don't have to create your own autorelease pool blocks. Often, the only one you will ever see in an application is the one that wraps the main application entry point in the main function. For example, an iOS application's main function usually looks like this:

```
int main(int argc, char *argv[]) {
    @autoreleasepool {
        return UIApplicationMain(argc,
                                  argv,
```

```
                                     nil,
                                     @"EOCAppDelegate");

        }
}
```

Technically, this autorelease pool block is unnecessary. The end of
the block coincides with the application terminating, at which point
the operating system releases all memory used by the application.
Without it, any objects autoreleased by the UIApplicationMain function would not have a pool to go into and would log a warning saying
just that. So this pool can be thought of as an outer catch-all pool.

The braces in the following code define the scope of the autorelease
pool. A pool is created at the first brace and is automatically drained
at the end of the scope. Any object autoreleased within the scope is
therefore sent the release message at the end of the scope. Autorelease pools can be nested. When an object is autoreleased, it is added
to the innermost pool. For example:

```
@autoreleasepool {
    NSString *string = [NSString stringWithFormat:@"1 = %i", 1];
    @autoreleasepool {
        NSNumber *number = [NSNumber numberWithInt:1];
    }
}
```

In this example, two objects are created using class factory methods,
which return objects autoreleased (see Item 30). The NSString object
will be added to the outer autorelease pool, and the NSNumber object
will be added to the inner autorelease pool. This nesting of autorelease pools can be taken advantage of to allow the control of the high
memory mark of an application.

Consider the following portion of code:

```
for (int i = 0; i < 100000; i++) {
    [self doSomethingWithInt:i];
}
```

If the doSomethingWithInt: method creates temporary objects, they
will likely make their way into the autorelease poOOol. These objects
may be temporary strings, for example. Even though they are not
used after the end of the method, these objects may still be alive
because they are in the autorelease pool, ready to be released and
subsequently deallocated. But the pool is not drained until the next
time around that thread's event loop. This means that as the for loop
executes, more and more objects will be created and added to the

autorelease pool. Eventually, once it has finished, the objects will be released. But throughout the execution of the loop, the memory footprint of the application will have been increasing steadily and then would suddenly come back down as all the temporary objects are finally released.

This situation is not ideal, especially if the length of such a loop is arbitrary, depending on user input. Consider reading in a set of objects from a database, for example. Such code may look like this:

```
NSArray *databaseRecords = /* … */;
NSMutableArray *people = [NSMutableArray new];
for (NSDictionary *record in databaseRecords) {
    EOCPerson *person = [[EOCPerson alloc]
                                initWithRecord:record];
    [people addObject:person];
}
```

The initializer for EOCPerson may create extra temporary objects, just as in the earlier example. If the number of records is large, so too is the number of temporary objects kept alive for longer than is strictly necessary. This is where adding in an autorelease pool can help. If the inner part of the loop is wrapped in an autorelease pool block, anything autoreleased inside the loop is added to that pool rather than the thread's main pool. For example:

```
NSArray *databaseRecords = /* … */;
NSMutableArray *people = [NSMutableArray new];
for (NSDictionary *record in databaseRecords) {
    @autoreleasepool {
        EOCPerson *person =
            [[EOCPerson alloc] initWithRecord:record];
        [people addObject:person];
    }
}
```

With this new autorelease pool added, the high-memory waterline of the application is lowered during the loop's execution. The high-memory waterline refers to the highest memory footprint of an application during a certain period. Adding in an autorelease pool block can reduce this footprint because some objects will be deallocated at the end of the block. These are the temporary objects as described earlier.

Autorelease pools can be thought of as being in a stack. When an autorelease pool is created, it is pushed onto the stack; when it is drained, it is pulled off the stack. When an object is autoreleased, it is put into the topmost pool in the stack.

The need to make this additional pool optimization depends entirely on your application. It is certainly not something that should be done without first monitoring the memory footprint to decide whether a problem needs addressing. Autorelease pool blocks do not incur too much overhead, but they do incur at least some overhead, so if the extra autorelease pool can be avoided, it should be.

If you were an Objective-C programmer before the transition to ARC, you will remember the old syntax that used an object called NSAutoreleasePool. This special object wasn't the same as a normal object, designed to represent an autorelease pool just like the new block syntax. Instead of draining the pool every time round a for loop, this object was more heavyweight, and it was usual to create one pool and drain it every so often, like this:

```
NSArray *databaseRecords = /* … */;
NSMutableArray *people = [NSMutableArray new];
int i = 0;

NSAutoreleasePool *pool = [[NSAutoreleasePool alloc] init];
for (NSDictionary *record in databaseRecords) {
    EOCPerson *person = [[EOCPerson alloc]
                              initWithRecord:record];
    [people addObject:person];

    // Drain the pool only every 10 cycles
    if (++i == 10) {
        [pool drain];
    }
}

// Also drain at the end in case the loop is not a multiple of 10
[pool drain];
```

This style of code is no longer necessary. Along with the new syntax, ARC brought much more lightweight autorelease pools. So if you have code that used to drain every *n* iterations of a loop, you can replace it with an autorelease pool block surrounding the contents of the for loop, meaning that a pool is created and drained for every single iteration.

Another benefit of the @autoreleasepool syntax is that every autorelease pool has an associated scope, which helps avoid accidentally using an object that was deallocated by an autorelease pool draining. For example, consider the following code in the old style:

```
NSAutoreleasePool *pool = [[NSAutoreleasePool alloc] init];
id object = [self createObject];
[pool drain];
[self useObject:object];
```

This is slightly exaggerated, but it explains the point. The call to useObject: is passing a potentially deallocated object. However, the same code in the new style would look like this:

```
@autoreleasepool {
    id object = [self createObject];
}
[self useObject:object];
```

This time, the code would not even compile, because the object variable is not valid outside of its enclosing scope, so it cannot be used in the call to useObject:.

Things to Remember

✦ Autorelease pools are arranged in a stack, with an object being added to the topmost pool when it is sent the autorelease message.

✦ Correct application of autorelease pools can help reduce the high-memory waterline of an application.

✦ Modern autorelease pools using the new @autoreleasepool syntax are cheap.

Item 35: Use Zombies to Help Debug Memory-Management Problems

Debugging memory-management issues can be painful. Sending a message to a deallocated object is completely unsafe, as one would expect. But sometimes it works, and sometimes it doesn't. It all depends on whether the memory where the object used to reside has been overwritten. Whether or not the memory is reused is nondeterministic, so a crash may happen only occasionally. Other times, the memory will be only partially reused, so certain bits of the object are still valid. Yet other times, the memory will by sheer fluke have been overwritten with another valid, live object. In these cases, the runtime will send the message to the new object, to which it may or may not respond. If it does, the app won't crash, but you'll wonder why objects you didn't expect to be receiving messages are. If it doesn't respond to that selector, the application will usually crash.

Fortunately, Cocoa's "zombies" feature can come in handy. When this debugging feature is enabled, the runtime turns all deallocated instances into a special zombie object rather than deallocating them. The core memory where the object is located is not made available for reuse; therefore, nothing will ever overwrite it. When it receives any message, a zombie object throws an exception saying exactly what message was sent and what the object used to be when it was still alive. Using zombies is the best way to debug memory-management problems.

The feature is turned on by setting the NSZombieEnabled environment variable to YES. For example, if you're using bash and running an application on Mac OS X, you would do something like this:

```
export NSZombieEnabled="YES"
./app
```

When a message is sent to a zombie, a message will be printed to the console, and the application will terminate. The message will look like this:

```
*** -[CFString respondsToSelector:]: message sent to
deallocated instance 0x7ff9e9c080e0
```

It is also possible to turn on the option in Xcode such that the environment variable is automatically set when the application is run from within Xcode. To do this, you edit the application's scheme, select the Run configuration, then the Diagnostics tab, and finally turn on Enable Zombie Objects. Figure 5.7 shows the dialog that you should see in Xcode, with the option to enable zombies turned on.

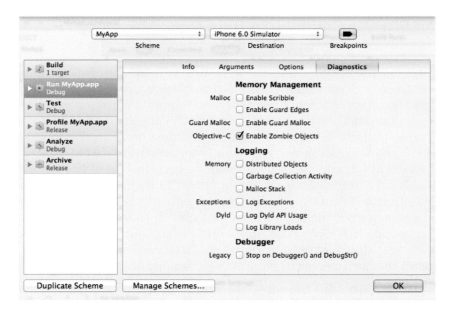

Figure 5.7 Enabling zombie objects from Xcode's scheme editor

So how does the zombies feature work? It is implemented deep within the Objective-C runtime and the Foundation and CoreFoundation frameworks. When an object is being deallocated, an additional step is made by using the environment variable if this feature is enabled. This extra step turns the object into a zombie rather than fully deallocating it.

To see what this extra step does, consider the following code:

```
#import <Foundation/Foundation.h>
#import <objc/runtime.h>

@interface EOCClass : NSObject
@end

@implementation EOCClass
@end

void PrintClassInfo(id obj) {
    Class cls = object_getClass(obj);
    Class superCls = class_getSuperclass(cls);
    NSLog(@"=== %s : %s ===",
            class_getName(cls), class_getName(superCls));
}

int main(int argc, char *argv[]) {
    EOCClass *obj = [[EOCClass alloc] init];
    NSLog(@"Before release:");
    PrintClassInfo(obj);

    [obj release];
    NSLog(@"After release:");
    PrintClassInfo(obj);
}
```

This code uses manual reference counting to make it easier to show what happens when an object becomes a zombie. ARC would ensure that the str object was alive for as long as it needed to be, meaning that it would never become a zombie in this simple scenario. That's not to say that objects can never become zombies under ARC. This type of memory bug can still occur with ARC but usually manifests itself through slightly more complex code.

The code in the example has a function to print out the class and superclass names of a given object. The code uses object_getClass(), a runtime function, rather than sending the class Objective-C message.

If the object is a zombie, sending any Objective-C message will cause the zombie error message to be printed out and the application to crash. The output of the code looks like this:

```
Before release:
=== EOCClass : NSObject ===
After release:
=== _NSZombie_EOCClass : nil ===
```

The object's class has changed from EOCClass to _NSZombie_EOCClass. But where did this class come from? It hasn't been defined in the code. Also, it would be fairly inefficient for the compiler to create an extra class for every class it finds, just in case zombies are enabled. What happens is that this _NSZombie_EOCClass is generated at run-time the first time an object of class EOCClass is turned into a zombie. This uses the powerful runtime functions that can manipulate the class list.

The zombie class is a duplicate of a template class called _NSZombie_. These zombie classes don't do much but simply act as a marker. You'll see how they act as a marker shortly. First, consider the following pseudocode showing how the zombie class is created if necessary and then how it is used to turn the deallocating object into a zombie.

```
// Obtain the class of the object being deallocated
Class cls = object_getClass(self);

// Get the class's name
const char *clsName = class_getName(cls);

// Prepend _NSZombie_ to the class name
const char *zombieClsName = "_NSZombie_" + clsName;

// See if the specific zombie class exists
Class zombieCls = objc_lookUpClass(zombieClsName);

// If the specific zombie class doesn't exist,
// then it needs to be created
if (!zombieCls) {
    // Obtain the template zombie class called _NSZombie_
    Class baseZombieCls = objc_lookUpClass("_NSZombie_");

    // Duplicate the base zombie class, where the new class's
    // name is the prepended string from above
    zombieCls = objc_duplicateClass(baseZombieCls,
                                    zombieClsName, 0);
```

```
}

// Perform normal destruction of the object being deallocated
objc_destructInstance(self);

// Set the class of the object being deallocated
// to the zombie class
objc_setClass(self, zombieCls);

// The class of 'self' is now _NSZombie_OriginalClass
```

This routine is what becomes NSObject's dealloc method. When it sees that the NSZombieEnabled environment variable is set, the runtime swizzles (see Item 13) the dealloc method for a version that performs the preceding code. At the end of this routine, the class of the object has been changed to _NSZombie_OriginalClass, where OriginalClass is the name of the class that once was.

Crucially, the memory the object lives in is not freed (through a call to free()); therefore, the memory will not be available for use again. Although this is leaking memory, this is a debugging tool only and would never be turned on for production-running applications, so it doesn't matter.

But why create a new class for each class that is turned into a zombie? This is done so that the original class can be determined when a message is sent to a zombie. If all zombies were of class _NSZombie_, the original class name would be lost. Creating a new class is done by using the runtime's function objc_duplicateClass(), which copies the entire class but gives it a new name. The superclass, instance variables, and methods of the duplicate class will be identical to the one being copied. Another way to achieve the same goal of maintaining the old class name would be to create the new class as inheriting from _NSZombie_ rather than copying it. However, the functions to do this are less efficient than performing a direct copy.

The zombie class comes into action within the forwarding routines (see Item 12). The _NSZombie_ class (and therefore all its copies) do not implement any methods. The class does not have a superclass and is therefore a root class, just like NSObject, with a single instance variable, called isa, which all Objective-C root classes must have. This lightweight class does not implement any methods, so whenever it is sent any message, it will go through the full forwarding mechanism (see Item 12).

At the heart of the full forwarding mechanism is ___forwarding___, a function you may have seen in backtraces while debugging. One

of the first things that this function does is check the name of the
class of the object being sent a message. If this name is prefixed
with _NSZombie_, a zombie has been detected, and something special
happens. The application is killed at this point, after printing out a
message (shown at the start of this item) to indicate what message
was sent and to what type of class. That's where the fact that the
class name has the original class name within it comes in handy.
The _NSZombie_ is removed from the start of the zombie class name to
leave just the original name. Pseudocode showing what happens is as
follows:

```
// Obtain the object's class
Class cls = object_getClass(self);

// Get the class's name
const char *clsName = class_getName(cls);

// Check if the class is prefixed with _NSZombie_
if (string_has_prefix(clsName, "_NSZombie_") {
    // If so, this object is a zombie

    // Get the original class name by skipping past the
    // _NSZombie_, i.e. taking the substring from character 10
    const char *originalClsName = substring_from(clsName, 10);

    // Get the selector name of the message
    const char *selectorName = sel_getName(_cmd);

    // Log a message to indicate which selector is
    // being sent to which zombie
    Log("*** -[%s %s]: message sent to deallocated instance %p",
        originalClsName, selectorName, self);

    // Kill the application
    abort();
}
```

The action of this routine can be seen if the example is extended to
attempt to message the zombie EOCClass object:

```
EOCClass *obj = [[EOCClass alloc] init];
NSLog(@"Before release:");
PrintClassInfo(obj);

[obj release];
```

```
NSLog(@"After release:");
PrintClassInfo(obj);
```

```
NSString *desc = [obj description];
```

If this is run with zombies enabled, the following is seen on the console:

```
Before release:
=== EOCClass : NSObject ===
After release:
=== _NSZombie_EOCClass : nil ===
*** -[EOCClass description]: message sent to deallocated
instance 0x7fc821c02a00
```

As you can see, this clearly shows what selector was sent and the original class of the object, as well as the pointer value of the dead object that was messaged. This information can be used if you are in a debugger for further analysis, if required, and can prove invaluable with the correct tools, such as Instruments, which ships with Xcode.

Things to Remember

✦ When an object is deallocated, it can optionally be turned into a zombie instead of being deallocated. This feature is turned on by using the environment flag NSZombieEnabled .

✦ An object is turned into a zombie by manipulating its isa pointer to change the object's class to a special zombie class. A zombie class responds to all selectors by aborting the application after printing a message to indicate what message was sent to what object.

Item 36: Avoid Using retainCount

Objective-C uses reference counting for memory management (see Item 29). Each object has a counter that determines how many other things are interested in keeping it alive. When an object is created, the retain count is greater than zero. Retaining and releasing manipulate the count by incrementing and decrementing it, respectively. When the count reaches zero, the object is deallocated and destroyed.

A method defined by the NSObject protocol allows you to obtain the current retain count for an object:

```
- (NSUInteger)retainCount
```

However, ARC has deprecated this method. In fact, the compiler will throw an error if you try to call it when using ARC, just as it does with such methods as `retain`, `release`, and `autorelease`. Even though this method is officially deprecated, it is often misunderstood, and its use should be avoided. If you are not using ARC, which you really should be, it's still possible to use this method without getting a compiler error. So it is still important to understand why this method is to be avoided.

It may seem as though this method does a reasonable and useful job. It returns the retain count, after all, which is clearly an important piece of information about every object. The problem is, though, that the absolute retain count is often completely irrelevant and not what you need to know. Even if you use this method only for debug purposes, it's usually not at all helpful.

The first important reason this method is not useful is that its value is the retain count at a given time. Because this value does not include any decrements that are going to happen during a subsequent autorelease pool drain (see Item 34), the value is not necessarily a true representation of the count. Therefore, the following code is very bad:

```
while ([object retainCount]) {
    [object release];
}
```

The first reason this code is wrong is that it will keep dropping the retain count until the object is deallocated, without regard for any autoreleases that may be pending. If the object was also in an autorelease pool at the time, when that pool is drained, the object is further released, and a crash will certainly occur.

Second, the code is dangerous because `retainCount` will never return 0; an optimization within the release behavior of objects means that an object is deallocated when it is released if its retain count is 1. Otherwise, the decrement happens. Therefore, the retain count should never officially reach 0. Unfortunately, this code does sometimes work, largely through sheer luck rather than judgment. Modern runtimes usually simply crash when the `while` loop iterates after the object was eventually deallocated.

Such code should never be necessary. Memory management should be done before this sort of code would ever need to be implemented. There should never be unbalanced retains leaving objects with a positive retain count when you thought they should be deallocated. In such a scenario, the problem should be diagnosed by working out what is still retaining the object and why it hasn't released it.

You may also try to use the retain count and wonder why the value sometimes looks very large. For example, consider the following code:

```
NSString *string = @"Some string";
NSLog(@"string retainCount = %lu", [string retainCount]);

NSNumber *numberI = @1;
NSLog(@"numberI retainCount = %lu", [number retainCount]);

NSNumber *numberF = @3.141f;
NSLog(@"numberF retainCount = %lu", [numberFloat retainCount]);
```

The output of that code on Mac OS X 10.8.2, 64-bit compiled with Clang 4.1, is this:

```
string retainCount = 18446744073709551615
numberI retainCount = 9223372036854775807
numberF retainCount = 1
```

The first number is $2^{64} - 1$ and the second number is $2^{63} - 1$. The retain counts of these objects are both very large because they are representing singleton objects. NSString is implemented as a singleton object, if possible. It is possible if the string is a compile-time constant, as in the example. In this case, the compiler makes a special object, placing the data for the NSString object within the application binary, and uses that instead of creating an NSString object at runtime. NSNumber does a similar thing, using a concept known as tagged pointers for certain types of values. In this scheme, there is no NSNumber object; rather, the pointer value itself holds all the information about the number. The runtime then detects that a tagged pointer is being used during message dispatch (see Item 11) and manipulates the pointer value accordingly to behave as though there were a full NSNumber object. This optimization is done only for certain cases, though, which is why the floating-point number in the example has a retain count of 1, as it does not use this optimization.

In addition, the retain counts of singletons such as these never change. Retains and releases are no-ops. The fact that the retain count can behave like this and even that the two singletons return different values for the retain count should indicate again that it is not always a good value to consider. If you were relying on NSNumber objects to have incrementing and decrementing retain counts and then tagged pointers were implemented post facto, your code would be wrong.

But what if you want to use the retain count for debugging purposes? Even then, it is usually not helpful. The retain count might not be as accurate as you think, owing to the object's being in an autorelease pool. Also, other libraries can interfere with the retain count by retaining and/or releasing the object. If you inspect the count, you may incorrectly assume that it has changed because of your code rather than from deep within another library. Take, for example, the following code:

```
id object = [self createObject];
[opaqueObject doSomethingWithObject:object];
NSLog(@"retainCount = %lu", [object retainCount]);
```

What is the retain count? It could be anything. The call to doSomethingWithObject: may have added the object to multiple collections, retaining it in the process. Or the call may have retained the object multiple times and autoreleased it multiple times, some of which are still pending an autorelease pool drain. The retain count is therefore unlikely to be useful to you.

When can you use retainCount? The best answer: never, especially given that Apple has officially deprecated it when using ARC.

Things to Remember

✦ The retain count of an object might seem useful but usually is not, because the absolute retain count at any given time does not give a complete picture of an object's lifetime.

✦ When ARC came along, the retainCount method was deprecated, and using it causes a compiler error to be emitted.

Blocks and Grand Central Dispatch

Multithreaded programming is something that every developer is going to need to think about with modern application development. Even if you don't think that your application is multithreaded, it most probably is because system frameworks often use extra threads to get work done off the UI thread. There's nothing worse than an application that hangs because the UI thread is blocked. In Mac OS X, this results in the dreaded spinning beach ball; in iOS, your application may be terminated if it blocks for too long.

Fortunately, Apple has thought about multithreading in a whole new way. The core features of modern multithreading are blocks and Grand Central Dispatch (GCD). Although distinct and separate technologies, they were introduced together. Blocks provide lexical closures to C, C++, and Objective-C and are incredibly useful, mainly because they provide a mechanism to pass around code as if it were an object, to be run in a different context. Crucially, though, blocks can use anything from the scope in which they were defined.

GCD is the associated technology and provides an abstraction to threading, based on so-called dispatch queues. Blocks can be enqueued on these queues, and GCD handles all scheduling for you. It creates, reuses, and destroys background threads as it sees fit, based on system resources, to process each queue. Moreover, GCD provides easy-to-use solutions to common programming tasks, such as thread-safe single-code execution and running the tasks in parallel, based on available system resources.

Both blocks and GCD are a mainstay of modern Objective-C programming. Therefore, you need to understand how they work and what they provide.

Item 37: Understand Blocks

Blocks provide closures. This language feature was added as an extension to the GCC compiler and is available in all modern Clang versions (the compiler project used for Mac OS X and iOS development). The runtime component required for blocks to function correctly is available in all versions of Mac OS X since 10.4 and iOS since 4.0. The language feature is technically a C-level feature and therefore can be used in C, C++, Objective-C, and Objective-C++ code compiled under a supported compiler and run with the block runtime present.

Block Basics

A block is similar to a function but is defined inline to another function and shares the scope of that within which it is defined. The symbol used to denote a block is the caret, followed by a scope block that contains the block's implementation. For example, a simple block looks like this:

```
^{
    // Block implementation here
}
```

A block is simply another value and has an associated type. Just like an int, float, or Objective-C object, a block can be assigned to a variable and then used like any other variable. The syntax for a block type is similar to that of a function pointer. Following is a simple example of a block that takes no parameters and returns nothing:

```
void (^someBlock)() = ^{
    // Block implementation here
};
```

This block defines a variable whose name is someBlock. This might look strange because the variable name is right in the middle, but once you understand the syntax, it is easy to read. The structure of the block type syntax is as follows:

```
return_type (^block_name)(parameters)
```

To define a block that returns an int and takes two ints as parameters, you would use the following syntax:

```
int (^addBlock)(int a, int b) = ^(int a, int b){
    return a + b;
};
```

A block can then be used as if it were a function. So, for example, the addBlock could be used like this:

```
int add = addBlock(2, 5); //< add = 7
```

The powerful feature that blocks allow is capturing the scope in which they are declared. This means that any variables available to the scope in which the block is declared are also available inside the block. For example, you could define a block that used another variable like this:

```
int additional = 5;
int (^addBlock)(int a, int b) = ^(int a, int b){
    return a + b + additional;
};
int add = addBlock(2, 5); //< add = 12
```

By default, any variable captured by a block cannot be modified by the block. In the example, if the variable called additional were changed within the block, the compiler would issue an error. However, variables can be declared as modifiable by giving them the __block qualifier. For example, a block can be used in array enumeration (see Item 48) to determine how many numbers in an array are less than 2:

```
NSArray *array = @[@0, @1, @2, @3, @4, @5];
__block NSInteger count = 0;
[array enumerateObjectsUsingBlock:
    ^(NSNumber *number, NSUInteger idx, BOOL *stop){
        if ([number compare:@2] == NSOrderedAscending) {
            count++;
        }
    }];
// count = 2
```

This example also shows the use of an inline block. The block passed to the enumerateObjectsUsingBlock: method is not assigned to a local variable but rather declared inline to the method call. This commonly used coding pattern with blocks shows why they are so useful. Before blocks became part of the language, the preceding code would have to be done by passing a function pointer or selector name that the enumeration method could call. State would have to be passed in and out manually, usually through an opaque void pointer, thereby introducing additional code and splitting up the method somewhat. Declaring a block inline means that the business logic is all in one place.

When it captures a variable of object type, a block implicitly retains it. It will be released when the block itself is released. This leads to a point about blocks that is important to understand. A block itself can be considered an object. In fact, blocks respond to many of the selectors that other Objective-C objects do. Most important to understand is that a block is reference counted just like other objects. When the last reference to a block is removed, it is deallocated. In doing so, any objects that the block captures are released to balance out the block's retain of them.

If the block is defined in an instance method of an Objective-C class, the `self` variable is available along with any instance variables of the class. Instance variables are always writable and do not need to be explicitly declared with `__block`. But if an instance variable is captured by either reading or writing to it, the `self` variable is implicitly captured also, because the instance variable relates to that instance. For example, consider following block within a method on a class called EOCClass:

```
@interface EOCClass


- (void)anInstanceMethod {
    // …
    void (^someBlock)() = ^{
        _anInstanceVariable = @"Something";
        NSLog(@"_anInstanceVariable = %@", _anInstanceVariable);
    };
    // …
}


@end
```

The particular instance of EOCClass that had the `anInstanceMethod` method run on is referred to as the `self` variable. It is easy to forget that `self` is captured by this sort of block because it is not used explicitly in the code. However, accessing an instance variable is equivalent to the following:

```
self->_anInstanceVariable = @"Something";
```

This is why the `self` variable is captured. More often than not, properties (see Item 6) will be used to access instance variables, and in this case, the `self` variable is explicit:

```
self.aProperty = @"Something";
```

However, it is important to remember that self is an object and is therefore retained when it is captured by the block. This situation can often lead to retain cycles being introduced if the block is itself retained by the same object to which `self` refers. See Item 40 for more information.

The Guts of a Block

Every object in Objective-C occupies a certain region of memory. This memory region is a different size for every object, depending on the number of instance variables and associated data contained. A block too is an object itself, since the first variable within the region of memory that a block is defined in is a pointer to a Class object, called the isa pointer (see Item 14). The rest of the memory a block uses contains the various bits of information it needs to function correctly. Figure 6.1 shows the layout of a block in detail.

The most important thing to note in the layout is the variable called invoke, a function pointer to where the implementation of the block resides. The prototype of the function takes at least a void*, which is the block itself. Recall that blocks are a simple replacement for function pointers where state is passed using an opaque void pointer. The block is wrapping up what was previously done using standard C language features into a succinct and simple-to-use interface.

The descriptor variable is a pointer to a structure that each block has, declaring the overall size of the block object and function pointers for copy and dispose helpers. These helpers are run when a block is copied and disposed of, for example, to perform any retaining or releasing, respectively, of captured objects.

Finally, a block contains copies of all the variables it captures. These copies are stored after the descriptor variable and take up as much

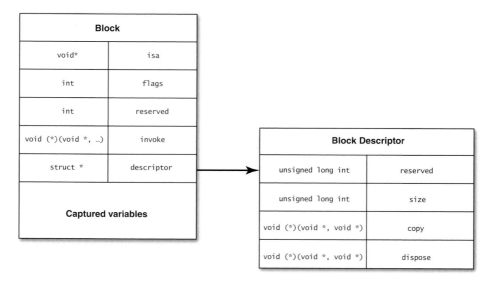

Figure 6.1 The memory layout of a block object

space as required to store all the captured variables. Note that this does not mean that objects themselves are copied but rather only the variables holding pointers. When the block is run, the captured variables are read from this region of memory, which is why the block needs to be passed as a parameter into the invoke function.

Global, Stack, and Heap Blocks

When blocks are defined, the region of memory they occupy is allocated on the stack. This means that the block is valid only within the scope in which it is defined. For example, the following code is dangerous:

```
void (^block)();
if ( /* some condition */ ) {
    block = ^{
        NSLog(@"Block A");
    };
} else {
    block = ^{
        NSLog(@"Block B");
    };
}
block();
```

The two blocks that are defined within the if and else statements are allocated within stack memory. When it allocates stack memory for each block, the compiler is free to overwrite this memory at the end of the scope in which that memory was allocated. So each block is guaranteed to be valid only within its respective if-statement section. The code would compile without error but at runtime may or may not function correctly. If it didn't decide to produce code that overwrote the chosen block, the code would run without error, but if it did, a crash would certainly occur.

To solve this problem, blocks can be copied by sending the block the copy message. In doing so, the block is copied from the stack to the heap. Once this has happened, the block can be used outside the scope in which it was defined. Also, once it has been copied to the heap, a block becomes a reference-counted object. Any subsequent copies do not perform a copy but instead simply increment that block's reference count. When a heap block is no longer referenced, it needs to be released either automatically, if using ARC, or through an explicit call to release, if using manual reference counting. When the reference count drops to zero, the heap block is deallocated just like any other object is. A stack block does not need to be explicitly released, as this is handled by virtue of the fact that stack memory is automatically reclaimed: the reason that the example code was dangerous.

With this in mind, you can simply apply a couple of copy method calls to make that code safe :

```
void (^block)();
if ( /* some condition */ ) {
    block = [^{
        NSLog(@"Block A");
    } copy];
} else {
    block = [^{
        NSLog(@"Block B");
    } copy];
}
block();
```

This code is now safe. If manual reference counting were used, the block too would need to be released after it is finished with.

Global blocks are another category, along with stack and heap blocks. Blocks that don't capture any state, such as variables from the enclosing scope, do not need any state to run. The entire region of memory these blocks use is known in full at compile time; so global blocks are declared within global memory rather than being created on the stack each time they are used. Also, it is a no-op to copy a global block, and a global block is never deallocated. Such blocks are, in effect, singletons. The following is a global block:

```
void (^block)() = ^{
    NSLog(@"This is a block");
};
```

All the information required to execute this block is known at compile time; therefore, it can be a global block. This is purely an optimization to reduce unnecessary work that might be done if such simple blocks were treated like more complex blocks that require work to be done when they are copied and disposed of.

Things to Remember

✦ Blocks are lexical closures for C, C++, and Objective-C.

✦ Blocks can optionally take parameters and optionally return values.

✦ Blocks can be stack allocated, heap allocated, or global. A stack-allocated block can be copied onto the heap, at which point it is reference counted just like standard Objective-C objects.

Item 38: Create `typedefs` for Common Block Types

Blocks have an inherent type; that is, they can be assigned to an appropriately typed variable. The type is made up of the parameters the block takes along and with the return type of the block. For example, consider the following block:

```
^(BOOL flag, int value){
    if (flag) {
        return value * 5;
    } else {
        return value * 10;
    }
}
```

This block takes two parameters of type `BOOL` and `int` and returns a value of type `int`. If it were to be assigned to a variable, this block would need to be appropriately typed. The type and assignment to the variable would look like this:

```
int (^variableName)(BOOL flag, int value) =
    ^(BOOL flag, int value){
        // Implementation
        return someInt;
    }
```

This looks quite different from a normal type but should look familiar if you're used to function pointers. The layout of the type is as follows:

```
return_type (^block_name)(parameters)
```

A block-variable definition is different from other types in that the variable name is in the middle of the type rather than on the right. This makes it quite difficult to remember the syntax and to read. For these reasons, it is a good idea to make type definitions for commonly used block types, especially if you are shipping an API that you expect others to use. However, it is possible to hide block types like this behind a name that is easy to read and indicates what the block is meant to do.

To hide the complicated block type, you use a language feature from C called type definitions. The keyword `typedef` allows you to define an easy-to-read name that becomes an alias for another type. For example, to define a new type for the block that returns an `int` and takes two parameters—a `BOOL` and an `int`—you would use the following type definition:

```
typedef int(^EOCSomeBlock)(BOOL flag, int value);
```

Just as the variable name of a block is in the middle prefixed by a caret, so too is the new type name. This adds a new type, called EOCSomeBlock, to the type system. So instead of creating a variable with a complicated type, you can simply use this new type:

```
EOCSomeBlock block = ^(BOOL flag, int value){
    // Implementation
};
```

This code is now much easier to read, as the variable definition is back to the type on the left and the variable name on the right, just like you're used to seeing with other variables.

Using this feature can make APIs that use blocks much easier to use. Any class that takes a block as a parameter to a method—for example, a completion handler for an asynchronous task—can make use of this feature to make it a lot easier to read. Consider, for example, a class that has a start method that takes a block as a handler to be run when the task finishes. Without making use of a type definition, the method signature may look like this:

```
- (void)startWithCompletionHandler:
            (void(^)(NSData *data, NSError *error))completion;
```

Note that the way the syntax for a block type is laid out is different again from that for defining a variable. It's much easier to read if the type in the method signature is a single word. So you can define a type definition and then use that instead:

```
typedef void(^EOCCompletionHandler)
                        (NSData *data, NSError *error);
- (void)startWithCompletionHandler:
            (EOCCompletionHandler)completion;
```

This is now much simpler to read and understand what the parameter is. Any good, modern Integrated Development Environment (IDE) will automatically expand the type definition, making this easy to use.

Using a type definition is also useful if you ever need to refactor to change the block's type signature. For example, if you decide that the completion handler block now needs to take an additional parameter to pass the time the task took, you can simply change the type definition:

```
typedef void(^EOCCompletionHandler)
        (NSData *data, NSTimeInterval duration, NSError *error);
```

Anywhere the type definition is used, such as method signatures, will now fail to compile in the same way, and you can go through and fix things. Without the type definition, you would find that you needed to change many types throughout your code. It would potentially be easy to miss one or two of these, leading to hard-to-find bugs.

It is usually best to define these type definitions along with the class that uses them. It is also prudent to prefix the new type's name with the class that uses the type definitions. This makes the block's use clear. If multiple type definitions end up being created for the same block signature type, fine. It's better to have more types than fewer.

An example of this point can be seen in the Accounts framework from Mac OS X and iOS. This framework defines, among others, the following block type definitions:

```
typedef void(^ACAccountStoreSaveCompletionHandler)
                          (BOOL success, NSError *error);
typedef void(^ACAccountStoreRequestAccessCompletionHandler)
                          (BOOL granted, NSError *error);
```

These block type definitions have the same signature but are used in distinct places. The name of the type and the name of the parameters in the signature make it easy for the developer to understand how the type is to be used. The developer could have defined a single type definition, perhaps called ACAccountStoreBooleanCompletionHandler, used in place of both of these. However, that would lose the clarity of how the block and parameters are used.

Similarly, if you have a few classes that perform a similar but distinct asynchronous task but that don't fit into a class hierarchy, each class should have its own completion handler type. The signature may be exactly the same for each one, but it's better to use a type definition for each class rather than a single one. On the other hand, if the classes fit into a hierarchy, you could define the type definition along with the base class and have each subclass use it.

Things to Remember

✦ Use type definitions to make it easier to use block variables.

✦ Always follow the naming conventions when defining new types such that you do not clash with other types.

✦ Don't be afraid to define multiple types for the same block signature. You may want to refactor one place that uses a certain block type by changing the block signature but not another.

Item 39: Use Handler Blocks to Reduce Code Separation

A common paradigm in programming a user interface is to perform tasks asynchronously. In this way, the thread that services user interface display and touches does not get blocked when long-running tasks happen, such as I/O or network activity. This thread is often referred to as the main thread. If such methods were synchronous, the user interface would be unresponsive while the task was occurring. In some circumstances, an application may be automatically terminated if it is unresponsive for a certain time. This is true of iOS applications; the system watchdog will terminate an application whose main thread is blocked for a certain period of time.

Asynchronous methods need a way to notify interested parties that they have finished. This can be achieved in several ways. A commonly used technique is having a delegate protocol (see Item 23) to which an object can conform. The object that is the delegate can be notified when pertinent things happen, such as completion of an asynchronous task.

Consider a class that fetches data from a URL. Using the Delegate pattern, the class may look like this:

```
#import <Foundation/Foundation.h>

@class EOCNetworkFetcher;
@protocol EOCNetworkFetcherDelegate <NSObject>
- (void)networkFetcher:(EOCNetworkFetcher*)networkFetcher
    didFinishWithData:(NSData*)data;
@end

@interface EOCNetworkFetcher : NSObject
@property (nonatomic, weak)
                    id <EOCNetworkFetcherDelegate> delegate;
- (id)initWithURL:(NSURL*)url;
- (void)start;
@end
```

A class might use this kind of API as follows:

```
- (void)fetchFooData {
    NSURL *url = [[NSURL alloc] initWithString:
                @"http://www.example.com/foo.dat"];
    EOCNetworkFetcher *fetcher =
        [[EOCNetworkFetcher alloc] initWithURL:url];
    fetcher.delegate = self;
```

```
    [fetcher start];
}

// …

- (void)networkFetcher:(EOCNetworkFetcher*)networkFetcher
      didFinishWithData:(NSData*)data
{
    _fetchedFooData = data;
}
```

This approach works and is not at all incorrect. However, blocks provide a much cleaner way to achieve the same thing. They can be used to tighten up an API like this and also make it much cleaner for a consumer to use. The idea is to define a block type that is used as the completion handler that is passed directly into the start method:

```
#import <Foundation/Foundation.h>

typedef void(^EOCNetworkFetcherCompletionHandler)(NSData *data);

@interface EOCNetworkFetcher : NSObject
- (id)initWithURL:(NSURL*)url;
- (void)startWithCompletionHandler:
            (EOCNetworkFetcherCompletionHandler)handler;
@end
```

This is very similar to using a delegate protocol but has an added bonus that the completion handler can be defined inline with the start method call, which greatly improves the readability of code using the network fetcher. For example, consider a class using the completion-block-style API:

```
- (void)fetchFooData {
    NSURL *url = [[NSURL alloc] initWithString:
                    @"http://www.example.com/foo.dat"];
    EOCNetworkFetcher *fetcher =
        [[EOCNetworkFetcher alloc] initWithURL:url];
    [fetcher startWithCompletionHandler:^(NSData *data){
        _fetchedFooData = data;
    }];
}
```

Comparing this to the code that uses the Delegate pattern should make clear that the block approach is much cleaner. The business logic for what happens when the asynchronous task has finished is sitting right next to the code that starts it. Also, because the block is declared in the same scope as the network fetcher is created, you have access to all the variables that are available in that scope. This is not useful in this simple example but can be extremely useful in more complex scenarios.

A downside to the Delegate approach is that if a class were to use multiple network fetchers to download different bits of data, it would need to switch in the delegate method, based on which network fetcher was calling back. Such code may look like this:

```
- (void)fetchFooData {
    NSURL *url = [[NSURL alloc] initWithString:
                    @"http://www.example.com/foo.dat"];
    _fooFetcher = [[EOCNetworkFetcher alloc] initWithURL:url];
    _fooFetcher.delegate = self;
    [_fooFetcher start];
}

- (void)fetchBarData {
    NSURL *url = [[NSURL alloc] initWithString:
                    @"http://www.example.com/bar.dat"];
    _barFetcher = [[EOCNetworkFetcher alloc] initWithURL:url];
    _barFetcher.delegate = self;
    [_barFetcher start];
}

- (void)networkFetcher:(EOCNetworkFetcher*)networkFetcher
     didFinishWithData:(NSData*)data
{
    if (networkFetcher == _fooFetcher) {
        _fetchedFooData = data;
        _fooFetcher = nil;
    } else if (networkFetcher == _barFetcher) {
        _fetchedBarData = data;
        _barFetcher = nil;
    }
    // etc.
}
```

In addition to making the delegate callback long, this code means that the network fetchers have to be stored as instance variables to be checked against. Doing so might be required anyway, for other reasons, such as to cancel them later, if required; more often than not, it is a side effect that can quickly clog up a class. The benefit of the block approach is that the network fetchers do not have to be stored, and no switching is required. Rather, the business logic of each completion handler is defined along with each fetcher, like this:

```
- (void)fetchFooData {
    NSURL *url = [[NSURL alloc] initWithString:
                        @"http://www.example.com/foo.dat"];
    EOCNetworkFetcher *fetcher =
        [[EOCNetworkFetcher alloc] initWithURL:url];
    [fetcher startWithCompletionHandler:^(NSData *data){
        _fetchedFooData = data;
    }];
}


- (void)fetchBarData {
    NSURL *url = [[NSURL alloc] initWithString:
                        @"http://www.example.com/bar.dat"];
    EOCNetworkFetcher *fetcher =
        [[EOCNetworkFetcher alloc] initWithURL:url];
    [fetcher startWithCompletionHandler:^(NSData *data){
        _fetchedBarData = data;
    }];
}
```

As an extension of this, many modern block-based APIs also use a block for error handling. Two approaches can be taken. With the first, a separate handler can be used for failure cases to success cases. With the second, the failure case can be wrapped up into the same completion block. Using a separate handler looks like this:

```
#import <Foundation/Foundation.h>

@class EOCNetworkFetcher;
typedef void(^EOCNetworkFetcherCompletionHandler)(NSData *data);
typedef void(^EOCNetworkFetcherErrorHandler)(NSError *error);

@interface EOCNetworkFetcher : NSObject
- (id)initWithURL:(NSURL*)url;
- (void)startWithCompletionHandler:
            (EOCNetworkFetcherCompletionHandler)completion
        failureHandler:
            (EOCNetworkFetcherErrorHandler)failure;
@end
```

Code that uses this style of API would look like this:

```
EOCNetworkFetcher *fetcher =
    [[EOCNetworkFetcher alloc] initWithURL:url];
```

```
[fetcher startWithCompletionHander:^(NSData *data){
    // Handle success
}
                    failureHandler:^(NSError *error){
    // Handle failure
}];
```

This style is good because it splits up the success and failure cases, meaning that consumer code too is logically split into success and failure, which helps readability. Also, it's possible for either failure or success to be ignored, if necessary.

The other style, putting the success and failure in a single block, looks like this:

```
#import <Foundation/Foundation.h>

@class EOCNetworkFetcher;
typedef void(^EOCNetworkFetcherCompletionHandler)
                        (NSData *data, NSError *error);

@interface EOCNetworkFetcher : NSObject
- (id)initWithURL:(NSURL*)url;
- (void)startWithCompletionHandler:
            (EOCNetworkFetcherCompletionHandler)completion;
@end
```

Code that uses this style of API would look like this:

```
EOCNetworkFetcher *fetcher =
    [[EOCNetworkFetcher alloc] initWithURL:url];
[fetcher startWithCompletionHander:
    ^(NSData *data, NSError *error){
        if (error) {
            // Handle failure
        } else {
            // Handle success
        }
    }];
```

This approach requires the error variable to be checked and puts all the logic in one place. The downside is that because all the logic is in one place, the block can become long and complicated. However, the upside of the single-block approach is that it is much more flexible. It's possible to pass an error, as well as data, for example. Consider that perhaps the network was able to download half the data and then an error occurred. Maybe in that case, you would pass back the data and the associated error. The completion handler can then determine the problem, handle it as appropriate, and may be able to do something useful with the part of the data that was successfully downloaded.

Another good reason for putting success and failure in the same block is that sometimes when processing the data of an otherwise successful response, the consumer detects an error. Perhaps the data returned was too short, for example. This situation may need to be handled in just the same way as the failure case from the network fetcher's perspective. In that case, having a single block means that processing can be done and that, if an error is found with the data, it can be handled along with the case in which a network fetcher error has been detected. If the success and failure cases are split into separate handlers, it becomes impossible to share the error-handling code of this scenario without deferring to a separate method, which defeats the point of using handler blocks to put business logic code all in one place.

Overall, I suggest using a single handler block for success and failure, which is also the approach that Apple seems to be taking in its APIs. For example, `TWRequest` from the Twitter framework and `MKLocalSearch` from the MapKit framework both use the approach of a single handler block.

Another reason to use handler blocks is for calling back at pertinent times. A consumer of the network fetcher may want to be told each time progress is made with the download, for example. This could be done with a delegate. But continuing the theme of using handler blocks instead, you could add a progress-handler block type and a property:

```
typedef void(^EOCNetworkFetcherCompletionHandler)
                                    (float progress);
@property (nonatomic, copy)
        EOCNetworkFetcherProgressHandler progressHandler;
```

This is a good pattern to follow, as it yet again allows all the business logic to be put in one place: where the network fetcher is created and the completion handler is defined.

Another consideration when writing handler-based APIs stems from the fact that some code is required to run on a certain thread. For instance, any UI work in both Cocoa and Cocoa Touch must happen on the main thread. This equates to the main queue in GCD-land. Therefore, it is sometimes prudent to allow the consumer of a handler-based API to decide on which queue the handler is run. One such

API is NSNotificationCenter, which has a method whereby you can register to be notified of a certain notification by the notification center's executing a certain block. It is possible, but not compulsory, to decide in what queue to schedule the block. If no queue is given, the default behavior is invoked, and the block is run on the thread that posted the notification. The method to add an observer looks like this:

```
- (id)addObserverForName:(NSString*)name
              object:(id)object
               queue:(NSOperationQueue*)queue
          usingBlock:(void(^)(NSNotification*))block
```

Here, an NSOperationQueue is passed in to denote the queue that the block should be run on when a notification is fired. Operation queues rather than the lower-level GCD queues are used, but the semantics are the same. (See Item 43 for more about GCD queues versus other tools.)

You could similarly design an API whereby an operation queue is passed in or even a GCD queue, if that is the level at which you want to pitch the API.

Things to Remember

✦ Use a handler block when it will be useful to have the business logic of the handler be declared inline with the creation of the object.

✦ Handler blocks have the benefit of being associated with an object directly rather than delegation, which often requires switching based on the object if multiple instances are being observed.

✦ When designing an API that uses handler blocks, consider passing a queue as a parameter, to designate the queue on which the block should be enqueued.

Item 40: Avoid Retain Cycles Introduced by Blocks Referencing the Object Owning Them

Blocks can very easily introduce retain cycles if they are not considered carefully. For example, the following class provides an interface for downloading a certain URL. A callback block, called a completion handler, can be set when the fetcher is started and is run when the download has finished. The completion handler needs to be stored in an instance variable in order to be available when the request-completion method is called.

```objc
// EOCNetworkFetcher.h
#import <Foundation/Foundation.h>

typedef void(^EOCNetworkFetcherCompletionHandler)(NSData *data);

@interface EOCNetworkFetcher : NSObject
@property (nonatomic, strong, readonly) NSURL *url;
- (id)initWithURL:(NSURL*)url;
- (void)startWithCompletionHandler:
            (EOCNetworkFetcherCompletionHandler)completion;
@end


// EOCNetworkFetcher.m
#import "EOCNetworkFetcher.h"

@interface EOCNetworkFetcher ()
@property (nonatomic, strong, readwrite) NSURL *url;
@property (nonatomic, copy)
          EOCNetworkFetcherCompletionHandler completionHandler;
@property (nonatomic, strong) NSData *downloadedData;
@end

@implementation EOCNetworkFetcher

- (id)initWithURL:(NSURL*)url {
    if ((self = [super init])) {
        _url = url;
    }
    return self;
}

- (void)startWithCompletionHandler:
        (EOCNetworkFetcherCompletionHandler)completion
{
    self.completionHandler = completion;
    // Start the request
    // Request sets downloadedData property
    // When request is finished, p_requestCompleted is called
}

- (void)p_requestCompleted {
    if (_completionHandler) {
        _completionHandler(_downloadedData);
    }
}

@end
```

Another class may create one of these network fetcher objects and use it to download data at a URL, like this:

```
@implementation EOCClass {
    EOCNetworkFetcher *_networkFetcher;
    NSData *_fetchedData;
}

- (void)downloadData {
    NSURL *url = [[NSURL alloc] initWithString:
                    @"http://www.example.com/something.dat"];
    _networkFetcher =
        [[EOCNetworkFetcher alloc] initWithURL:url];
    [_networkFetcher startWithCompletionHandler:^(NSData *data){
        NSLog(@"Request URL %@ finished", _networkFetcher.url);
        _fetchedData = data;
    }];
}

@end
```

This code looks fairly normal. But you may have failed to realize that a retain cycle is present. It stems from the fact that the completion-handler block references the self variable because it sets the _fetchedData instance variable (see Item 37 for more about captured variables). This means that the EOCClass instance that creates the network fetcher is retained by the block. This block is retained by the network fetcher, which is in turn retained by the same instance of EOCClass because it is held within a strong instance variable. Figure 6.2 illustrates this retain cycle.

This retain cycle can easily be fixed by breaking either the reference the _networkFetcher instance variable holds or the one the completionHandler property holds. This break would need to be done when the completion handler has finished in the case of this network fetcher, so the network fetcher is alive until it has finished. For example, the completion-handler block could be changed to this:

```
[_networkFetcher startWithCompletionHandler:^(NSData *data){
    NSLog(@"Request for URL %@ finished", _networkFetcher.url);
    _fetchedData = data;
    _networkFetcher = nil;
}
```

This retain-cycle problem is common in APIs that make use of completion callback blocks and is therefore important to understand. Often, the problem can be solved by clearing one of the references at

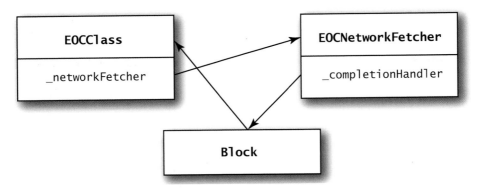

Figure 6.2 Retain cycle between the network fetcher and the class
that owns it

an opportune moment; however, it cannot always be guaranteed that
the moment will occur. In the example, the retain cycle is broken only
if the completion handler is run. If the completion handler was never
run, the retain cycle would never be broken, and leaks would occur.

Another potential retain cycle can be introduced with the completion-
handler block approach. This retain cycle occurs when the completion-
handler block references the object that ends up owning it. For example, to extend the previous example, instead of the consumer having
to keep a reference to the network fetcher while it is running, it has a
mechanism for staying alive itself. The network fetcher may do this by
adding itself to a global collection, such as a set, when it is started and
removing itself when it finishes. The consumer could then change its
code to the following:

```
- (void)downloadData {
    NSURL *url = [[NSURL alloc] initWithString:
                    @"http://www.example.com/something.dat"];
    EOCNetworkFetcher *networkFetcher =
        [[EOCNetworkFetcher alloc] initWithURL:url];
    [networkFetcher startWithCompletionHandler:^(NSData *data){
        NSLog(@"Request URL %@ finished", networkFetcher.url);
        _fetchedData = data;
    }];
}
```

Most networking libraries use this kind of approach, as it is annoying
to have to keep the fetcher object alive yourself. An example is the

TWRequest object from the Twitter framework. However, as the code for EOCNetworkFetcher stands, a retain cycle remains. It is more subtle than before, though, and stems from the fact that the completion-handler block references the request itself. The block therefore retains the fetcher, which in turn retains the block through the completionHandler property. Fortunately, the fix is simple. Recall that the completion handler was being kept in a property only so that it could be used later. The problem is that once the completion handler has been run, it no longer needs to hold onto the block. So the simple fix is to change the following method:

```
- (void)p_requestCompleted {
    if (_completionHandler) {
        _completionHandler(_downloadedData);
    }
    self.completionHandler = nil;
}
```

The retain cycle is then broken once the request has completed, and the fetcher object will be deallocated as necessary. Note that this is a good reason to pass the completion handler in the start method. If instead the completion handler were exposed as a public property, you couldn't just go and clear it when the request completed, as that would break the encapsulation semantics you have given the consumer by saying that the completion handler is public. In this case, the only way to break the retain cycle sensibly is by enforcing that the consumer clear the completionHandler property in the handler itself. But that is not very sensible, because you cannot assume that a consumer will do this and will instead blame you for the leaks.

Both of these scenarios are not uncommon. They are bugs that are easy to creep in when using blocks; similarly, they are just as easy to mitigate if you are careful. The key is to think about what objects a block may capture and therefore retain. If any of these can be an object that retains the block, either directly or indirectly, you will need to think about how to break the retain cycle at the correct moment.

Things to Remember

+ Be aware of the potential problem of retain cycles introduced by blocks that capture objects that directly or indirectly retain the block.

+ Ensure that retain cycles are broken at an opportune moment, but never leave responsibility to the consumer of your API.

Item 41: Prefer Dispatch Queues to Locks for Synchronization

Sometimes in Objective-C, you will come across code that you're having trouble with because it's being accessed from multiple threads. This situation usually calls for the application of some sort of synchronization through the use of locks. Before GCD, there were two ways to achieve this, the first being the built-in synchronization block:

```
- (void)synchronizedMethod {
    @synchronized(self) {
        // Safe
    }
}
```

This construct automatically creates a lock based on the given object and waits on that lock until it executes the code contained in the block. At the end of the code block, the lock is released. In the example, the object being synchronized against is self. This construct is often a good choice, as it ensures that each instance of the object can run its own synchronizedMethod independently. However, overuse of @synchronized(self) can lead to inefficient code, as each synchronized block will execute serially across all such blocks. If you overuse synchronization against self, you can end up with code waiting unnecessarily on a lock held by unrelated code.

The other approach is to use the NSLock object directly:

```
_lock = [[NSLock alloc] init];

- (void)synchronizedMethod {
    [_lock lock];
    // Safe
    [_lock unlock];
}
```

Recursive locks are also available through NSRecursiveLock, allowing for one thread to take out the same lock multiple times without causing a deadlock.

Both of these approaches are fine but come with their own drawbacks. For example, synchronization blocks can suffer from deadlock under extreme circumstances and are not necessarily efficient. Direct use of locks can be troublesome when it comes to deadlocks.

The alternative is to use GCD, which can provide locking in a much simpler and more efficient manner. Properties are a good example of where developers find the need to put synchronization, known as making the property atomic. This can be achieved through use of the atomic property attribute (see Item 6). Or, if the accessors need to be written manually, the following is often seen:

```
- (NSString*)someString {
    @synchronized(self) {
        return _someString;
    }
}

- (void)setSomeString:(NSString*)someString {
    @synchronized(self) {
        _someString = someString;
    }
}
```

Recall that @synchronized(self) is dangerous if overused, because all such blocks will be synchronized with respect to one another. If multiple properties do that, each will be synchronized with respect to all others, which is probably not what you want. All you really want is that access to each property be synchronized individually.

As an aside, you should be aware that although this goes some way to ensuring thread safety, it does not ensure absolute thread safety of the object. Rather, access to the property is atomic. You are guaranteed to get valid results when using the property, but if you call the getter multiple times from the same thread, you may not necessarily get the same result each time. Other threads may have written to the property between accesses.

A simple and effective alternative to synchronization blocks or lock objects is to use a serial synchronization queue. Dispatching reads and writes onto the same queue ensures synchronization. Doing so looks like this:

```
_syncQueue =
dispatch_queue_create("com.effectiveobjectivec.syncQueue", NULL);

- (NSString*)someString {
    __block NSString *localSomeString;
    dispatch_sync(_syncQueue, ^{
        localSomeString = _someString;
    });
    return localSomeString;
}
```

```
- (void)setSomeString:(NSString*)someString {
    dispatch_sync(_syncQueue, ^{
        _someString = someString;
    });
}
```

The idea behind this pattern is that all access to the property is synchronized because the GCD queue that both the setter and the getter
run on is a serial queue. Apart from the __block syntax in the getter, required to allow the block to set the variable (see Item 37), this
approach is much neater. All the locking is handled down in GCD,
which has been implemented at a very low level and has many optimizations made. Thus, you don't have to worry about that side of things
and can instead focus on writing your accessor code.

However, we can go one step further. The setter does not have to be
synchronous. The block that sets the instance variable does not need
to return anything to the setter method. This means that you can
change the setter method to look like this:

```
- (void)setSomeString:(NSString*)someString {
    dispatch_async(_syncQueue, ^{
        _someString = someString;
    });
}
```

The simple change from synchronous dispatch to asynchronous provides the benefit that the setter is fast from the caller's perspective,
but reading and writing are still executed serially with respect to each
another. One downside, though, is that if you were to benchmark this,
you might find that it's slower; with asynchronous dispatch, the block
has to be copied. If the time taken to perform the copy is significant
compared to the time the block takes to execute, it will be slower. So
in our simple example, it's likely to be slower. However, the approach
is still good to understand as a potential candidate if the block that is
being dispatched performs much heavier tasks.

Another way to make this approach even faster is to take advantage
of the fact that the getters can run concurrently with one another but
not with the setter. This is where the GCD approach comes into its
own. The following cannot be easily done with synchronization blocks
or locks. Instead of using a serial queue, consider what would happen
if you used a concurrent queue:

```
_syncQueue =
dispatch_get_global_queue(DISPATCH_QUEUE_PRIORITY_DEFAULT, 0);
```

```
- (NSString*)someString {
    __block NSString *localSomeString;
    dispatch_sync(_syncQueue, ^{
        localSomeString = _someString;
    });
    return localSomeString;
}

- (void)setSomeString:(NSString*)someString {
    dispatch_async(_syncQueue, ^{
        _someString = someString;
    });
}
```

As it stands, that code would not work for synchronization. All reads and writes are executed on the same queue, but that queue being concurrent, reads and writes can all happen at the same time. This is what we were trying to stop from happening in the first place! However, a simple GCD feature, called a barrier, is available and can solve this. The functions that a queue barrier blocks are as follows:

```
void dispatch_barrier_async(dispatch_queue_t queue,
                            dispatch_block_t block);
void dispatch_barrier_sync(dispatch_queue_t queue,
                           dispatch_block_t block);
```

A barrier is executed exclusively with respect to all other blocks on that queue. They are relevant only on concurrent queues, since all blocks on a serial queue are always executed exclusively with respect to one another. When a queue is processed and the next block is a barrier block, the queue waits for all current blocks to finish and then executes the barrier block. When the barrier block finishes executing, processing of the queue continues as normal.

Barriers can be used with the property example in the setter. If the setter uses a barrier block, reads of the property will still execute concurrently, but writes will execute exclusively. Figure 6.3 illustrates the queue with many reads and a single write queued.

The code to achieve this is simple:

```
_syncQueue =
dispatch_get_global_queue(DISPATCH_QUEUE_PRIORITY_DEFAULT, 0);

- (NSString*)someString {
    __block NSString *localSomeString;
    dispatch_sync(_syncQueue, ^{
```

```
        localSomeString = _someString;
    });
    return localSomeString;
}

- (void)setSomeString:(NSString*)someString {
    dispatch_barrier_async(_syncQueue, ^{
        _someString = someString;
    });
}
```

Concurrent Queue

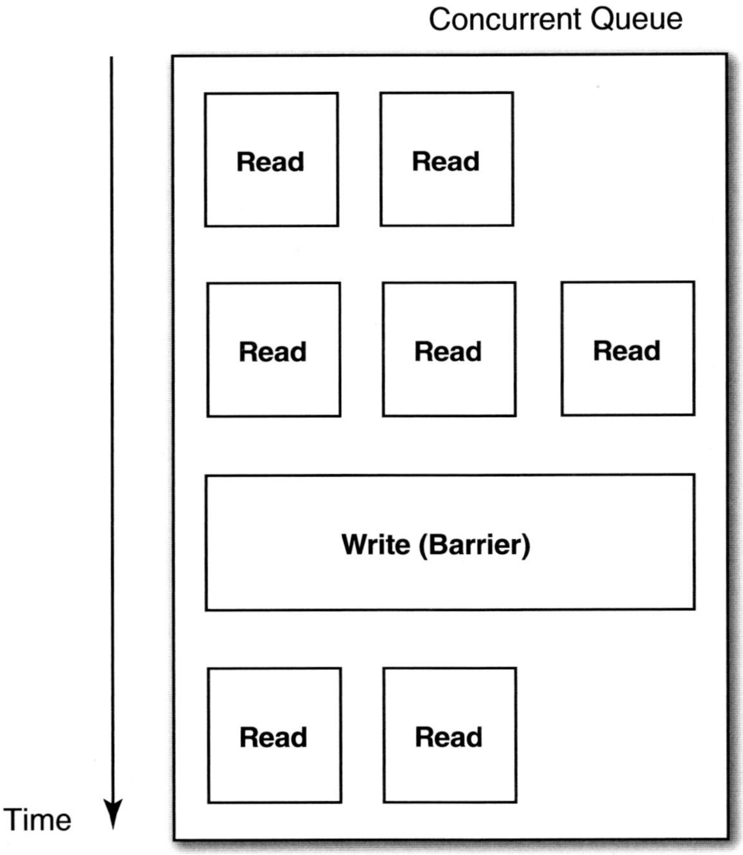

Figure 6.3 Concurrent queue with reads as normal blocks and writes as barrier blocks. Reads are executed concurrently; writes are executed exclusively, as they are barriers.

If you were to benchmark this, you would certainly find it quicker than using a serial queue. Note that you could also use a synchronous barrier in the setter, which may be more efficient for the same reason as explained before. It would be prudent to benchmark each approach and choose the one that is best for your specific scenario.

Things to Remember

✦ Dispatch queues can be used to provide synchronization semantics and offer a simpler alternative to @synchronized blocks or NSLock objects.

✦ Mixing synchronous and asynchronous dispatches can provide the same synchronized behavior as with normal locking but without blocking the calling thread in the asynchronous dispatches.

✦ Concurrent queues and barrier blocks can be used to make synchronized behavior more efficient.

Item 42: Prefer GCD to performSelector and Friends

Thanks to the extremely dynamic nature of Objective-C (see Item 11), a few methods defined on NSObject allow you to call any method you wish. They allow delayed execution of a method call or specification of which thread it should be run on. They were once a very useful feature; now, however, technologies such as Grand Central Dispatch and blocks are making their use less important. Although you will often still see code using them, I encourage you to stay clear of them.

The most basic method in this family is performSelector:. It takes a single argument, which is the selector to perform, with the following signature:

```
- (id)performSelector:(SEL)selector
```

This is equivalent to calling the selector directly. So the following two lines of code are equivalent:

```
[object performSelector:@selector(selectorName)];
[object selectorName];
```

It might seem as though this is redundant. It would be if this were the only way the method could be used. However, its real power comes from the fact that the selector can be decided at runtime. Such dynamic binding on top of dynamic binding means that you can do something like this:

```
SEL selector;
if ( /* some condition */ ) {
    selector = @selector(foo);
} else if ( /* some other condition */ ) {
    selector = @selector(bar);
} else {
    selector = @selector(baz);
}
[object performSelector:selector];
```

This code is extremely flexible and can often be used to simplify complex code. Another use is to store a selector that should be performed after an event has happened. In either case, the compiler doesn't know until runtime which selector is going to be performed. But the cost of this feature is that if you compile this under ARC, the compiler emits the following warning:

```
warning: performSelector may cause a leak because its selector
is unknown [-Warc-performSelector-leaks]
```

You probably weren't expecting that! If you were, you probably know why you should be careful with these methods. This message may look strange to you, and you're wondering why a leak is mentioned. After all, you were simply trying to call a method. The reason is that the compiler doesn't know what selector is going to be invoked and therefore doesn't know the method signature, the return type, or even if there is a returned value. Also, the compiler doesn't know the method name and therefore cannot apply ARC's memory-management rules to determine whether the return value should be released. For this reason, ARC plays it safe and doesn't add a release. However, the result might be a memory leak, as the object might be being returned as a retained object.

Consider the following code:

```
SEL selector;
if ( /* some condition */ ) {
    selector = @selector(newObject);
} else if ( /* some other condition */ ) {
    selector = @selector(copy);
} else {
    selector = @selector(someProperty);
}
id ret = [object performSelector:selector];
```

This is a slight variation on the preceding example to show the problem. In the case of the first two selectors, the ret object would need to be released by this code; with the third selector, it would not. This is true not only in an ARC world but also in a non-ARC world, which is strictly following the method-naming guidelines. Without ARC (and therefore no compiler warning), the ret object would need to be released if either of the first two conditions were true but not otherwise. This could easily be overlooked, and even a static analyzer would not help detect the subsequent memory leak. This is one reason for treating the performSelector family of methods with caution.

Another reason these methods are not ideal is that the return type can be only void or an object type. The performSelector method's return type is id, although it's also valid that the selector being performed returns void. Although intricate casting can use selectors that return other values, such as integers or floats, it can be fragile. It's technically possible to return any type that has the same size as a pointer, as the id type is a pointer to any Objective-C object: on 32-bit architectures, any type that is 32 bits wide; on 64-bit architectures, any type that is 64 bits wide. If the return type is a C struct, the performSelector method cannot be used.

A couple of other performSelector variants that can pass arguments with the message are defined as follows:

```
- (id)performSelector:(SEL)selector
        withObject:(id)object
- (id)performSelector:(SEL)selector
        withObject:(id)objectA
        withObject:(id)objectB
```

For example, these variants can be used to set a property called value on an object:

```
id object = /* an object with a property called 'value' */;
id newValue = /* new value for the property */;
[object performSelector:@selector(setValue:)
        withObject:newValue];
```

These methods may seem useful, but they have serious limitations. The objects being passed in must be objects, as the type is always id. So if the selector takes an integer or a float, these methods cannot be used. In addition, the selector can take a maximum of two parameters, using the method performSelector:withObject:withObject:. There are no equivalent methods to perform selectors that take more than two parameters.

One of the other features of the performSelector family of methods is the fact that the selector can be run after a delay or on another thread. Some of the more common of these methods are as follows:

```
- (void)performSelector:(SEL)selector
         withObject:(id)argument
         afterDelay:(NSTimeInterval)delay
- (void)performSelector:(SEL)selector
           onThread:(NSThread*)thread
         withObject:(id)argument
      waitUntilDone:(BOOL)wait
- (void)performSelectorOnMainThread:(SEL)selector
                    withObject:(id)argument
                 waitUntilDone:(BOOL)wait
```

However, these methods soon become too constraining. For example, there is no method to perform a given selector that takes two arguments after a delay. The threading methods are not very generic, for the same reason. Code that wants to make use of these methods often packs multiple arguments into a dictionary and unpacks in the called method, thereby adding overhead and the potential for bugs.

All these limitations are solved by using one of the alternatives. The main alternative is using blocks (see Item 37). Furthermore, using blocks with Grand Central Dispatch (GCD) enables you to achieve all the threading-related reasons for using one of the performSelector methods. Performing after a delay can be achieved with dispatch_after, and performing on another thread can be achieved with dispatch_sync and dispatch_async.

For example, to perform a task after a delay, you should prefer the latter to the former:

```
// Using performSelector:withObject:afterDelay:
[self performSelector:@selector(doSomething)
         withObject:nil
         afterDelay:5.0];


// Using dispatch_after
dispatch_time_t time = dispatch_time(DISPATCH_TIME_NOW,
                              (int64_t)(5.0 * NSEC_PER_SEC));
dispatch_after(time, dispatch_get_main_queue(), ^(void){
   [self doSomething];
});
```

To perform a task on the main thread:

```
// Using performSelectorOnMainThread:withObject:waitUntilDone:
[self performSelectorOnMainThread:@selector(doSomething)
                    withObject:nil
                 waitUntilDone:NO];
```

```
// Using dispatch_async
// (or if waitUntilDone is YES, then dispatch_sync)
dispatch_async(dispatch_get_main_queue(), ^{
    [self doSomething];
});
```

Things to Remember

◆ The performSelector family of methods is potentially dangerous with respect to memory management. If it has no way of determining what selector is going to be performed, the ARC compiler cannot insert the appropriate memory-management calls.

◆ The family of methods is very limited with respect to the return type and the number of parameters that can be sent to the method.

◆ The methods that allow performing a selector on a different thread are better replaced with certain Grand Central Dispatch (GCD) calls using blocks.

Item 43: Know When to Use GCD and When to Use Operation Queues

GCD is a fantastic technology, but it is sometimes better to use other tools that come as part of the standard system libraries. Knowing when to use each tool is important; using the wrong tool can lead to code that's difficult to maintain.

The synchronization mechanisms of GCD (see Item 41) can hardly be rivaled. The same goes for single-time code execution through the use of dispatch_once (see Item 45). However, using GCD is not always the best approach for executing tasks in the background. A separate but related technology, NSOperationQueue, allows you to queue operations (subclasses of NSOperation) that can optionally run concurrently. The similarity to GCD's dispatch queues is not a coincidence. Operation queues came before GCD, but there is no doubt that GCD is based on the principles made popular by operation queues. In fact, from iOS 4 and Mac OS X 10.6 onward, operation queues use GCD under the hood.

The first difference to note is that GCD is a pure C API, whereas operation queues are Objective-C objects. In GCD, the task that is queued is a block, which is a fairly lightweight data structure (see Item 37). Operations, on the other hand, are Objective-C objects and are therefore more heavyweight. That said, GCD is not always the approach of choice. Sometimes, this overhead is minimal, and the benefits of using full objects far outweigh the downsides.

Through the use of the NSBlockOperation or NSOperationQueue's addOperationWithBlock: method, the syntax of operation queues can look very similar to plain GCD. Here are some of the benefits of NSOperation and NSOperationQueue:

✦ Cancelling operations

With operation queues, this is simple. When run, the cancel method on NSOperation sets internal flags within the operation to tell it not to run, although it cannot cancel an operation that has already started. On the other hand, GCD queues have no way of cancelling a block once it is scheduled. The architecture is very much "fire and forget." Implementing cancelling at the application level, however, would be possible but would require writing a lot of code that has already been written in the form of operations.

✦ Operation dependencies

An operation can have dependencies on as many other operations as it wishes. This enables you to create a hierarchy of operations dictating that certain operations can execute only after another operation has completed successfully. For example, you may have operations to download and process files from a server that requires a manifest file to be downloaded first before others can be processed. The operation to download the manifest file first could be a dependency of the subsequent download operations. If the operation queue were set to allow concurrent execution, the subsequent downloads could execute in parallel but only after the dependent operation had completed.

✦ Key-Value Observing of operation properties

Operations have many properties that are appropriate for KVO, such as isCancelled to determine whether it has been cancelled and isFinished to determine whether it has finished. Using KVO can be useful if you have code that wants to know when a certain task changes state and gives much finer-grained control than GCD over the tasks that are operating.

✦ Operation priorities

An operation has an associated priority that ranks it against other operations in a queue. Higher-priority operations are executed before lower-priority ones. The scheduling algorithm is opaque but most certainly will have been carefully thought out. GCD has no direct way of achieving the same thing. It does have queue priorities, but they set a priority for the entire queue rather than individual blocks. Writing your own scheduler on top of this is not something you really want to do. Priorities are therefore a useful feature of operations.

Operations also have an associated thread priority, which determines at what priority the thread will execute when the operation runs. You could do this yourself with GCD, but operations make it as simple as setting a property.

✦ Reuse of operations

Unless you use one of the built-in concrete subclasses of NSOperation, such as NSBlockOperation, you must create your own subclass. This class, being a normal Objective-C object, can store whatever information you want. When it runs, it has full use of this information and any methods that have been defined on the class. This makes it much more powerful than a simple block that is queued on a dispatch queue. These operation classes can be reused throughout your code, thereby following the "Don't Repeat Yourself" (DRY) principle of software development.

As you can see, there are many good reasons to use operation queues over dispatch queues. Operation queues mostly provide instant solutions to many of the things you might want to do when executing tasks. Instead of writing complex schedulers, or cancel semantics or priorities yourself, you get them for free when using operation queues.

One API that makes use of operation queues rather than dispatch queues is NSNotificationCenter, which has a method where you can register to observe a notification through a block instead of calling a selector. The method prototype looks like this:

```
- (id)addObserverForName:(NSString*)name
                  object:(id)object
                   queue:(NSOperationQueue*)queue
              usingBlock:(void(^)(NSNotification*))block
```

Instead of taking an operation queue, this method could have taken a dispatch queue on which to queue the notification-handler block. But clearly, the design decision was made to make use of the higher-level Objective-C API. In this case, there is little difference between the two in terms of efficiency. The decision was possibly made because using a dispatch queue would introduce an unnecessary dependency on GCD; remember that blocks are not GCD, so the block itself does not introduce this dependency. Or perhaps the developers wanted to keep it all in Objective-C.

You will often hear that you should always use the highest-level API possible, dropping down only when truly necessary. I subscribe to this mantra but with caution. Just because it can be done with the high-level Objective-C variant does not necessarily mean that it's better. Benchmarking is always the best way to know for sure what is best.

Things to Remember

+ Dispatch queues are not the only solution to multithreading and task management.

+ Operation queues provide a high-level, Objective-C API that can do most of what plain GCD can do. These queues can also do much more complex things that would require additional code on top of GCD.

Item 44: Use Dispatch Groups to Take Advantage of Platform Scaling

Dispatch groups are a GCD feature that allows you to easily group tasks. You can then wait on that set of tasks to finish or be notified through a callback when the set of tasks has finished. This feature is very useful for several reasons, the first and most interesting of which is when you want to perform multiple tasks concurrently but need to know when they have all finished. An example of this would be performing a task, such as compressing a set of files.

A dispatch group is created with the following function:

```
dispatch_group_t dispatch_group_create();
```

A group is a simple data structure with nothing distinguishing it, unlike a dispatch queue, which has an identifier. You can associate tasks with a dispatch group in two ways. The first is to use the following function:

```
void dispatch_group_async(dispatch_group_t group,
                          dispatch_queue_t queue,
                          dispatch_block_t block);
```

This is a variant of the normal dispatch_async function but takes an additional group parameter, which specifies the group with which to associate the block to execute. The second way to associate a task with a dispatch group is to use the following pair of functions:

```
void dispatch_group_enter(dispatch_group_t group);
void dispatch_group_leave(dispatch_group_t group);
```

The former causes the number of tasks the group thinks are currently running to increment; the latter does the opposite. Therefore, for each call to dispatch_group_enter, there must be an associated dispatch_group_leave. This is similar to reference counting (see Item

29), whereby retains and releases must be balanced to avoid leaks. In the case of dispatch groups, if an enter is not balanced with a leave, the group will never finish.

The following function can be used to wait on a dispatch group to finish:

```
long dispatch_group_wait(dispatch_group_t group,
                         dispatch_time_t timeout);
```

This takes the group to wait on and a timeout value. The timeout specifies how long this function should block while waiting for the group to finish. If the group finishes before the timeout, zero is returned; otherwise, a nonzero value is returned. The constant DISPATCH_TIME_FOREVER can be used as the timeout value to indicate that the function should wait forever and never time out.

The following function is an alternative to blocking the current thread to wait for a dispatch group to finish:

```
void dispatch_group_notify(dispatch_group_t group,
                           dispatch_queue_t queue,
                           dispatch_block_t block);
```

Slightly different from the wait function, this function allows you to specify a block that will be run on a certain queue when the group is finished. Doing so can be useful if the current thread should not be blocked, but you still need to know when all the tasks have finished. In both Mac OS X and iOS, for example, you should never block the main thread, as that's where all UI drawing and event handling are done.

An example of using this GCD feature is to perform a task on an array of objects and then wait for all tasks to finish. The following code does this:

```
dispatch_queue_t queue =
  dispatch_get_global_queue(DISPATCH_QUEUE_PRIORITY_DEFAULT, 0);
dispatch_group_t dispatchGroup = dispatch_group_create();
for (id object in collection) {
    dispatch_group_async(dispatchGroup,
                         queue,
                         ^{ [object performTask]; });
}

dispatch_group_wait(dispatchGroup, DISPATCH_TIME_FOREVER);
// Continue processing after completing tasks
```

If the current thread should not be blocked, you can use the notify function instead of waiting:

```
dispatch_queue_t notifyQueue = dispatch_get_main_queue();
dispatch_group_notify(dispatchGroup,
                    notifyQueue,
                    ^{
                    // Continue processing after completing tasks
                    });
```

The queue on which the notify callback should be queued is entirely dependent on circumstances. Here, I've shown it being the main queue, which would be a fairly common use case. But it could also be any custom serial queue or one of the global concurrent queues.

In this example, the queue dispatched onto was the same one for all tasks. But this doesn't have to be the case. You may want to put some tasks at a higher priority but still group them all into the same dispatch group and be notified when all have finished:

```
dispatch_queue_t lowPriorityQueue =

  dispatch_get_global_queue(DISPATCH_QUEUE_PRIORITY_LOW, 0);
dispatch_queue_t highPriorityQueue =
  dispatch_get_global_queue(DISPATCH_QUEUE_PRIORITY_HIGH, 0);
dispatch_group_t dispatchGroup = dispatch_group_create();

for (id object in lowPriorityObjects) {
    dispatch_group_async(dispatchGroup,
                    lowPriorityQueue,
                    ^{ [object performTask]; });
}

for (id object in highPriorityObjects) {
    dispatch_group_async(dispatchGroup,
                    highPriorityQueue,
                    ^{ [object performTask]; });
}

dispatch_queue_t notifyQueue = dispatch_get_main_queue();
dispatch_group_notify(dispatchGroup,
                    notifyQueue,
                    ^{
                    // Continue processing after completing tasks
                    });
```

Instead of submitting tasks to concurrent queues as in the preceding examples, you may instead use dispatch groups to track multiple tasks submitted to different serial queues. However, a group is not particularly useful if all tasks are queued on the same serial queue. Because the tasks will all execute serially anyway, you could simply queue another block after queuing the tasks, which is the equivalent of a dispatch group's notify callback block:

```
dispatch_queue_t queue =
dispatch_queue_create("com.effectiveobjectivec.queue", NULL);

for (id object in collection) {
    dispatch_async(queue,
                   ^{ [object performTask]; });
}

dispatch_async(queue,
              ^{
                  // Continue processing after completing tasks
              });
```

This code shows that you don't always need to use something like dispatch groups. Sometimes, the desired effect can be achieved by using a single queue and standard asynchronous dispatch.

Why did I mention performing tasks based on system resources? Well, if you look back to the example of dispatching onto a concurrent queue, it should become clear. GCD automatically creates new threads or reuses old ones as it sees fit to service blocks on a queue. In the case of concurrent queues, this can be multiple threads, meaning that multiple blocks are executed concurrently. The number of concurrent threads processing a given concurrent queue depends on factors, mostly based on system resources, that GCD decides. If the CPU has multiple cores, a queue having a lot of work to do will likely be given multiple threads on which to execute. Dispatch groups provide an easy way to perform a given set of tasks concurrently and be told when that group of tasks has finished. Through the nature of GCD's concurrent queues, the tasks will be executed concurrently and based on available system resources. This leaves you to code your business logic and not have to write any kind of complex scheduler to handle concurrent tasks.

The example of looping through a collection and performing a task on each item can also be achieved through the use of another GCD function, as follows:

```
void dispatch_apply(size_t iterations,
                    dispatch_queue_t queue,
                    void(^block)(size_t));
```

This function performs a given number of iterations of a block, each time passing an incrementing value from zero to the number of iterations minus one. It is used like this:

```
dispatch_queue_t queue =
    dispatch_queue_create("com.effectiveobjectivec.queue", NULL);
dispatch_apply(10, queue, ^(size_t i){
    // Perform task
});
```

In effect, this is equivalent to a simple for loop that iterates from 0 to 9, like this:

```
for (int i = 0; i < 10; i++) {
    // Perform task
}
```

The key thing to note with dispatch_apply is that the queue could be a concurrent queue. If so, the blocks will be executed in parallel according to system resources, just like the example of dispatch groups. If the collection in that example were an array, it could be rewritten using dispatch_apply like this:

```
dispatch_queue_t queue =
    dispatch_get_global_queue(DISPATCH_QUEUE_PRIORITY_DEFAULT, 0);

dispatch_apply(array.count, queue, ^(size_t i){
    id object = array[i];
    [object performTask];
});
```

Once again, this example shows that dispatch groups are not always necessary. However, dispatch_apply blocks until all iterations have finished. For this reason, if you try to run blocks on the current queue (or a serial queue above the current queue in the hierarchy), a deadlock will result. If you want the tasks to be executed in the background, you need to use dispatch groups.

Things to Remember

✦ Dispatch groups are used to group a set of tasks. You can optionally be notified when the group finishes executing.

✦ Dispatch groups can be used to execute multiple tasks concurrently through a concurrent dispatch queue. In this case, GCD handles the scheduling of multiple tasks at the same time, based on system resources. Writing this yourself would require a lot of code.

Item 45: Use dispatch_once for Thread-Safe Single-Time Code Execution

The Singleton design pattern—no stranger in the Objective-C world—is usually achieved through a class method called something like sharedInstance, which returns the singleton instance of a class instead of specifically allocating a new instance each time. A common implementation of the shared-instance method for a class called EOCClass is the following:

```
@implementation EOCClass

+ (id)sharedInstance {
    static EOCClass *sharedInstance = nil;
    @synchronized(self) {
        if (!sharedInstance) {
            sharedInstance = [[self alloc] init];
        }
    }
    return sharedInstance;
}

@end
```

I have found that the Singleton pattern generates hot debate, especially in Objective-C. Thread safety is the primary candidate for debate. The preceding code creates the singleton instance enclosed in a synchronization block to make it thread safe. For better or worse, the pattern is commonly used, and such code is commonplace.

However, GCD introduced a feature that makes singleton instances much easier to implement. The function is as follows:

```
void dispatch_once(dispatch_once_t *token,
                   dispatch_block_t block);
```

This function takes a special dispatch_once_t type, which I will call the "token," and a block. The function ensures that for a given token, the block is executed once and only once. The block is always executed the first time and, most important, is entirely thread safe. Note that the token passed in needs to be exactly the same one for each block that should be executed once. This usually means declaring the token variable in static or global scope.

Rewriting the singleton shared-instance method with this function looks like this:

```
+ (id)sharedInstance {
    static EOCClass *sharedInstance = nil;
    static dispatch_once_t onceToken;
    dispatch_once(&onceToken, ^{
        sharedInstance = [[self alloc] init];
    });
    return sharedInstance;
}
```

Using dispatch_once simplifies the code and ensures thread safety entirely, so you don't even have to think about locking or synchronization. All that is handled in the depths of GCD. The token has been declared static because it needs to be exactly the same token each time. Defining the variable in static scope means that the compiler ensures that instead of creating a new variable each time the sharedInstance method is run, only a single variable is reused each time.

Furthermore, dispatch_once is more efficient. Instead of using a heavyweight synchronization mechanism, which acquires a lock every time the code is run, it uses atomic access to the dispatch token to indicate whether the code has been run yet. A simple benchmark on my 64-bit, Mac OS X 10.8.2 machine, accessing the sharedInstance method using the @synchronized approach versus the dispatch_once approach, showed an almost doubled speedup using dispatch_once.

Things to Remember

✦ Thread-safe single-code execution is a common task. GCD provides an easy-to-use tool for this with the dispatch_once function.

✦ The token should be declared in static or global scope such that it is the same token being passed in for each block that should be executed once.

Item 46: Avoid dispatch_get_current_queue

When using GCD and especially when dispatching onto various queues, it is common to need to determine which queue is currently being executed. For example, UI work in both Mac OS X and iOS needs to be performed on the main thread, which equates to the main queue in GCD. Sometimes, it seems necessary to determine whether the current code is being executed on the main queue. Reading through the documentation, you would come across the following function:

```
dispatch_queue_t dispatch_get_current_queue()
```

This is documented to return the current queue that is being executed. That is exactly what the function does, but it should be treated with caution. In fact, it is now officially deprecated in iOS as of version 6.0. But it is not deprecated in Mac OS X as of version 10.8. Nevertheless, it should still be avoided on Mac OS X.

A typical antipattern that has become a common use of this method is to check the current queue against a specific queue to try to work around a deadlock that can occur if dispatching synchronously. Consider the following accessor methods, which use a queue to synchronize access to an instance variable (see Item 41):

```
- (NSString*)someString {
    __block NSString *localSomeString;
    dispatch_sync(_syncQueue, ^{
        localSomeString = _someString;
    });
    return localSomeString;
}

- (void)setSomeString:(NSString*)someString {
    dispatch_async(_syncQueue, ^{
        _someString = someString;
    });
}
```

A problem you may encounter with this pattern is a deadlock in the getter, if the getter is called from the same queue as the queue used for synchronization (_syncQueue in the example), because dispatch_sync won't return until the block has executed in full. But if the target queue for the block is the current queue, the block will never get a chance to run, because dispatch_sync will continue to block, waiting for the queue to become available to run the target block. This is an example of a method that is not reentrant.

Having read the documentation for dispatch_get_current_queue, you may think that it would be safe to make the method reentrant by checking whether the current queue is the synchronization queue and, if so, simply execute the block directly rather than dispatching, as follows:

```
- (NSString*)someString {
    __block NSString *localSomeString;
    dispatch_block_t accessorBlock = ^{
        localSomeString = _someString;
    };
```

```
    if (dispatch_get_current_queue() == _syncQueue) {
        accessorBlock();
    } else {
        dispatch_sync(_syncQueue, accessorBlock);
    }

    return localSomeString;
}
```

This would probably work for you under simple circumstances. However, it is dangerous and can still deadlock. To see why, consider the following scenario with two serial dispatch queues:

```
dispatch_queue_t queueA =
    dispatch_queue_create("com.effectiveobjectivec.queueA", NULL);
dispatch_queue_t queueB =
    dispatch_queue_create("com.effectiveobjectivec.queueB", NULL);

dispatch_sync(queueA, ^{
    dispatch_sync(queueB, ^{
        dispatch_sync(queueA, ^{
            // Deadlock
        });
    });
});
```

This will always deadlock at the inner dispatch onto _queueA because it will wait for the outer dispatch_sync to finish, which itself won't finish until the inner dispatch_sync finishes: hence deadlock. Now consider putting in the same check using dispatch_get_current_queue:

```
dispatch_sync(queueA, ^{
    dispatch_sync(queueB, ^{
        dispatch_block_t block = ^{ /* … */ };
        if (dispatch_get_current_queue() == queueA) {
            block();
        } else {
            dispatch_sync(queueA, block);
        }
    });
});
```

However, this too will deadlock, since dispatch_get_current_queue returns the current queue, which in the preceding example will be _queueB. So the synchronous dispatch onto _queueA will still be done, resulting in deadlock, just as before.

In this scenario, the correct solution is that the accessor does not need to be made reentrant. Rather, you should ensure that the queue used for synchronization never tries to access the property; never call someString. The queue should be used only for synchronization of the property. Dispatch queues are fairly lightweight, so it's fine to create multiple queues to ensure that the synchronization queue is used solely for synchronization of that one property.

The preceding example may seem slightly contrived, but another thing to be aware of with queues can make this problem occur when you didn't think it would. Queues are arranged into a hierarchy, meaning that blocks enqueued on one queue are executed within their parent queue. The final queue in a hierarchy is always one of the global concurrent queues. To illustrate a simple hierarchy, see Figure 6.4.

Blocks enqueued on either queue B or queue C are subsequently scheduled to run on serial A. So blocks queued on queues A, B, and C will be executed exclusively with respect to one another. However, blocks enqueued on queue D will run concurrently with those enqueued on queue A (and therefore B and C) because the target queue of A and D is a concurrent one. Concurrent queues execute blocks in parallel on multiple threads, if necessary, depending on system resources, such as the number of cores the CPU has.

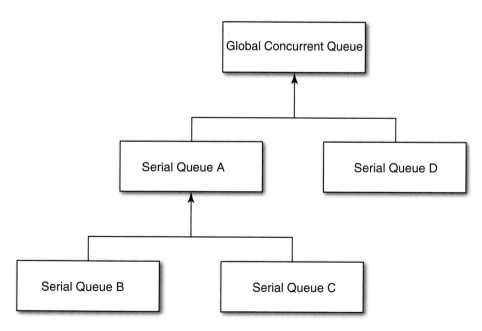

Figure 6.4 Dispatch queue hierarchy

Because of queue hierarchies, the equality check of the current queue with the queue about to be dispatched synchronously may not always work. A block enqueued on queue C, for instance, will return queue C for the current queue, so it may think it can safely dispatch synchronously onto queue A. In fact, this would result in a deadlock as before.

This problem may occur if an API allows you to specify what queue to schedule callback blocks on, but a serial synchronization queue is used internally, with its target set to the callback queue. Code in the consumer of such an API would be incorrect to assume that the current queue, as returned by dispatch_get_current_queue in callback blocks, will always equal the queue it gave. In fact, the internal synchronization queue would be returned instead.

To solve this problem, the best approach is to use the queue-specific data functions of GCD, which allow you to associate arbitrary data with a queue as a key-value pair. Most important, if no data is associated for a certain key when retrieving data, the system walks up the hierarchy until it either finds data or the root is reached. It may not be obvious how this can be used, so consider this example:

```
dispatch_queue_t queueA =
    dispatch_queue_create("com.effectiveobjectivec.queueA", NULL);
dispatch_queue_t queueB =
    dispatch_queue_create("com.effectiveobjectivec.queueB", NULL);
dispatch_set_target_queue(queueB, queueA);

static int kQueueSpecific;
CFStringRef queueSpecificValue = CFSTR("queueA");
dispatch_queue_set_specific(queueA,
                            &kQueueSpecific,
                            (void*)queueSpecificValue,
                            (dispatch_function_t)CFRelease);

dispatch_sync(queueB, ^{
    dispatch_block_t block = ^{ NSLog(@"No deadlock!"); };

    CFStringRef retrievedValue =
                    dispatch_get_specific(&kQueueSpecific);
    if (retrievedValue) {
        block();
    } else {
        dispatch_sync(queueA, block);
    }
});
```

In this example, two queues are created. The target queue of queue B is set to queue A, whose target queue stays as the default priority global concurrent queue. Then a queue-specific value is set on queue A, using the following function:

```
void dispatch_queue_set_specific(dispatch_queue_t queue,
                                 const void *key,
                                 void *context,
                                 dispatch_function_t destructor);
```

This takes the target queue to set the data on, followed by the key and the value. Both the key and the value are opaque void pointers. For the keys, the important thing to remember is that they are compared by the pointer value, not by the contents. So queue-specific data behaves differently from NSDictionary objects, which compare object equality of keys. Queue-specific data behaves more like associated references (see Item 10). Values (called context in the function prototype) are also opaque void pointers. So they can be absolutely anything you want. However, you have to perform any memory management you want on the object. This makes it very difficult to use Objective-C objects as the value under ARC. In the example, a CoreFoundation string is used as the value because ARC does not take care of memory management of any CoreFoundation object. Such objects therefore make for good queue-specific data because they can be toll-free bridged to their Objective-C Foundation classes as required.

The final argument to the function is the destructor function, which is run whenever the object held for a given key is removed either because the queue is deallocated or a new value is set for that key. The dispatch_function_t type is defined like so:

```
typedef void (*dispatch_function_t)(void*)
```

The destructor must therefore be a function that takes a single pointer as its only argument and returns void. In the example, CFRelease is given, which is an example of such a function, although it could also have been a user-defined function that in turn called CFRelease to clean up the value and perform any other necessary cleanup.

Queue-specific data therefore provides a simple-to-use mechanism to get around one of the common pitfalls of dispatch_get_current_queue. Other common uses of dispatch_get_current_queue might include debugging. In these circumstances, it is safe to use the deprecated method so long as that code is not compiled into release builds. If a specific requirement for accessing the current queue is not covered by other functions, it is best to file a feature request with Apple.

Things to Remember

- ✦ The `dispatch_get_current_queue` function does not in general perform how you would expect. It has been deprecated and should now be used only for debugging.

- ✦ Dispatch queues are organized into a hierarchy; therefore, the current queue cannot be described simply by a single queue object.

- ✦ Queue-specific data can be used to solve the usual reason for using `dispatch_get_current_queue`, which is to avoid deadlocks owing to nonreentrant code.

The System Frameworks

Although it is possible to use Objective-C without using any of the system frameworks, doing so is extremely uncommon. Even the standard root class, NSObject, is part of the Foundation framework rather than part of the language itself. If you didn't want to use Foundation, you would have to write your own root class, as well as your own collections, event loops, and other useful classes. Furthermore, you cannot use Objective-C for developing Mac OS X and iOS applications without using the system frameworks. They are powerful but have come through years of development to where they are today. Therefore, you may find some parts that feel old and are awkward to work with, but you may also find hidden gems.

Item 47: Familiarize Yourself with the System Frameworks

When writing an application in Objective-C, you will almost certainly use the system frameworks, which provide many of the common classes, such as collections, that you need to be able to write applications. If you don't understand what the system frameworks provide, you may end up writing something that has already been written. When they upgrade their operating systems, users of your application obtain the latest versions of the system frameworks. So if you use classes from these frameworks, you benefit from any improvements made to them, without having to update your application.

A framework is a set of code packaged as a dynamic library along with header files describing its interface. Sometimes, a third-party framework built for iOS uses a static library, since iOS applications are not allowed to ship dynamic libraries with them. These are not true frameworks but are often referred to as such. However, all system frameworks use dynamic libraries on iOS still.

If you're developing a graphical application for Mac OS X or iOS, you will come across the framework called Cocoa, which is also referred to as Cocoa Touch for iOS. Cocoa is not a framework in itself but rather a collection of other frameworks commonly used when creating applications.

The main framework you will come across is called Foundation, where classes such as NSObject, NSArray, and NSDictionary are found. The class prefix used throughout the Foundation framework is NS, which was first formulated when Objective-C was being used for work on the NeXTSTEP operating system. The Foundation framework truly is the foundation of all Objective-C applications; without it, most of this book would be irrelevant.

Foundation provides not only core features that you would expect, such as collections, but also complex features, such as string processing. For example, NSLinguisticTagger provides the ability to parse a string and find all the nouns, verbs, pronouns, and so on. In short, Foundation goes far beyond the basics.

Alongside Foundation is another framework: CoreFoundation. Although not technically Objective-C, CoreFoundation is another important framework to be familiar with when writing Objective-C applications and is a C API that mirrors much of the functionality of the Foundation framework. The CoreFoundation and Foundation frameworks are closely linked in more than name. A feature known as toll-free bridging allows seamless casting from the C data structures of CoreFoundation to the Objective-C objects of Foundation, and vice versa. For example, a string from Foundation is an NSString, which can be cast to its equivalent in CoreFoundation: CFString. Toll-free bridging works through some rather intricate code that makes CoreFoundation objects appear to the runtime as though they are Objective-C objects. Unfortunately, toll-free bridging is very complex, so replicating it yourself in your own code is tricky. This feature should be used, but copied only if you really know what you're doing.

Along with Foundation and CoreFoundation are many other system libraries. They include but are not limited to the following:

+ **CFNetwork** This provides C-level networking facilities for talking to networks through an easy-to-use abstraction over BSD sockets. Foundation wraps parts of this framework to provide an Objective-C interface for networking, such as NSURLConnection for downloading data from a URL.

+ **CoreAudio** This provides a C-level API for interfacing with audio hardware on a device. This is one of the harder frameworks to work with, owing to the complex nature of audio processing. Fortunately, Objective-C abstractions can be used make audio processing easier.

+ **AVFoundation** This provides Objective-C objects for dealing with audio and video playback and recording, such as UI view classes for presenting video.

+ **CoreData** This provides Objective-C interfaces for persisting objects to a database. CoreData handles data fetching and saving and can be used cross-platform between Mac OS X and iOS.

+ **CoreText** This provides a C interface for high-performance text typesetting and rendering.

Other frameworks are available, but looking at the few listed here highlights an important feature of programming in Objective-C: Often, you will need to drop down to use C-level APIs. APIs written in C benefit from the speed improvement of bypassing the Objective-C runtime. Of course, more care needs to be taken with memory management in those APIs, since ARC (see Item 30) is available only to Objective-C objects. Being familiar with the basics of C is important if you need to use one of these frameworks.

You will likely be writing Mac OS X or iOS applications that make use of the UI frameworks. The core UI frameworks, called AppKit and UIKit, respectively, both provide Objective-C classes built on top of Foundation and CoreFoundation. They provide UI elements and the glue to put everything together to create an application. Underneath these main UI frameworks are the CoreAnimation and CoreGraphics frameworks.

CoreAnimation is written in Objective-C and provides the tools that the UI frameworks use to render graphics and perform animations. You may never need to drop down to this level, but it is good to know that it is there. CoreAnimation is not a framework on its own but rather is part of the QuartzCore framework. However, CoreAnimation should still be considered as a first-class citizen.

CoreGraphics is written in C and provides data structures and functions that are essential for 2D rendering. For example, this is where the CGPoint, CGSize, and CGRect data structures are defined, and all are used by the UIKit class UIView to indicate where views should be positioned relative to one another.

Many other frameworks are built on top of the UI frameworks, such as MapKit, which provides mapping functionality to iOS, or the Social framework, which provides social networking facilities to both Mac

OS X and iOS. You will usually work with these frameworks and the core UI framework for the platform on which you are working.

Overall, many frameworks come as standard with Mac OS X and iOS installations. So, if you need to write a new utility class, for example, consider searching for it first in the system frameworks. Often, it will have already been written for you.

Things to Remember

+ Many system frameworks are available to you. The most important ones, Foundation and CoreFoundation, provide the core functionality on which much of an application is built.

+ Frameworks exist for many common tasks, such as audio and video processing, networking, and data managing.

+ Remember that frameworks written in pure C rather than Objective-C are just as important to you, so to be a good Objective-C developer, you should understand the core concepts of C.

Item 48: Prefer Block Enumeration to for Loops

Enumerating a collection is a very common task in programming, and modern Objective-C has many ways to do so, ranging from standard C loops to NSEnumerator in Objective-C 1.0 and fast enumeration in Objective-C 2.0. The addition of blocks (see Item 37) to the language brought a few new methods that developers sometimes overlooked. These methods allow you to enumerate a collection by passing a block that should be run for each item in the collection and are usually much easier to use, as I will explain.

The collections presented in this item—NSArray, NSDictionary, and NSSet—are the ones most commonly used. Additionally, custom collections can all be made to support any of the enumeration techniques outlined, although explaining how is beyond the scope of this item.

For Loops

The first method for enumerating a collection is the good, old-fashioned for loop, which harks back to Objective-C's roots in the C language. This method is very basic and therefore quite limiting. The usual idea is to do something like this:

```
NSArray *anArray = /* … */;
for (int i = 0; i < anArray.count; i++) {
    id object = anArray[i];
```

```
    // Do something with 'object'
}
```

This is acceptable but becomes more complicated for a dictionary or a set:

```
// Dictionary
NSDictionary *aDictionary = /* … */;
NSArray *keys = [aDictionary allKeys];
for (int i = 0; i < keys.count; i++) {
    id key = keys[i];
    id value = aDictionary[key];
    // Do something with 'key' and 'value'
}

// Set
NSSet *aSet = /* … */;
NSArray *objects = [aSet allObjects];
for (int i = 0; i < objects.count; i++) {
    id object = objects[i];
    // Do something with 'object'
}
```

By definition, dictionaries and sets are unordered, so there's no way to directly access the value at a certain integer index. Therefore, you need to ask for all the keys for the dictionary or all the objects for a set; in both cases, the ordered array returned can then be enumerated instead to access the values. Creating this extra array is extra work and causes an extra object to be created that retains the objects in the collection. Of course, those objects will be released when the array is released, but it's more unnecessary method calls. All the other enumeration techniques mitigate needing to create an extra intermediate array.

Enumerating backward can be achieved with a for loop by starting at the count of objects minus one, decrementing the counter on each iteration, and stopping when the counter equals zero. This is much easier.

Objective-C 1.0 Enumeration Using NSEnumerator

The NSEnumerator object is an abstract base class that defines only two methods for concrete subclasses to implement:

```
- (NSArray*)allObjects
- (id)nextObject
```

The key method is nextObject, which returns the next object in the enumeration. Each time the method is invoked, internal data structures are updated such that the next invocation returns the next object. After all the objects in the enumeration have been returned, nil is returned, signaling the end of enumeration.

All the built-in collection classes within the Foundation framework implement enumeration in this way. For example, enumerating an array is done like this:

```
NSArray *anArray = /* … */;
NSEnumerator *enumerator = [anArray objectEnumerator];
id object;
while ((object = [enumerator nextObject]) != nil) {
    // Do something with 'object'
}
```

This is similar to a standard for loop but is more work. The only real benefit is that enumerating any collection is made with similar syntax. For example, consider the equivalent for a dictionary and a set:

```
// Dictionary
NSDictionary *aDictionary = /* … */;
NSEnumerator *enumerator = [aDictionary keyEnumerator];
id key;
while ((key = [enumerator nextObject]) != nil) {
    id value = aDictionary[key];
    // Do something with 'key' and 'value'
}

// Set
NSSet *aSet = /* … */;
NSEnumerator *enumerator = [aSet objectEnumerator];
id object;
while ((object = [enumerator nextObject]) != nil) {
    // Do something with 'object'
}
```

The dictionary enumeration is slightly different because a dictionary has keys and values, so the value has to be pulled out of the dictionary given the key. The additional benefit to NSEnumerator is that different types of enumerators are often available. For example, with an array, there is a reverse enumerator; if that is used instead, the collection is iterated in reverse. For example:

```
NSArray *anArray = /* … */;
NSEnumerator *enumerator = [anArray reverseObjectEnumerator];
```

```
id object;
while ((object = [enumerator nextObject]) != nil) {
    // Do something with 'object'
}
```

This is much easier to read than the equivalent syntax of reverse enumerating using a for loop.

Fast Enumeration

Fast enumeration was introduced with Objective-C 2.0. Fast enumeration is similar to enumeration using NSEnumerator, except that the syntax is much more condensed, adding a keyword, in, to the for-loop syntax. This keyword greatly condenses the syntax for enumerating a collection, such as an array:

```
NSArray *anArray = /* … */;
for (id object in anArray) {
    // Do something with 'object'
}
```

This is much simpler! It works by using a protocol called NSFastEnumeration, to which an object can conform in order to indicate that it supports fast enumeration. The protocol defines a single method:

```
- (NSUInteger)countByEnumeratingWithState:
                        (NSFastEnumerationState*)state
                      objects:(id*)stackbuffer
                        count:(NSUInteger)length
```

Explaining how this works in full is beyond the scope of this item. However, decent tutorials on the Internet explain this topic well. The important thing to note is that this method allows the class to return multiple objects at the same time, which means that the enumeration loop can be more efficient.

Enumerating dictionaries and sets is just as simple:

```
// Dictionary
NSDictionary *aDictionary = /* … */;
for (id key in aDictionary) {
    id value = aDictionary[key];
    // Do something with 'key' and 'value'
}

// Set
NSSet *aSet = /* … */;
```

```
for (id object in aSet) {
    // Do something with 'object'
}
```

Reverse enumeration can be achieved by noting that NSEnumerator objects also implement NSFastEnumeration. So to reverse iterate through an array, you can do the following:

```
NSArray *anArray = /* … */;
for (id object in [anArray reverseObjectEnumerator]) {
    // Do something with 'object'
}
```

This method of enumeration is the best so far in terms of syntax and efficiency, but enumerating a dictionary still requires an additional step if you want both the key and the value. Also, the index of enumeration is not easily accessible, unlike a traditional for loop. The index is often useful to have during an iteration, as many algorithms will make use of it.

Block-Based Enumeration

Block-based methods are the final type of enumeration available in modern Objective-C. The most basic method for enumerating an array is as follows, defined on NSArray:

```
- (void)enumerateObjectsUsingBlock:
            (void(^)(id object, NSUInteger idx, BOOL *stop))block
```

The other methods in this family can take options to control the enumeration and are discussed later.

For the array and the set, the block that is performed for each iteration takes the object at that iteration, the index into the iteration, and a pointer to a Boolean. The first two parameters are self-explanatory. The third provides a mechanism for halting the enumeration.

For example, you can enumerate an array with this method as follows:

```
NSArray *anArray = /* … */;
[anArray enumerateObjectsUsingBlock:
    ^(id object, NSUInteger idx, BOOL *stop){
        // Do something with 'object'
        if (shouldStop) {
            *stop = YES;
        }
    }];
```

This syntax is slightly more verbose than fast enumeration but is clean, and you get both the index of iteration and the object. This method also provides a clean way to stop the enumeration, if you wish, through the stop variable, although a break can achieve the same thing in the other methods of enumeration and is just as clean.

It's not just arrays that can be enumerated in this way. The same block-enumeration method exists in NSSet and a slightly different one in NSDictionary:

```
- (void)enumerateKeysAndObjectsUsingBlock:
                    (void(^)(id key, id object, BOOL *stop))block
```

Therefore, enumerating dictionaries and sets is just as simple:

```
// Dictionary
NSDictionary *aDictionary = /* … */;
[aDictionary enumerateKeysAndObjectsUsingBlock:
    ^(id key, id object, BOOL *stop){
        // Do something with 'key' and 'object'
        if (shouldStop) {
            *stop = YES;
        }
    }];

// Set
NSSet *aSet = /* … */;
[aSet enumerateObjectsUsingBlock:
    ^(id object, BOOL *stop){
        // Do something with 'object'
        if (shouldStop) {
            *stop = YES;
        }
    }];
```

The big win here is that you get a lot more information directly in the block. In the case of arrays, you get the index of enumeration. The same goes for ordered sets (NSOrderedSet). In the case of a dictionary, you get both the key and the value without any additional work, thereby saving the extra cycles required to obtain the value for a given key. Instead, the dictionary can give both at the same time, which is highly likely to be far more efficient, since keys and values will be stored together in a dictionary's internal data structures.

Another benefit is that you can change the method signature of the block to limit the need for casting; in effect, you push the cast into the block-method signature. Consider the code for enumerating a dictionary with fast enumeration. If the objects in the dictionary are known to you as strings, you may do this:

```
for (NSString *key in aDictionary) {
    NSString *object = (NSString*)aDictionary[key];
    // Do something with 'key' and 'object'
}
```

With the block-based method, you can do the cast in the block-method signature like so:

```
NSDictionary *aDictionary = /* … */;
[aDictionary enumerateKeysAndObjectsUsingBlock:
    ^(NSString *key, NSString *obj, BOOL *stop){
        // Do something with 'key' and 'obj'
    }];
```

This works because the id type is rather special and can be overridden like this. If the original block signature had defined key and object as NSObject*, you wouldn't be able to do this trick. This technique is more useful than it seems at first glance. Giving the exact type of an object allows the compiler to help you by throwing an error if a method you call on the object doesn't exist. If you can guarantee what type of objects are in a certain collection, indicating the type in this way should always be done.

The ability to reverse enumerate is not lost. Arrays, dictionaries, and sets all implement a variant of the preceding method, allowing you to pass an options mask:

```
- (void)enumerateObjectsWithOptions:
            (NSEnumerationOptions)options
                usingBlock:
            (void(^)(id obj, NSUInteger idx, BOOL *stop))block
- (void)enumerateKeysAndObjectsWithOptions:
            (NSEnumerationOptions)options
                usingBlock:
            (void(^)(id key, id obj, BOOL *stop))block
```

The NSEnumerationOptions type is an enum whose values you can bitwise OR together to indicate how the enumeration should behave. For example, you can request that iteration be concurrent, meaning that the blocks for each iteration will be executed in parallel if that is possible with current system resources. This is achieved through the NSEnumerationConcurrent option. Underneath, this option uses GCD to handle concurrent execution, most likely making use of dispatch groups (see Item 44). However, the implementation is not relevant here. Asking for reverse iteration is achieved through the NSEnumerationReverse option. Note that this is available only for situations in which it makes sense, such as arrays or ordered sets.

Overall, block enumeration has all the benefits of the other methods combined, and more. It is slightly more verbose than fast enumeration. But the benefits of having the index of enumeration, both the key and the value in dictionary enumeration, and the option to perform iterations concurrently are worth the extra source code.

Things to Remember

✦ Enumerating collections can be achieved in four ways. The for loop is the most basic, followed by enumeration using NSEnumerator and fast enumeration. The most modern and advanced way is using the block-enumeration methods.

✦ Block enumeration allows you to perform the enumeration concurrently, without any additional code, by making use of GCD. This cannot as easily be achieved with the other enumeration techniques.

✦ Alter the block signature to indicate the precise types of objects if you know them.

Item 49: Use Toll-Free Bridging for Collections with Custom Memory-Management Semantics

The collection classes that come with the Objective-C system libraries are fairly extensive: arrays, dictionaries, and sets. The Foundation framework defines Objective-C classes for these and other types of collections. Similarly, the CoreFoundation framework defines C APIs for manipulating data structures that represent these and other types of collections. For example, NSArray is Foundation's Objective-C class for an array, and CFArray is CoreFoundation's equivalent. These two ways of creating an array may seem distinct, but a powerful feature called toll-free bridging allows you to cast between the two classes seamlessly.

Toll-free bridging allows you to cast between Objective-C classes defined in Foundation and C data structures defined in CoreFoundation and vice versa, of course. I refer to the C-level APIs as data structures rather than classes or objects because they are not the same as classes or objects from Objective-C. For example, CFArray is referenced by a CFArrayRef, which is a pointer to a struct __CFArray. This struct is manipulated by using such functions as CFArrayGetCount to obtain the size of the array. This is distinct from its Objective-C counterpart, where you create an NSArray object and call methods, such as count, on that object to obtain the size of the array.

A simple toll-free bridging example is as follows:

```
NSArray *anNSArray = @[@1, @2, @3, @4, @5];
CFArrayRef aCFArray = (__bridge CFArrayRef)anNSArray;
NSLog(@"Size of array = %li", CFArrayGetCount(aCFArray));
// Output: Size of array = 5
```

The __bridge within the cast tells ARC (see Item 30) what to do with
the Objective-C object that forms part of the cast. A __bridge on its
own means that ARC still has ownership of the Objective-C object. A
__bridge_retained, conversely, means that ARC will hand over owner-
ship of the object. If this were used in the preceding example, we would
be responsible for adding in a CFRelease(aCFArray) after the array had
finished with it. Similarly, the opposite is done with __bridge_transfer.
For example if a CFArrayRef is being cast to an NSArray* and you want
ARC to take ownership of the object, you use this type of cast. These
three types of casting are known as bridged casts.

But, you may be wondering, why you would ever want to use this
feature in a purely Objective-C application? Well, Foundation's
Objective-C classes can do some things that CoreFoundation's C data
structures cannot, and vice versa. One major problem that crops up
with Foundation's dictionary, for example, is that keys are copied and
values are retained. These semantics cannot be altered unless you
use the power of toll-free bridging.

The CoreFoundation dictionary type is called CFDictionary. The
mutable counterpart is called CFMutableDictionary. When creating a
CFMutableDictionary, you can specify custom memory-management
semantics to apply to both keys and values by using the following
method:

```
CFMutableDictionaryRef CFDictionaryCreateMutable(
    CFAllocatorRef allocator,
    CFIndex capacity,
    const CFDictionaryKeyCallBacks *keyCallBacks,
    const CFDictionaryValueCallBacks *valueCallBacks
)
```

The first parameter defines the allocator to use. This part of Core-
Foundation is slightly alien if you have spent most of your time in
Objective-C land. An allocator is responsible for allocating and deallocating the memory required to hold the data structures for CoreFoundation objects. Usually, you would pass NULL here to use the default
allocator.

The second parameter simply defines how big to make the dictionary
initially. This doesn't put a cap on the maximum size but rather is a
hint to the allocator about how much memory to allocate to start. If

you know that you're going to create a dictionary with ten objects, you would pass 10.

The final parameters are the interesting ones. They define the callbacks that will be run when various things happen to the keys and values stored in the dictionary. These parameters are both pointers to structures, which look like this:

```
struct CFDictionaryKeyCallBacks {
    CFIndex version;
    CFDictionaryRetainCallBack retain;
    CFDictionaryReleaseCallBack release;
    CFDictionaryCopyDescriptionCallBack copyDescription;
    CFDictionaryEqualCallBack equal;
    CFDictionaryHashCallBack hash;
};

struct CFDictionaryValueCallBacks {
    CFIndex version;
    CFDictionaryRetainCallBack retain;
    CFDictionaryReleaseCallBack release;
    CFDictionaryCopyDescriptionCallBack copyDescription;
    CFDictionaryEqualCallBack equal;
};
```

The version parameter should be set to 0 at present. This has always been the case, but the value is there in case Apple decides to change the structure. This parameter can be used to check compatibility between newer and older versions. The rest of the structures are all function pointers, defining which functions should be run when each of the tasks needs to be done. For example, the retain function is called on each key and value added to the dictionary. The type of this parameter is as follows:

```
typedef const void* (*CFDictionaryRetainCallBack) (
    CFAllocatorRef allocator,
    const void *value
);
```

So it is a pointer to a function that takes a CFAllocatorRef and a const void*. The value passed in to the function is the key or the value that wants to be added to the dictionary. A void* is returned, which is the value that ends up being put into the dictionary. You could write your own callback as follows:

```
const void* CustomCallback(CFAllocatorRef allocator,
                           const void *value)
```

```
{
    return value;
}
```

This simply returns the value unaltered. So in this case, if a dictionary were created with this function for the retain callback, keys and values would not be retained. By coupling this with toll-free bridging, you can create an NSDictionary object that behaves differently from one created simply in Objective-C.

A full example of how this can be effective is as follows:

```
#import <Foundation/Foundation.h>
#import <CoreFoundation/CoreFoundation.h>

const void* EOCRetainCallback(CFAllocatorRef allocator,
                              const void *value)
{
    return CFRetain(value);
}

void EOCReleaseCallback(CFAllocatorRef allocator,
                        const void *value)
{
    CFRelease(value);
}

CFDictionaryKeyCallBacks keyCallbacks = {
    0,
    EOCRetainCallback,
    EOCReleaseCallback,
    NULL,
    CFEqual,
    CFHash
};

CFDictionaryValueCallBacks valueCallbacks = {
    0,
    EOCRetainCallback,
    EOCReleaseCallback,
    NULL,
    CFEqual
};

CFMutableDictionaryRef aCFDictionary =
    CFDictionaryCreateMutable(NULL,
```

```
                                      0,
                                      &keyCallbacks,
                                      &valueCallbacks);

NSMutableDictionary *anNSDictionary =
    (__bridge_transfer NSMutableDictionary*)aCFDictionary;
```

In the callbacks, NULL is specified for the copyDescription callback because the default is fine. The equal and hash callbacks are set to CFEqual and CFHash, respectively, because they use the same method as the default NSMutableDictionary implementation. CFEqual will end up calling NSObject's isEqual: method, and CFHash will end up calling NSObject's hash method. This is yet more power of toll-free bridging.

The retain and release callbacks of both the keys and the values are set to the EOCRetainCallback and EOCReleaseCallback functions, respectively. But what use is that? Recall that NSMutableDictionary copies its keys and retains its values by default. What if the objects you want to use as keys cannot be copied? In that case, you cannot use them in a normal NSMutableDictionary, because doing so will result in a runtime error like this:

```
*** Terminating app due to uncaught exception
'NSInvalidArgumentException', reason: '-[EOCClass
copyWithZone:]: unrecognized selector sent to instance
0x7fd069c080b0'
```

That error means that the class does not support the NSCopying protocol, because copyWithZone: is not implemented. By dropping down to the CoreFoundation level and creating the dictionary there, you can alter the memory-management semantics and create a dictionary that retains rather than copies the keys.

A similar approach could be used to create an array or a set that doesn't retain the objects it holds. This might be useful if, by having an array that retains certain objects, you introduce a retain cycle. Note, however, that this scenario could possibly be solved better in another way. Creating an array that doesn't retain its objects is fraught with danger. If one of the objects happens to be deallocated but is still in the array, the application will likely crash if that object is accessed.

Things to Remember

✦ Toll-free bridging allows you to cast between Foundation's Objective-C objects and CoreFoundation's C data structures.

✦ Dropping down to CoreFoundation to create a collection allows you to specify various callbacks that are used when the collection handles its contents. Casting this through toll-free bridging allows you to end up with an Objective-C collection that has custom memory-management semantics.

Item 50: Use `NSCache` Instead of `NSDictionary` for Caches

A common problem encountered when developing a Mac OS X or an iOS application that downloads images from the Internet is deciding what to do about caching them. A good first approach is to use a dictionary to store in memory images that have been downloaded, such that they don't need to be downloaded again if they are requested later. A naïve developer will simply use an `NSDictionary` (or rather a mutable one) because that's a commonly used class. However, an even better class, called `NSCache`, is also part of the Foundation framework and has been designed exactly for this task.

The benefit of `NSCache` over an `NSDictionary` is that as system memory becomes full, the cache is automatically pruned. When using a dictionary, you often end up having to write pruning code yourself by hooking into system notifications for low memory. However, `NSCache` offers this automatically; because it is part of the Foundation framework, it will be able to hook in deeper to the system than you could yourself. An `NSCache` will also prune the least recently used objects first. Writing the code to support this yourself with a dictionary would be quite complex.

Also, an `NSCache` does not copy keys but rather retains them. This is something that can be controlled on `NSDictionary` but requires more complex code (see Item 49). A cache usually would rather not copy the keys because often, the key will be an object that does not support copying. Since `NSCache` doesn't copy by default, it makes it an easier class to work with in these situations. Also, `NSCache` is thread safe. This is certainly not true of an `NSDictionary`, which means that you can poke away at an `NSCache` from multiple threads at the same time without having to introduce any locks of your own. This is usually useful for a cache because you may want to read from it in one thread, and, if a certain key doesn't exist, you may download the data for that key. The callbacks for downloading may be in a background thread, so you end up adding to the cache in this other thread.

You can control when a cache will prune its contents. Two user-controllable metrics alongside the system resources are a limit on both the number of objects in the cache and the overall "cost" of the objects. Each object can optionally be given a cost when added to the cache. When the total number of objects exceeds the count limit or the total cost exceeds the cost limit, the cache may evict objects, just as it does when the available system memory becomes tight. However, it is important to note that it *may* evict rather than it *will* evict. The order in which objects are evicted is implementation specific. In particular, this means that manipulating the cost metric in order to force eviction in a certain order is a bad idea.

The cost metric should be used only when adding an object to the cache if calculating the cost is very cheap. If calculating it is expensive, you may find that using the cache becomes suboptimal, since you are having to calculate this additional factor each time an object is cached. After all, caches are meant to help with making an application more responsive. For example, having to go to the disk to find the size of a file or to a database to determine the cost would be bad ideas. However, an example of a good cost to use is if NSData objects are added to the cache; in that case, you can use the size of that data as the cost. This is already known to the NSData object, and so calculating it is as simple as reading a property.

The following is an example of using a cache:

```
#import <Foundation/Foundation.h>

// Network fetcher class
typedef void(^EOCNetworkFetcherCompletionHandler)(NSData *data);
@interface EOCNetworkFetcher : NSObject
- (id)initWithURL:(NSURL*)url;
- (void)startWithCompletionHandler:
                (EOCNetworkFetcherCompletionHandler)handler;
@end

// Class that uses the network fetcher and caches results
@interface EOCClass : NSObject
@end

@implementation EOCClass {
    NSCache *_cache;
}

- (id)init {
    if ((self = [super init])) {
        _cache = [NSCache new];
```

```objc
        // Cache a maximum of 100 URLs
        _cache.countLimit = 100;

        /**
         * The size in bytes of data is used as the cost,
         * so this sets a cost limit of 5MB.
         */
        _cache.totalCostLimit = 5 * 1024 * 1024;
    }
    return self;
}

- (void)downloadDataForURL:(NSURL*)url {
    NSData *cachedData = [_cache objectForKey:url];
    if (cachedData) {
        // Cache hit
        [self useData:cachedData];
    } else {
        // Cache miss
        EOCNetworkFetcher *fetcher =
            [[EOCNetworkFetcher alloc] initWithURL:url];
        [fetcher startWithCompletionHandler:^(NSData *data){
            [_cache setObject:data forKey:url cost:data.length];
            [self useData:data];
        }];
    }
}

@end
```

In this example, the URL to be retrieved is used as the cache key. When there is a cache miss, the data is downloaded and added to the cache. The cost is calculated as the data's length. When the cache is created, the total number of objects that can be cached is set to 100, and the overall cost is set to a value that equates to 5MB because the unit of cost is the size in bytes.

Another class that can be used effectively alongside NSCache is called NSPurgeableData, an NSMutableData subclass that implements a protocol called NSDiscardableContent. This protocol defines an interface for objects whose memory can be discarded, if required. This means that the memory backing NSPurgeableData is freed when system resources are getting low. The method called isContentDiscarded, part of the NSDiscardableContent protocol, returns whether the memory has been freed.

If a purgeable data object needs to be accessed, you call beginContent
Access to tell it that it should not be discarded now. When you are done
with it, you call endContentAccess to tell it that it is free to be discarded,
if desired. These calls can be nested, so you can think of them as just
like a reference count being incremented and decremented. Only when
the reference count is zero can the object be discarded.

If NSPurgeableData objects are added to an NSCache, a purgeable data object that is purged is automatically removed from the
cache. This can optionally be turned on or off through the cache's
evictsObjectsWithDiscardedContent property.

The preceding example could therefore be changed to make use of
purgeable data, like so:

```
- (void)downloadDataForURL:(NSURL*)url {
    NSPurgeableData *cachedData = [_cache objectForKey:url];
    if (cachedData) {
        // Stop the data being purged
        [cacheData beginContentAccess];

        // Use the cached data
        [self useData:cachedData];

        // Mark that the data may be purged again
        [cacheData endContentAccess];
    } else {
        // Cache miss
        EOCNetworkFetcher *fetcher =
            [[EOCNetworkFetcher alloc] initWithURL:url];
        [fetcher startWithCompletionHandler:^(NSData *data){
            NSPurgeableData *purgeableData =
                [NSPurgeableData dataWithData:data];
            [_cache setObject:purgeableData
                    forKey:url
                       cost:purgeableData.length];

            // Don't need to beginContentAccess as it begins
            // with access already marked

            // Use the retrieved data
            [self useData:data];

            // Mark that the data may be purged now
            [purgeableData endContentAccess];
```

```
        }];
    }
}
```

Note that when a purgeable data object is created, it is returned with a +1 purge reference count, so you do not need to specifically call beginContentAccess on it, but you must balance the +1 with a call to endContentAccess.

Things to Remember

✦ Consider using NSCache in the place of NSDictionary objects being used as caches. Caches provide optimal pruning behavior, thread safety, and don't copy keys, unlike a dictionary.

✦ Use the count limit and cost limits to manipulate the metrics that define when objects are pruned from the cache. But never rely on those metrics to be hard limits; they are purely guidance for the cache.

✦ Use NSPurgeableData objects with a cache to provide autopurging data that is also automatically removed from the cache when purged.

✦ Caches will make your applications more responsive if used correctly. Cache only data that is expensive to recalculate, such as data that needs to be fetched from the network or read from disk.

Item 51: Keep initialize and load Implementations Lean

Sometimes, a class needs to perform some initialization before it can be used successfully. In Objective-C, objects inheriting from the NSObject root class, which is the vast majority of classes, have a couple of methods available to them to perform this task.

The first of these methods is called load, and its prototype is as follows:

```
+ (void)load
```

It is called once and only once for every class and category that is added to the runtime. This happens when the library containing the class or category is loaded, generally at application launch, and is certainly the case for any code written for iOS. Mac OS X applications are generally freer to use features such as dynamic loading, and it's therefore possible that a library will be loaded after application launch. The load method for a category is always called after the class that the category is on.

The problem with the load method is that the runtime is in a fragile state at the time it is run. All superclasses' load methods are guaranteed to be run before those of any class; also, any load methods from classes in dependent libraries are guaranteed to be run first. Within any given library, however, you cannot assume the order in which classes are loaded. Therefore, it is unsafe to use another class in a load method. For example, consider the following code:

```
#import <Foundation/Foundation.h>
#import "EOCClassA.h" //< From the same library

@interface EOCClassB : NSObject
@end

@implementation EOCClassB
+ (void)load {
    NSLog(@"Loading EOCClassB");
    EOCClassA *object = [EOCClassA new];
    // Use 'object'
}
@end
```

It is safe to use NSLog and the associated NSString that is being logged, since we know that the Foundation framework has already loaded by the time the load method is run. However, it is unsafe to use EOCClassA from EOCClassB's load method, since you cannot know deterministically whether EOCClassA has been loaded by the time EOCClassB's load method is invoked. For all you know, in its own load method, EOCClassA may perform some important work that must be done before an instance can be used.

An important thing to note is that load does not follow the normal inheritance rules for methods. A class that does not implement load is not called, regardless of whether any of its superclasses do. Also, load can appear in a category and the class itself. Both implementations will be called, with the class's coming before the category's.

You should also make sure that an implementation of load is lean, meaning that as little as possible is done, because the entire application will be blocked while loading is taking place. If a load method does some heavy lifting, the application will be unresponsive for that period. You should not attempt to wait on any locks or call methods that may themselves call locks. In essence, you should do very little. In fact, load is almost never the right solution to perform tasks that have to happen before a class is used. Its only real use is for debugging, perhaps when used in a category if you want to check that the category has been successfully loaded. Perhaps the method was of use historically, but it's safe to say that any modern Objective-C code base does not need to be concerned with it.

The other way to perform class initialization is by overriding the following method:

```
+ (void)initialize
```

This method is called on every class, once and only once, before the class is used. The method is called by the runtime and should never be invoked directly. It is similar to load but subtly different in a few important ways. First, it is called lazily, meaning that it is called only before the class is used for the first time. Thus, a certain class's initialize method will never be run if the class is never used. However, this does mean that there is no period when all initialize implementations are run, unlike load, which blocks the application until all have finished.

The second difference from load is that the runtime is in a normal state during execution and therefore it is safe to use and call any method on any class from a runtime integrity point of view. Also, the runtime ensures that initialize is executed in a thread-safe environment, meaning that only the thread executing initialize is allowed to interact with the class or instances of the class. Other threads will block until initialize is completed.

The final difference is that initialize is sent just like any other message; if a class doesn't implement it but its superclass does, that implementation will be run. This might sound obvious, but it is often overlooked. Consider the following two classes:

```
#import <Foundation/Foundation.h>

@interface EOCBaseClass : NSObject
@end

@implementation EOCBaseClass
+ (void)initialize {
    NSLog(@"%@ initialize", self);
}
@end

@interface EOCSubClass : EOCBaseClass
@end

@implementation EOCSubClass
@end
```

Even though it does not implement initialize, EOCSubClass will still be sent the message. All superclasses' initialize implementations are called first as well. So the first time EOCSubClass is used, you would see the following output:

```
EOCBaseClass initialize
EOCSubClass initialize
```

That may surprise you, but it makes perfect sense. Normal inheritance rules apply to initialize just like other methods (apart from load!), so the implementation from EOCBaseClass is run once when EOCBaseClass is initialized and again when EOCSubClass is initialized, since EOCSubClass does not override it. This is why it is common to see initialize implementations look like this:

```
+ (void)initialize {
    if (self == [EOCBaseClass class]) {
        NSLog(@"%@ initialized", self);
    }
}
```

With this check in place, it is only when the desired class is initialized that the initialization work is done. If this is applied to the earlier example, instead of two log lines being printed, only one is:

```
EOCBaseClass initialize
```

All this leads on to the main point about both load and initialize as hinted at earlier. Implementations of both should be lean. They should be limited to setting up state that is required for the class to operate correctly but not do any work that may take a long time or take out locks. In the case of load, the reasons are as covered earlier; the reasons for keeping initialize lean are similar. First, nobody wants an application that hangs. A class will be initialized the first time it is used and this can be from any thread. If this happens to be the UI thread, that will block while the initialization is taking place, causing an unresponsive application. It's sometimes hard to predict which thread will first use a class, and it's certainly not ideal to attempt to force a certain thread to be the one that causes a class to be initialized.

Second, you do not control when a class will be initialized. It is guaranteed to be before a class is used for the first time, but relying on its being at any given time is dangerous. The runtime may be updated in future to subtly change the way in which classes are initialized, and your assumptions about exactly when a class is initialized may become invalid.

Finally, if you make implementations complex, you may start using, either directly or indirectly, other classes from your class. If these classes have not yet been initialized, they will be forced to initialize as well. However, the first class's initializer won't have finished running. If the other class relies on certain data in the first class being initialized, that data may not have been initialized yet by the time the other class's initialize runs. For example:

```objc
#import <Foundation/Foundation.h>

static id EOCClassAInternalData;
@interface EOCClassA : NSObject
@end

static id EOCClassBInternalData;
@interface EOCClassB : NSObject
@end

@implementation EOCClassA

+ (void)initialize {
    if (self == [EOCClassA class]) {
        [EOCClassB doSomethingThatUsesItsInternalData];
        EOCClassAInternalData = [self setupInternalData];
    }
}

@end

@implementation EOCClassB

+ (void)initialize {
    if (self == [EOCClassB class]) {
        [EOCClassA doSomethingThatUsesItsInternalData];
        EOCClassBInternalData = [self setupInternalData];
    }
}

@end
```

If EOCClassA is initialized first, it has not set up its internal data by the time EOCClassB calls doSomethingThatUsesItsInternalData on EOCClassA. In reality, the problem will not be as apparent as it is here and may involve more than two classes. It may therefore be harder to track down why something isn't working properly.

So the purpose of initialize is for setting up internal data. You should try not to call any methods, even those on the class itself. If you do and later down the line end up adding functionality to the method it calls, you may end up with the problems described. Keep the initializer for setting up global state that cannot be initialized at compile time. The following example illustrates this:

```
// EOCClass.h
#import <Foundation/Foundation.h>

@interface EOCClass : NSObject
@end

// EOCClass.m
#import "EOCClass.h"

static const int kInterval = 10;
static NSMutableArray *kSomeObjects;

@implementation EOCClass

+ (void)initialize {
    if (self == [EOCClass class]) {
        kSomeObjects = [NSMutableArray new];
    }
}

@end
```

The integer can be defined at compile time, but the mutable array cannot, since it is an Objective-C object and therefore needs the runtime to be active before an instance can be created. Note that some Objective-C objects can be created at compile time, such as NSString instances. But the compiler would throw an error if you attempted the following:

```
static NSMutableArray *kSomeObjects = [NSMutableArray new];
```

Bear these thoughts in mind if you find yourself writing a load or initialize method. Keeping implementations lean can save hours of debugging. If you do find yourself wanting to do more than initialize global state, consider creating a method that performs this, and mandate that consumers call it before they use the class. Such examples would be singleton classes that perform additional work when they are first accessed.

Things to Remember

✦ Classes go through a load phase in which they have the load method called on them if it has been implemented. This method may also be present in categories whereby the class load always happens before the category load. Unlike other methods, the load method does not participate in overriding.

✦ Before a class is used for the first time, it is sent the initialize method. This method does participate in overriding, so it is usually best to check which class is being initialized.

✦ Both implementations of load and initialize should be kept lean, which helps to keep applications responsive and reduces the likelihood that interdependency cycles will be introduced.

✦ Keep initialize methods for setting up global state that cannot be done at compile time.

Item 52: Remember that NSTimer Retains Its Target

Timers are a useful object to have at your disposal. The Foundation framework contains a class called NSTimer that can be scheduled to run either at an absolute date and time or after a given delay. Timers can also repeat and therefore have an associated interval to define how frequently they should fire. You may use one to fire every 5 seconds to handle polling of a resource, for example.

Timers are associated with a run loop, and the run loop handles when it should fire. When a timer is created, it can either be prescheduled in the current run loop, or you can create it and schedule it yourself. Either way, the timer will fire only if it is scheduled in a run loop. For example, the method to create a timer that is prescheduled is as follows:

```
+ (NSTimer *)scheduledTimerWithTimeInterval:
                        (NSTimeInterval)seconds
                            target:(id)target
                          selector:(SEL)selector
                          userInfo:(id)userInfo
                           repeats:(BOOL)repeats
```

This method can be used to create a timer that fires after a certain time interval. Optionally, it can repeat until it is manually stopped at a later time. The target and the selector specify which selector should be called on which object when the timer fires. The timer retains its target and will release it when the timer is invalidated. A timer is invalidated either through a call to invalidate or when it fires. If a timer is set to repeat, you invalidate the timer when you want to stop it.

Because the timer retains its target, repeating timers can often cause problems in applications. This means that you can often get into a retain-cycle situation with repeating timers. To see why, consider this example:

```objc
#import <Foundation/Foundation.h>

@interface EOCClass : NSObject
- (void)startPolling;
- (void)stopPolling;
@end

@implementation EOCClass {
    NSTimer *_pollTimer;
}

- (id)init {
    return [super init];
}

- (void)dealloc {
    [_pollTimer invalidate];
}

- (void)stopPolling {
    [_pollTimer invalidate];
    _pollTimer = nil;
}

- (void)startPolling {
    _pollTimer =
    [NSTimer scheduledTimerWithTimeInterval:5.0
                                     target:self
                                   selector:@selector(p_doPoll)
                                   userInfo:nil
                                    repeats:YES];
}

- (void)p_doPoll {
    // Poll the resource
}

@end
```

Can you spot the problem here? Consider what happens if an instance of this class is created and polling is started. The timer is created, which retains the instance because the target is self. However, the timer is also retained by the instance because it is set as an instance variable. (Recall that with ARC, Item 30, this means that it is retained.) This sets up a retain cycle, which would be fine if the retain cycle were broken at some point. The only way it can be broken is if the instance variable is changed or the timer is invalidated. So the only way it is broken is if stopPolling is called or the instance is deallocated. You cannot assume that stopPolling will be called unless you control all the code that uses this class. Even then, it is not good practice to require that a method be called to avoid a leak. Also, there is a chicken-and-egg situation with the other way the timer is invalidated through deallocation. The instance will not be deallocated, because its retain count will never drop to zero while the timer is valid. And the timer will stay valid until it is invalidated. Figure 7.1 illustrates this.

Once the final reference to an instance of EOCClass is removed, it will continue to stay alive, thanks to the timer retaining it. The timer will never be released, because the instance holds a strong reference to it. Worse still, this instance will be lost forever because there are no more references to it other than through the timer. But you don't have any references to the timer other than through the instance. This is a leak. It's a particularly bad leak because the polling will continue to occur

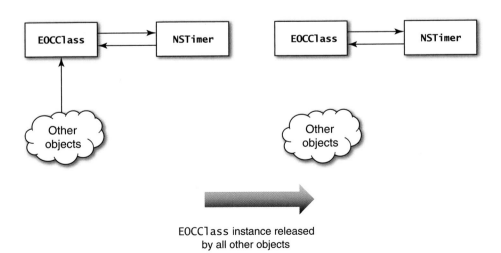

Figure 7.1 Retain cycle because timer retains its target, which in turn retains the timer

forever. If polling is downloading data from a network, data will continue to be downloaded forever, further adding to the potential leak.

Little can be done to alleviate this problem by using timers on their own. You could mandate that stopPolling be called before all other objects release an instance. However, there is no way to check for this, and if the class forms part of a public API that you expose to other developers, you cannot guarantee that they will call it.

One way to solve this problem is to use blocks. Although timers do not currently support blocks directly, the functionality can be added like this:

```
#import <Foundation/Foundation.h>

@interface NSTimer (EOCBlocksSupport)

+ (NSTimer*)eoc_scheduledTimerWithTimeInterval:
                          (NSTimeInterval)interval
                                   block:(void(^)())block
                                 repeats:(BOOL)repeats;

@end

@implementation NSTimer (EOCBlocksSupport)

+ (NSTimer*)eoc_scheduledTimerWithTimeInterval:
                          (NSTimeInterval)interval
                                   block:(void(^)())block
                                 repeats:(BOOL)repeats
{
    return [self scheduledTimerWithTimeInterval:interval
                                 target:self
                     selector:@selector(eoc_blockInvoke:)
                               userInfo:[block copy]
                                repeats:repeats];
}

+ (void)eoc_blockInvoke:(NSTimer*)timer {
    void (^block)() = timer.userInfo;
    if (block) {
        block();
    }
}

@end
```

The reason for doing this to solve the retain-cycle problem will become clear shortly. The block that is to be run when the timer fires is set as the userInfo parameter of the timer. This is an opaque value that the timer retains while it is valid. A copy of the block needs to be taken to ensure that it is a heap block (see Item 37); otherwise, it may be invalid when we come to execute it later. The target of the timer is now the NSTimer class object, a singleton, and it therefore does not matter if it is retained by the timer. A retain cycle remains here, but since the class object never needs to be deallocated, it doesn't matter.

On its own, this solution does not solve the problem but merely provides the tools with which to solve the problem. Consider changing the problematic code to use this new category:

```
- (void)startPolling {
    _pollTimer =
    [NSTimer eoc_scheduledTimerWithTimeInterval:5.0
                                          block:^{
                                              [self p_doPoll];
                                          }
                                        repeats:YES];
}
```

If you think about this one carefully, you'll note that there is still a retain cycle. The block retains the instance because it captures self. In turn, the timer retains the block through the userInfo parameter. Finally, the timer is retained by the instance. However, the retain cycle can be broken through the use of weak references (see Item 33):

```
- (void)startPolling {
    __weak EOCClass *weakSelf = self;
    _pollTimer =
    [NSTimer eoc_scheduledTimerWithTimeInterval:5.0
                                          block:^{
                          EOCClass *strongSelf = weakSelf;
                          [strongSelf p_doPoll];
                                          }
                                        repeats:YES];
}
```

This code uses a useful pattern of defining a weak self variable, which is captured by the block instead of the normal self variable. This means that self won't be retained. However, when the block is executed, a strong reference is immediately generated, which will ensure that the instance is guaranteed to be alive for the duration of the block.

With this pattern, if the instance of EOCClass has its last reference to it from outside released, it will be deallocated. The invalidation of the timer during deallocation (check back to the original example) ensures that the timer will no longer run again. Using a weak reference ensures more safety; if the timer does run again for any reason, perhaps because you have forgotten to invalidate it during deallocation, weakSelf will be nil once in the block.

Things to Remember

✦ An NSTimer object retains its target until the timer is invalidated either because it fires or through an explicit call to invalidate.

✦ Retain cycles are easy to introduce through the use of repeating timers and do so if the target of a timer retains the timer. This may happen directly or indirectly through other objects in the object graph.

✦ An extension to NSTimer to use blocks can be used to break the retain cycle. Until this is made part of the public NSTimer interface, the functionality must be added through a category.

Index